W9-AGG-785

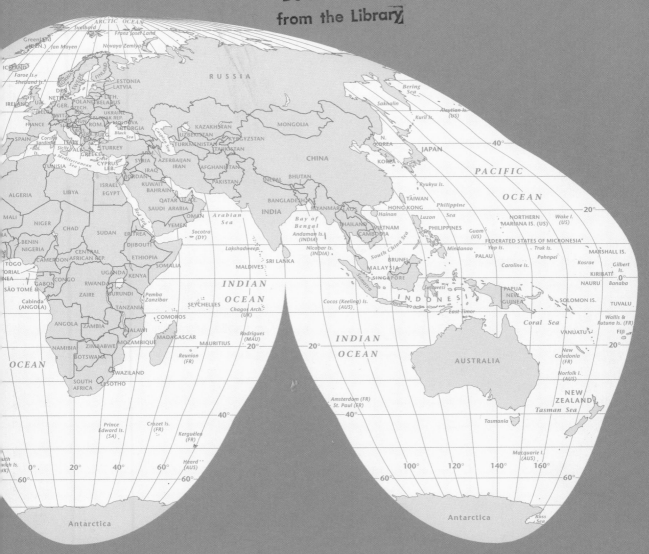

Junior
Worldmark
Encyclopedia
of the
Nations

VOLUME **1**

Junior Worldmark Encyclopedia of the Nations

An imprint of Gale Research
An ITP Information/Reference Group Company

Changing the Way the World Learns

NEW YORK • LONDON • BONN • BOSTON • DETROIT
MADRID • MELBOURNE • MEXICO CITY • PARIS
SINGAPORE • TOKYO • TORONTO • WASHINGTON
ALBANY NY • BELMONT CA • CINCINNATI OH

VOLUME 1

Afghanistan to
Brunei Darussalam

JUNIOR WORLDMARK ENCYCLOPEDIA OF THE NATIONS

Timothy L. Gall and Susan Bevan Gall, *Editors*
Rosalie Wieder, *Senior Editor*
Deborah Baron and Daniel M. Lucas, *Associate Editors*
Brian Rajewski and Deborah Rutti, *Graphics and Layout*
Cordelia R. Heaney, *Editorial Assistant*
Dianne K. Daeg de Mott, Janet Fenn, Matthew Markovich,
    Ariana Ranson, and Craig Strasshofer, *Copy Editors*
Janet Fenn and Matthew Markovich, *Proofreaders*

U•X•L Staff

Jane Hoehner, *U•X•L Developmental Editor*
Sonia Benson and Rob Nagel, *Contributors*
Thomas L. Romig, *U•X•L Publisher*
Mary Beth Trimper, *Production Director*
Evi Seoud, *Assistant Production Manager*
Shanna Heilveil, *Production Associate*
Cynthia Baldwin, *Product Design Manager*
Barbara J. Yarrow, *Graphic Services Supervisor*
Mary Krzewinski, *Cover Designer*
Margaret McAvoy-Amoto, *Permissions Associate (Pictures)*

Library of Congress Cataloging-in-Publication Data
Junior Worldmark encyclopedia of the nations / edited by Timothy Gall
    and Susan Gall.
        p.   cm.
    Includes bibliographical references and index.
    ISBN 0-7876-0741-X (set)
    1. Geography--Encyclopedias, Juvenile. 2. History--Encyclopedias,
Juvenile. 3. Economics--Juvenile literature. 4. Political science--
Encyclopedia, Juvenile. 5. United Nations--Encyclopedias,
Juvenile. I. Gall, Timothy L. II. Gall, Susan B.
G63.J86   1995
910'.3--dc20   95-36739
                                                                CIP

ISBN 0-7876-0741-X (set)
ISBN 0-7876-0742-8 (vol. 1)   ISBN 0-7876-0743-6 (vol. 2)   ISBN 0-7876-0744-4 (vol. 3)
ISBN 0-7876-0745-2 (vol. 4)   ISBN 0-7876-0746-0 (vol. 5)   ISBN 0-7876-0747-9 (vol. 6)
ISBN 0-7876-0748-7 (vol. 7)   ISBN 0-7876-0749-5 (vol. 8)   ISBN 0-7876-0750-9 (vol. 9)

U•X•L is an imprint of Gale Research Inc.,
an International Thomson Publishing Company.
ITP logo is a trademark under license.

CONTENTS

READER'S GUIDE

Junior Worldmark Encyclopedia of the Nations presents profiles of 193 countries of the world, arranged alphabetically from Afghanistan to Zimbabwe, in 9 volumes. *Junior Worldmark* is based on the 8th edition of the reference work, *Worldmark Encyclopedia of the Nations*. The *Worldmark* design organizes facts and data about every country in a common structure. Every profile contains a map, showing the country and its location in the world.

For this edition of *Worldmark,* facts were updated and many new graphical elements were added, including photographs, pie charts, bar charts, and line graphs. The photographs accompanying the fact-filled text were chosen to show people engaged in activities of everyday life. Whenever possible, photographs include young people or families at home, at school, or at work. In some cases—notably Somalia and Bosnia—the photographs poignantly illustrate the often tragic circumstances that many children face in their everyday lives.

The *Junior Worldmark* structure—35 numbered headings—allows students to compare two or more countries in a variety of ways. To further the opportunity for comparisons, most country profiles feature up to four graphical presentations of data: Growth Rate of the Economy, Components of the Economy, Yearly Balance of Trade, and a standard table comparing selected social indicators.

The table entitled Selected Social Indicators offers a snapshot of the country and its development in relation to the other nations of the world. Included are data for eight key characteristics—per capita gross national product, population growth rate (overall and in urban areas), life expectancy, population per physician, pupils per teacher in primary schools, illiteracy rate, and per capita energy consumption. The country's statistics are compared to the averages for low-income countries, high-income countries, and the United States.

Because of differences in exchange rates, economic systems, and government reporting procedures, it is difficult—in some cases impossible—to find data for all of the categories listed in the articles. If a country profile lacks any of the graphical elements, in most cases it was due to lack of reliable statistical information.

The statistics, however, are more than complete enough to paint a disturbing picture of the great discrepancy in wealth between the industrialized nations and those of most of the rest of the world. As every Selected Social Indicators table illustrates, almost 60% of the world's 5.5 billion people live in countries where the yearly per capita gross national product averages $380. In the United States, that figure is almost $25,000.

Because many terms used in this encyclopedia will be new to students, each volume includes a comprehensive glossary. A keyword index to all nine volumes appears in Volume 9.

Profile Features

Each country profile begins by defining eight ways that the country is known to its neighbors and to the rest of the world:

Country names are reported in three forms. The first, the common name, is the name most English-speaking people use when talking about the country. In smaller type below the common name is the official name, in English. Finally, the name, in the language of the country, appears in italic type below the official name.

Capitals are named in the common English-language form, with the native language (if available) following in parentheses.

National emblems and flags are provided in black and white; the flag is also described in text appearing to the right of the flag. (A key to the flag color symbols appears on page xii in this volume and on page vi in volumes 2–9.)

National Anthem. The title of the national anthem is provided in the native language (with English translation in parentheses). Some anthems are untitled. In those cases, the first line of the anthem is provided in the native language (with English translation in parentheses).

Monetary Unit of the country is described, with information about its history where available. Exchange rates are provided to give the student a relative idea of the value of the currency as of mid-1994, and to enable broad comparisons between currencies of different countries. For up-to-the-minute information on exchange rates, the student should consult a newspaper or bank.

Weights and measures vary around the world, and *Junior Worldmark* reports on the system used by each country.

Holidays listed are official public holidays celebrated by the government and its citizens. A movable holiday falls on a different date each year, like Labor Day (first Monday in September) in the United States.

Time is standard time given by time zone in relation to Greenwich mean time (GMT). The world is divided into 24 time zones, each one hour apart. The Greenwich meridian, which is 0 degrees, passes through Greenwich, England, a suburb of London. Greenwich is at the center of the initial time zone, known as Greenwich mean time (GMT). All times given are converted from noon in this zone. The time reported for the country is the official time zone.

The body of each country's profile is arranged in 35 numbered headings.

1 LOCATION AND SIZE. The country is located on its continent in the world. Statistics are given on area and boundary length. Size comparisons are made to states of the United States, and a descriptive location for the capital is provided.

2 TOPOGRAPHY. Dominant geographic features including terrain and major rivers and lakes are described.

3 CLIMATE. Temperature and rainfall are given for the various regions of the country in both English and metric units.

4 PLANTS AND ANIMALS. Described here are the plants and animals native the country.

5 ENVIRONMENT. Destruction of natural resources—forests, water supply, air—is described here. Statistics on solid waste production and endangered and extinct species are also included.

6 POPULATION. Census statistics from the country, from the United Nations, and from the United States are provided. Population density and major urban populations are summarized.

7 MIGRATION. This section describes movements of the country's people, both within the country, and emigration to other nations of the world. Also described is the country's policy on refugees and immigration from other countries.

8 ETHNIC GROUPS. The major ethnic groups are ranked in percents. Where appropriate, some description of the influence or history of ethnicity is provided.

9 LANGUAGES. The official language is listed, along with other languages spoken in the country.

10 RELIGIONS. The population is broken down according to religion.

11 TRANSPORTATION. Statistics on roads, railways, waterways, and air traffic, along with a listing of key ports for international trade and travel, are provided.

12 HISTORY. Concise summary of the country's history from ancient times (where appropriate) to the present.

13 GOVERNMENT. The form of government is described, and the process of governing is summarized.

14 POLITICAL PARTIES. Descriptions of the political parties of significance through history where appropriate, and of influence in the mid-1990s.

15 JUDICIAL SYSTEM. Structure of the court system and the jurisdiction of courts in each category is provided.

16 ARMED FORCES. Statistics on troops and weapons are provided, along with description of the structure of the military.

17 ECONOMY. This section summarizes the key elements of the economy and describes key trading alliances. In most countries, two graphical presentations of data accompany the text. These are a bar graph showing the yearly growth rate of the country's economy from 1985 to 1993, and a pie chart illustrating the percentage of the economy devoted to agriculture, industry, and services.

18 INCOME. Gross national product, total and per person in US$, along with the average inflation rate since 1985.

19 INDUSTRY. Key industries are listed, and important aspects of industrial development in the country are described.

20 LABOR. Statistics on the civilian labor force, including numbers of workers, percent of workers by industry segment, employment outlook including unemployment statistics, wage rates where available.

21 **AGRICULTURE.** Statistics on key agricultural crops for internal consumption and export are provided.

22 **DOMESTICATED ANIMALS.** Statistics on livestock—cattle, hogs, sheep, etc.—and the land area devoted to raising them are given.

23 **FISHING.** The relative significance of fishing to the country is provided, with statistics on fish and seafood products.

24 **FORESTRY.** Land area classified as forest is given, along with a listing of key forest products and a description of government policy toward forest land.

25 **MINING.** Description of mineral deposits and statistics on related mining activity and export are provided.

26 **FOREIGN TRADE.** Value of exports and imports in US$, with key products, are listed. For most countries, a graph illustrates the trend in balance of trade (exports minus imports) since 1988.

27 **ENERGY AND POWER.** Description of the country's power resources, including electricity produced and oil reserves and production, are provided.

28 **SOCIAL DEVELOPMENT.** Government social programs are described and statistics given. Included are insurance for elderly, unemployed, disabled, and children. The status of women is summarized.

29 **HEALTH.** Statistics and description on such public health factors as life expectancy, principal causes of death, access to safe drinking water, numbers of hospitals and medical facilities appear here.

30 **HOUSING.** Housing shortages and government programs to build housing are described. Statistics on numbers of dwellings, percentage with water, plumbing, and electricity are provided.

31 **EDUCATION.** Statistical data on literacy, compulsory education, and primary and secondary schools are given. Major universities are listed, and government programs to foster education are described.

32 **MEDIA.** The state of telecommunications—television, radio, telephone—and print media is summarized.

33 **TOURISM AND RECREATION.** Under this heading, the student will find a summary of the importance of tourism to the country, and factors affecting the tourism industry (such as war or natural disasters). Key tourist attractions are listed.

34 **FAMOUS PEOPLE.** In this section, a few of the best-known citizens of a country are listed. When a person is noted in a country that is not the country of his of her birth, the birthplace is given.

35 **BIBLIOGRAPHY.** The bibliographic listings at the end of each country profile are provided as a guide for further reading. Wherever possible, sources are included that are likely to be available in a medium-size public school or public library. These include many references to recent articles from *National Geographic* magazine.

GLOSSARY. Appearing in every volume of *Junior Worldmark Encyclopedia of the*

Nations, the glossary expands upon information given in the body of the profile to further define terms and concepts.

INDEX. A keyword index to all nine volumes appears in Volume 9.

Acknowledgments

Junior Worldmark Encyclopedia of the Nations draws on the eighth edition of the *Worldmark Encyclopedia of the Nations.* Readers are directed to that work for a complete list of contributors, too numerous to list here. Special acknowledgment goes to the government officials throughout the world who gave their cooperation to this project, and to the Cleveland Council on World Affairs, and its president Ambassador Charles F. Dunbar, for guidance and direction in preparation of *Worldmark Encyclopedia of the Nations,* 8th edition.

Photographs

The photographs in *Junior Worldmark* were assembled with assistance from the following: Cynthia Bassett, Photographer; Marcia Lein-Schiff, AP/Wide World Photos; and Susan D. Rock, Photographer.

Advisors

The following persons were consulted on the content and structure of this encyclopedia. Their insights, opinions, and suggestions led to many enhancements and improvements in the presentation of the material.

Mary Alice Anderson, Media Specialist, Winona Middle School, Winona, Minnesota

Pat Baird, Library Media Specialist and Department Chair, Shaker Heights Middle School, Shaker Heights, Ohio

Pat Fagel, Library Media Specialist, Shaker Heights Middle School, Shaker Heights, Ohio

Nancy Guidry, Young Adult Librarian, Santa Monica Public Library, Santa Monica, California

Ann West LaPrise, Children's Librarian, Redford Branch, Detroit Public Library, Detroit, Michigan

Nancy C. Nieman, Teacher, U.S. History, Social Studies, Journalism, Delta Middle School, Muncie, Indiana

Madeline Obrock, Library Media Specialist, Woodbury Elementary School, Shaker Heights, Ohio

Ernest L. O'Roark, Teacher, Social Studies, Martin Luther King Middle School, Germantown, Maryland

Ellen Stepanian, Director of Library Services, Shaker Heights Board of Education, Shaker Heights, Ohio

Mary Strouse, Library Media Specialist, Woodbury Elementary School, Shaker Heights, Ohio

Comments and Suggestions

We welcome your comments on the *Junior Worldmark Encyclopedia of the Nations* as well as your suggestions for features to be included in future editions. Please write: Editors, Junior Worldmark Encyclopedia of the Nations, U•X•L, 835 Penobscot Building, Detroit, Michigan 48226-4094; or call toll-free: 1-800-877-4253.

Guide to Country Articles

Every country profile in this encyclopedia includes the same 35 headings. Also included in every profile is a map (showing the country and its location in the world), the country's flag and seal, and a table of data on the country. The country articles are organized alphabetically in nine volumes. A glossary of terms is included in each of the nine volumes. This glossary defines many of the specialized terms used throughout the encyclopedia. A keyword index to all nine volumes appears at the end of Volume 9.

Flag Color Symbols

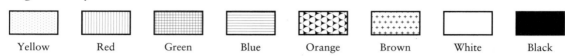

Yellow   Red   Green   Blue   Orange   Brown   White   Black

Alphabetical listing of sections

Agriculture	21	Income	18	
Armed Forces	16	Industry	19	
Bibliography	35	Judicial System	15	
Climate	3	Labor	20	
Domesticated Animals	22	Languages	9	
Economy	17	Location and Size	1	
Education	31	Media	32	
Energy and Power	27	Migration	7	
Environment	5	Mining	25	
Ethnic Groups	8	Plants and Animals	4	
Famous People	34	Political Parties	14	
Fishing	23	Population	6	
Foreign Trade	26	Religions	10	
Forestry	24	Social Development	28	
Government	13	Topography	2	
Health	29	Tourism/Recreation	33	
History	12	Transportation	11	
Housing	30			

Sections listed numerically

1	Location and Size.	19	Industry
2	Topography	20	Labor
3	Climate	21	Agriculture
4	Plants and Animals	22	Domesticated Animals
5	Environment	23	Fishing
6	Population	24	Forestry
7	Migration	25	Mining
8	Ethnic Groups	26	Foreign Trade
9	Languages	27	Energy and Power
10	Religions	28	Social Development
11	Transportation	29	Health
12	History	30	Housing
13	Government	31	Education
14	Political Parties	32	Media
15	Judicial System	33	Tourism/Recreation
16	Armed Forces	34	Famous People
17	Economy	35	Bibliography
18	Income		

Abbreviations and acronyms to know

GMT= Greenwich mean time. The prime, or Greenwich, meridian passes through Greenwich, England (near London), and marks the center of the initial time zone for the world. The standard time of all 24 time zones relate to Greenwich mean time. Every profile contains a map showing the country and its location in the world.

These abbreviations are used in references to famous people:
b.=born
d.=died
fl.=flourished (lived and worked)
r.=reigned (for kings, queens, and similar monarchs)

A dollar sign ($) stands for US$ unless otherwise indicated.

AFGHANISTAN

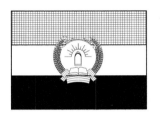

Islamic State of Afghanistan

Jamhurriyati Afghanistan

CAPITAL: Kabul.

FLAG: The national flag has three equal horizontal stripes of green, white, and black. In the center is the national coat of arms.

ANTHEM: *Esllahte Ardi (Land Reform),* beginning "So long as there is the earth and the heavens."

MONETARY UNIT: The afghani (Af) is a paper currency of 100 puls. There are coins of 25 and 50 puls and 1, 2, and 5 afghanis, and notes of 10, 20, 50, 100, 500, and 1,000 afghanis. Af1 = $0.0198 (or $1 = Af50.60).

WEIGHTS AND MEASURES: The metric system is the legal standard, although some local units are still in use.

HOLIDAYS: Now Rooz (New Year's Day), 21 March; Anniversary of the Saur Revolution, 27 April; May Day, 1 May; Independence Day, 18 August. Movable religious holidays include First Day of Ramadan, 'Id al-Fitr, 'Id al-'Adha', 'Ashura, and Milad an-Nabi. The Afghan calendar year begins on 21 March; the Afghan year 1366 began on 21 March 1987.

TIME: 4:30 PM = noon GMT.

1 LOCATION AND SIZE

Afghanistan is a landlocked country in South Asia. With a total area of 647,500 square kilometers (250,001 square miles), Afghanistan is slightly smaller than the state of Texas. It has a total boundary length of 5,529 kilometers (3,436 miles).

The capital city of Afghanistan, Kabul, is located in the east central part of the country.

2 TOPOGRAPHY

The Hindu Kush mountain range rises to more than 6,100 meters (20,000 feet) in the northern corner of the Vakhan panhandle in the northeast and continues in a southwesterly direction. It divides the northern provinces from the rest of the country. Central Afghanistan is a plateau with an average elevation of 1,800 meters (6,000 feet). Southwestern Afghanistan is a desert.

The four major river systems are the Amu Darya (Oxus) in the north; the Harirud and Morghab in the west; the Helmand in the southwest; and the Kabul in the east. There are few lakes.

3 CLIMATE

Wide temperature variations are usual from season to season and from day to night. Summer temperatures in Kabul may range from 16°C (61°F) at sunrise to 38°C (100°F) by noon, while the mean January temperature is 0°C (32°F). The maximum summer temperature in Jalalabad is about 46°C (115°F). Rainfall averages about 25 to 30 centimeters (10 to 12 inches).

4 PLANTS AND ANIMALS

There are over 3,000 plant species, including hundreds of varieties of trees, shrubs, vines, flowers, and fungi. The country is particularly rich in medicinal plants, such as rue, wormwood, and asafetida. Native animals include the fox, lynx, wild dog, bear, mongoose, shrew, hedgehog, hyena, jerboa, hare, and wild varieties of cats, asses, mountain goats, and mountain sheep. Trout is the most common fish. There are more than 100 kinds of wildfowl and birds.

5 ENVIRONMENT

Afghanistan's most serious ecological problems are loss of forest land and the effects of war. Neglect and damage caused by large-scale bombing have destroyed productive agricultural areas. A major earthquake and flash floods in 1991 added to the destruction. Afghanistan has responded to its fuel needs by cutting down already scarce forests. As of 1994, less than 3% of Afghanistan was forest land. By 1994, 13 species of mammals, 13 species of birds, and 4 plant species of were endangered.

6 POPULATION

As of 1991, population estimates ranged from 12 to 19 million. However, the official government estimate was 16,433,000 (excluding the 15% who are nomads, a wandering people). The United Nations projected a population of 26,767,000 for the year 2000. However, due to continuous warfare since 1979, experts question the reliability of population estimates for the last decade, as well as future projections. Afghanistan's estimated population density (excluding nomads) was 26 persons per square kilometer (65 persons per square mile) in 1991. Kabul, the capital, had a population of 1,424,400 in 1988.

7 MIGRATION

Following the Soviet invasion of Afghanistan in December 1979, a massive emigration of Afghans took place. According to the UNHCR (the United Nations High Commissioner for Refugees), there were 3,098,000 Afghan refugees (18.8% of the estimated population) across the Pakistani border by the end of 1992. The number in Iran was 3,186,600. By March 1993, an estimated 2 million refugees had returned—1.8 million from Pakistan and 200,000 from Iran. Afghanistan was harboring about 90,000 refugees from Tajikstan in 1993.

8 ETHNIC GROUPS

The Pashtoons (also written as Pushtun, Pukhtun, or Pathan), numbering about 43%, are often referred to as "true Afghans." They are divided into two major groups, the Durranis and the Ghilzais.

The Tajiks, of Iranian descent, comprise nearly 25% of the population and the Hazaras about 5%. Turkic and Turko-Mongol groups include the Uzbeks, who number about 6% of the population. Other groups include the Aimaks, Farsiwans (Persians), and Brahiu.

AFGHANISTAN

0   50   100   150 Miles

0   50   100   150 Kilometers

KYRGYSTAN

CHINA

UZBEKISTAN

⊛ Dushanbe

TAJIKISTAN

PAMIRS

TURKMENISTAN

Termez

Amu Dar'ya

Balkh

Sheberghān

Kondūz

Tāloqān

Panj

Kcwkcheh

Feyzābād

Khorugh

Qal'eh-ye Panjeh

Vākhān

Sar-e Pol

Mazār-e Sharif

Dowlatābād

Baghlān

HINDU KUSH

Nowshāk 24,557 ft. 7485 m.

Meymaneh

Qonduz

IRAN

Towraghondi

Morghāb

Chārīkar

Asmār

Tayyebāt

PAROPAMISUS MTS.

Kūh-e Fūlādī 16,847 ft. 5135 m.

Kabul

Kabul

Konar

Herāt

Harirūd

Chaghcharān

Kowt-e 'Ashrow

Jalālābād

Peshawar

Khyber Pass

Islāmābād

Baraki

Shindand

Farāh

Helmand

Gardēyz

Ghaznī

Khowst

Zareh Sharan

Farāh

Arghandāb

Qalāt

Hāmūn-e Sabērī

Zaranj

Lashkar Gāh

Qandahār

Zābol

Rīgestān Desert

Khojak Pass

PAKISTAN

Helmand

Afghanistan

Gowd-e Zereh

Quetta

Chagai Hills

N W E S

LOCATION: 29°28′ to 38°30′ N; 60°30′ to 74°53′E. **BOUNDARY LENGTHS:** China, 76 kilometers (47 miles); Iran, 936 kilometers (582 miles); Pakistan, 2,430 kilometers (1,511 miles); Tajikistan, 1,206 kilometers (750 miles); Turkmenistan, 744 kilometers (463 miles); Uzbekistan, 137 kilometers (85mi).

9 LANGUAGES

Both Pashtu and Dari (Afghan Persian) are the official languages of the country. Dari is the principal language of government, business, and culture. The Turkic languages include Uzbek, Turkoman, and Kirghiz.

10 RELIGIONS

Almost all Afghans are Muslims. More than 75% are Sunni Muslims. The rest are Shiites, including some Isma'ilis. In 1992, an Islamic State was proclaimed, and Islam became the official religion, as it had been before the Soviet invasion in 1979.

11 TRANSPORTATION

Afghanistan has an estimated 21,000 kilometers (13,000 miles) of roads. However, due to the ongoing war, two-thirds of all paved roads were unusable by the early 1990s. In 1992 there were 40,000 passenger cars and 35,000 trucks and buses in use.

The Khyber Pass in Pakistan is the best known of the passes providing land access to Afghanistan. However, most of the country's trade moves through the former USSR. There were only three short lines of railway in the country in 1991. There are no navigable rivers except for the Amu Darya, on Turkmenistan's border. Kabul and Qandahar have airports capable of receiving international flights.

12 HISTORY

Afghanistan has existed as a nation for less than three centuries. Previously, the area was made up of various kingdoms, going as far back as the Persian rule of Darius I in the 6th century BC and, 300 years later, Alexander the Great. Toward the middle of the 3rd century BC, Buddhism spread to Afghanistan from India.

Beginning in the 7th century, Muslim invaders brought Islam to the region, and it eventually became the main cultural influence. The region came under the control of a series of Arab and Turkic kingdoms until it was invaded by the Mongols under Genghis Khan in 1219. It was then ruled by Mongols and Uzbeks for several centuries.

The formation of a unified Afghanistan under the Persian commander Ahmad Shah Abdali in the 18th century marks Afghanistan's beginning as a distinct nation. His descendant, Dost Muhammad, was defeated by the British in the two Afghan Wars (1838–42) and (1877–79). Abdur Rahman Khan, recognized as emir by the British in 1880, established a central administration, and supported the British interest in a neutral Afghanistan to help prevent the expansion of Russian influence.

In 1907, an agreement between the British and Russians guaranteed the independence of Afghanistan (and Tibet) under British influence, and Afghanistan remained neutral in both World Wars. The Treaty of Rawalpindi (1919) gave the government of Afghanistan the freedom to conduct its own foreign affairs.

Muhammad Zahir Shah, who ascended the throne in 1933, continued the modernization efforts begun by his father, Muhamad Nadir Shah. He governed for the next 40 years. In 1964, a new constitution was introduced, converting Afghanistan into a constitutional monarchy, and a year later the country's first general election was held.

In July 1973, Muhammad Daoud Khan, the king's first cousin, seized power, establishing a republic and appointing himself president and prime minister. He abolished the monarchy, dissolved the legislature, and suspended the constitution. Daoud ruled as a dictator until 1977, when the newly convened Loya Jirga (Grand National Assembly) elected him president for a six-year term.

Afghanistan Under PDPA Rule

On 27 April 1978, Daoud was removed from the throne and executed in a bloody coup d'état (military takeover), and the pro-Soviet Democratic Republic of Afghanistan emerged. Soon after the takeover, rural Afghan groups took up arms against the new government. These groups came to be known as the mujahidin guerrillas.

Meanwhile, the two main groups of the ruling People's Democratic Party of Afghanistan (PDPA) had become involved in a bitter power struggle. By the end of 1979, two prime ministers had been forcibly removed from power, and 4,000 to 5,000 Soviet troops had been airlifted into the capital city of Kabul to maintain order.

The Soviet presence increased to about 85,000 troops in late January 1980, and by spring, the first clashes between Soviet troops and the mujahidin had occurred. Throughout the early and mid-1980s, the mujahidin resistance continued to build. Much of the countryside remained under mujahidin control, while in Kabul, Soviet advisers assumed control of most Afghan government agencies.

By late 1987, more than a million Afghans had lost their lives in the struggle. Soviet troop strength in Afghanistan at the end of 1987 was about 120,000.

International efforts to bring about a political solution to the war were pursued within the UN framework from 1982 onward. In April 1988, the USSR agreed to pull its troops out of Afghanistan within nine months. The Russians com-

Photo credit: AP/Wide World Photos

These women wear clothes that represent the change in the lives of Afghan women since the civil war; the one on the right wears the traditional veiled chadri, the other a spangled party dress.

pleted the removal of their forces on schedule, but the Soviet-backed Najibullah government remained in power until April 1992, when Najibullah fled Kabul as mujahidin forces closed in on the city.

With the fall of the Najibullah government, the Seven Party Alliance (SPA) of Islamic groups announced plans to set up an Afghan Interim Government (AIG) in charge of preparing the way for elections. Since then, differences within the SPA/AIG leadership have prevented the creation of a genuine interim government and the country remains in a state of civil war.

[13] GOVERNMENT

No new constitution has been drafted since the end of the Najibullah government. While the Afghan Interim Government (AIG) headed by Burhanuddin Rabbani is officially in control, multiple small kingdoms exist throughout the country, and there is no real central authority.

[14] POLITICAL PARTIES

There are currently some 10 Islamic parties active in the struggle for power in Afghanistan, including the Jamiat-i-Islami (JI), the Hizbi-Islami, and the Ittihad-i-Islami Barai Azadi Afghanistan. In addition, remnants of the Khalq and Parchem factions of the former PDPA/Wattan Party are still active.

[15] JUDICIAL SYSTEM

The ongoing civil war has disrupted government functions to such an extent that there is no functioning central legal system. Some local and provincial courts continue to operate. These courts apply rule based on the Shari'a (Islamic law) and traditional tribal law.

[16] ARMED FORCES

The regular armed forces may have had 45,000 men in 1993 following the collapse of the Soviet-supported Najibullah regime. The victorious mujahidin factions keep their own armies, armed with Russian vehicles and weapons. These forces number at least 40,000. There is no reliable estimate on military expenses.

Photo credit: AP/Wide World Photos

A refugee boy carries a suitcase to his new home in an apartment building that was abandoned during the war.

[17] ECONOMY

Afghanistan's economy has been ruined by over 15 years of war. By 1991, wheat output—the mainstay of the agricultural economy—had dropped to less than half of prewar levels. Exports had dropped to about a third of those recorded ten years earlier. With the growth of open conflict between rival mujahidin factions, what little is left of the country's resources is rapidly being destroyed. Three separate economic systems are emerging in the west, east, and northern parts of the country. They are encouraged by undercover support for local leaders by Iran, Pakistan and the Central Asian republics.

18 INCOME

In 1990 the gross domestic product (GDP) was reported to be $2.27 billion. The per person national product was estimated to be $200 in 1989.

19 INDUSTRY

Still in an early stage of growth before the outbreak of war, Afghan industry has struggled ever since. The few industries that continued production through the 1980s remained limited to processing local materials.

The main modern industry is cotton textile production. There are also small woolen and rayon textile industries. Other industries are wheat flour processing, cement, raisin cleaning and fruit preservation, leather tanning, preparation of casings, sugar refining, and vegetable oil extraction.

Carpet making is the most important handicraft industry. Other handicrafts include feltmaking and the weaving of cotton, wool, and silk cloth.

20 LABOR

Afghanistan's labor force was estimated at 5 million in 1980, with about two-thirds engaged in agriculture and animal husbandry. More recent estimates are not available. The textile industry is the largest employer of industrial labor.

21 AGRICULTURE

Normally, Afghanistan grew about 95% of its needs in wheat and rye, and more than met its needs in rice, potatoes, beans, nuts, and seeds. It depended on imports only for sugar and edible fats and oils. Agricultural production, however, is now a fraction of its potential. In some regions, it has all but stopped due to destruction caused by the war and the migration of Afghans out of the country.

Crop production includes wheat, fruits, corn, vegetables, rice, barley, and seed cotton. Pistachios and almonds are widely grown and exported. Agricultural products accounted for about 36% of Afghanistan's exports in 1992.

22 DOMESTICATED ANIMALS

The availability of land suitable for grazing has made animal husbandry an important part of the economy. Natural pastures cover some 3 million hectares (7.4 million acres) but are being overgrazed. In 1992 there were an estimated 13.5 million sheep, and 2.1 million goats.

Much of Afghanistan's livestock was removed from the country by early waves of refugees who fled to Pakistan and Iran. Indications are that livestock products since the mid-1980s no longer approach prewar totals.

23 FISHING

Fish does not constitute a significant part of the Afghan diet. The average annual catch is about 1,500 tons.

Selected Social Indicators

These statistics are estimates for the period 1988 to 1993. For comparison purposes, data for the United States and averages for low-income countries and high-income countries are also given.

Indicator	Afghanistan	Low-income countries	High-income countries	United States
Per capita gross national product†	**$200**	$380	$23,680	$24,740
Population growth rate	**4.5%**	1.9%	0.6%	1.0%
Population growth rate in urban areas	**6.4%**	3.9%	0.8%	1.3%
Population per square kilometer of land	**26**	78	25	26
Life expectancy in years	**44**	62	77	76
Number of people per physician	**6,690**	>3,300	453	419
Number of pupils per teacher (primary school)	**49**	39	<18	20
Illiteracy rate (15 years and older)	**71%**	41%	<5%	<3%
Energy consumed per capita (kg of oil equivalent)	**145**	364	5,203	7,918

† The gross national product (GNP) is the total dollar value of all goods and services produced by a country in a year. The per capita GNP is calculated by dividing a country's GNP by its population. The World Bank defines low-income countries as those with a per capita GNP of $695 or less. High-income countries have a per capita GNP of $8,626 or more. Less than 14% of the world's 5.5 billion people live in high-income countries, while almost 60% live in low-income countries.   > = greater than   < = less than

Sources: World Bank, Social Indicators of Development 1995, Baltimore: Johns Hopkins University Press, 1995. Central Intelligence Agency, World Fact Book, Washington, D.C.: Government Printing Office, 1994.

24 FORESTRY

The once rich forests have been greatly depleted by the war. In 1991, about 6.7 million cubic meters of roundwood were produced.

25 MINING

Afghanistan has valuable deposits of barite, beryl, chrome, coal, copper, iron, lapis lazuli, lead, mica, natural gas, petroleum, salt, silver, sulfur, and zinc. Deposits of lapis lazuli in the northeast are mined in small quantities.

26 FOREIGN TRADE

As reconstruction efforts proceeded in many of the country's provinces, trade flows appeared to recover somewhat by the late 1980s. Exports for 1990/91 were up by 3.4% from the year before, though still totaling only $243 million. Imports totaled $737 million in 1990/91, much of this comprised of fuel and food.

In 1989/90, Afghanistan's main export markets included Germany, the United Kingdom, India, Pakistan and the United States. Major suppliers included Japan, Singapore, Germany, the UK and the US. In the early 1990s, smuggled trade with the Central Asian republics and border regions of Pakistan is reported to have expanded considerably.

27 ENERGY AND POWER

In 1991, production of electricity totaled 1,015 million kilowatt hours. Natural gas reserves are estimated to total 120 billion cubic meters. Production rose to an annual average of 2.6 billion cubic meters during 1987–91. As of 1991, a new 72-collector solar installation was completed in Kabul at a cost of $364 million.

28 SOCIAL DEVELOPMENT

Social welfare in Afghanistan has traditionally relied on family and tribal organization. Disabled people are cared for in social welfare centers in the provincial capitals.

In the 1980s, the Communist regime approved a wider role for women than the traditional one which limits them mostly to the home and the fields, but the victory of the mujahidin has turned back this trend.

29 HEALTH

Even before the war disrupted medical services, health conditions in Afghanistan were inadequate by western standards. Since 1980, volunteer medical programs from France, Sweden, the US, and other countries have provided medical services to war-ravaged areas of Afghanistan. In 1991, there were 2,233 doctors. In 1992, only 29% of the population had access to health services. In 1992, estimated life expectancy was 44 years—one of the lowest in the world. From 1978 to 1991, there were over 1,500,000 war-related deaths.

30 HOUSING

The war has severely damaged or destroyed countless houses. According to an official report, there were 200,000 dwellings in Kabul in the mid-1980s. The latest available figures for 1980–88 show a total housing stock of 3,500,000 with 4.4 people per dwelling.

31 EDUCATION

Adult literacy in 1990 was estimated at 45.1% for men and 14.9% for women. Education is free at all levels. Officially, primary education is compulsory and lasts for eight years, while secondary education lasts for a further four years. In 1989 an estimated 726,287 pupils were enrolled in primary schools.

By 1988 a total of five universities were established in Afghanistan, beside eight vocational colleges and fifteen technical colleges. Teacher-training institutes have been established in the provinces of Balkh and Qandahar.

32 MEDIA

Radio and television broadcasting originates in Kabul. In 1991, there were 1,890,000 radios and 147,000 television sets in the country. Over 31,700 telephones were in use. The only Afghan newspapers and magazines permitted are operated by the government. In 1991 there were 14 daily newspapers and 3 regular periodicals. The major newspapers, all headquartered in Kabul, (with estimated 1991 circulations) were *Anis* (3,700), published in Dari and Pashto; *Hiwad* (4,600), in Dari and Pashto; *Sarbaz* (5,000); and *Kabul New Times* (1,500), in English.

High school students are seated on the floor of a gymnasium as they register for classes.

33 TOURISM AND RECREATION

The tourist industry, developed with government help in the early 1970s, has been negligible since 1979 due to internal political instability.

34 FAMOUS AFGHANS

The most renowned ruler of medieval Afghanistan, Mahmud of Ghazni (971?–1030), was the Turkish creator of an empire stretching from Iran to India. Jalal ud-Din Rumi (1207–73), who stands at the summit of Persian poetry, was born in Balkh. The founder of the state of Afghanistan was Ahmad Shah Abdali (1724–73).

Muhammad Zahir Shah (b.1914) was king from 1933 until he was deposed by a military takeover in July 1973. Lieutenant General Sardar Muhammad Daoud Khan (1909–78), cousin and brother-in-law of King Zahir, was the leader of the takeover and the founder and first president of the Republic of Afghanistan.

35 BIBLIOGRAPHY

Afghanistan—In Pictures. Minneapolis: Lerner Publications, 1989.

Clifford, Mary Louise. *The Land and People of Afghanistan*. New York: Lippincott, 1989.

Jones, Schuyler. *Afghanistan*. Santa Barbara, Calif.: Clio Press, 1992.

Mackenzie, Richard. "Afghanistan's Uneasy Peace." *National Geographic*, October 1993, 58–89.

ALBANIA

Republic of Albania
Republika e Shqipërisë

CAPITAL: Tiranë (Tirana).

FLAG: The flag consists of a red background at the center of which is a black double-headed eagle.

ANTHEM: *Hymni i Flamúrit (Anthem of the Flag)* begins "Rreth flamúrit të për bashkuar" ("The flag that united us in the struggle").

MONETARY UNIT: The lek (L) of 100 qindarka is a convertible paper currency. There are coins of 5, 10, 20, 50 qindarka, and 1 lek, and notes of 1, 3, 5, 10, 25, 50, 100, and 500 leks. L1 = $0.1483 (or $1 = L6.743).

WEIGHTS AND MEASURES: The metric system is the legal standard.

HOLIDAYS: New Year's Day, 1 January; Small Bayram, end of Ramadan, 3 March*; International Women's Day, 8 March; Catholic Easter, 14–17 April; Orthodox Easter, 23 April; Great Bayram, Feast of the Sacrifice, 10 May*; Independence Day, 28 November; Christmas Day, 25 December.

*These holidays are dependent on the Islamic lunar calendar and may vary by one or two days from the dates given.

TIME: 1 PM = noon GMT.

1 LOCATION AND SIZE

Albania is located on the west coast of the Balkan Peninsula opposite the "heel" of the Italian "boot," from which it is separated by the Strait of Otranto and the Adriatic Sea. Albania is slightly larger than the state of Maryland, with a total area of 28,750 square kilometers (11,100 square miles). Albania's capital city, Tiranë, is located in the west central part of the country.

2 TOPOGRAPHY

Albania is mostly mountainous, with 70% of the territory at elevations of more than 300 meters (1,000 feet). The rest of the country is made up of a coastal lowland and river valleys opening onto the coastal plain. The highest peak, Korab (2,751 meters/9,026 feet) lies in eastern Albania. The most important rivers—the Drin, the Buna, the Mat, the Shkumbin, the Seman, and the Vijosë—empty into the Adriatic sea.

3 CLIMATE

The average annual temperature is 15°C (59°F). Rainy winters (with frequent cyclones) and dry, hot summers are typical of the coastal plain. Summer rainfall is more frequent and winters colder in the mountains. Annual precipitation ranges from about 100 centimeters (40 inches) on the coast to more than 250 centimeters (100 inches) in the mountains.

4 PLANTS AND ANIMALS

The dry lowlands are home to a bush-shrub known as maquis. There are some woods in the low-lying regions, and larger forests of oak, beech, and other species begin at 910 meters (2,986 feet). Black pines and other evergreens are found at higher elevations in the northern part of the country. There are few wild animals, even in the mountains, but wild birds still abound in the lowland forests.

5 ENVIRONMENT

Destruction of the forests is Albania's main environmental problem, in spite of government forest programs. Albania's endangered species include the Baltic sturgeon, Dalmatian pelican, Mediterrranean monk seal, and the white-headed duck. The Dalmation pelican is the largest member of the pelican family and has a wingspan of 10 to 11 feet.

6 POPULATION

Albania's population in mid-1994 was estimated at 3,514,140. The projection for the year 2000 was 3,589,000. Average population density was 116 persons per square kilometer (317 persons per square mile). Tiranë, the capital and principal city, had a population of 251,000 in 1991.

7 MIGRATION

Albania has been largely isolated from the rest of Europe, so migration has been very limited. In the early 1990s, about 2 million Albanians lived in the former Yugoslavia. Many Albanians and people of Albanian descent live in Greece, Italy, and Macedonia.

8 ETHNIC GROUPS

Usually thought of as descendants of the ancient Illyrians, the Albanians make up about 98% of the population. It is estimated that there are over 300,000 Greeks in Albania, together with 4,500 Macedonians, and small numbers of Gypsies, Vlachs, Bulgarians, and Serbs. The Albanians themselves fall into two major groups: the Ghegs in the north and the Tosks in the south, divided by the Shkumbin River.

9 LANGUAGES

Albanian (Shqip) is a member of the Indo-European family of languages. It was not until 1908 that a written Latin alphabet was established for Albanian. There are two distinct dialects—Gheg, spoken in the north; and Tosk, spoken in the south. Greek is spoken by a minority in the southeast border area.

10 RELIGIONS

In 1967, the government closed more than 2,100 mosques, churches, and monasteries, and declared the country an atheistic (denying the existence of God) state. In 1991, Albania ended its official opposition to religious activities, and churches and mosques were allowed to reopen. Today, the percentage of Muslims is 65%; Eastern Orthodox, 20%; and Roman Catholic, 13%.

11 TRANSPORTATION

Many roads are unsuitable for motor transport. Bicycles and donkeys are common. In 1991, there were 16,700 kilometers (10,377 miles) of road. The railroads had a total length of 509 kilometers (316 miles).

Albania's rivers are not navigable, but there is some local shipping on lakes Skadarsko, Ohridsko, and Prespanko. Durrës is the principal port for foreign trade. Tiranë's international airport connects Albania with major cities throughout the world.

12 HISTORY

Origins and the Middle Ages

The Albanians are descended from ancient Illyrian or Thracian tribes that may have come to the Balkan Peninsula even before the Greeks. An Illyrian kingdom was formed in the 3rd century BC and conquered by Rome in 167 BC. Present-day Albania was raided by Slav invaders in the 6th century AD and taken over by Bulgaria in the 9th century. Some independent kingdoms existed briefly during the second half of the 14th century.

From the Ottomans to Independence

By 1479, the Turks gained complete control of the area. Over the following centuries Islam spread throughout most of the country. Turkish rule continued through the 19th century. However, during this period nationalistic feelings grew, and often erupted into open rebellion against the Turks.

In November 1912, the National Assembly proclaimed Albania's independence. However, Albania became a principal battleground during World War I (1914–18) and by the time the war ended,

LOCATION: 39°38′ to 42°39′N; 19°16′ to 21°4′E.
BOUNDARY LENGTHS: Yugoslavia, 476 kilometers (296 miles); Greece, 256 kilometers (159 miles); coastline, 472 kilometers (293 miles). **TERRITORIAL SEA LIMIT:** 15 miles.

portions of Albania were under Italian, French, and Yugoslav control. Albania again asserted its independence in 1920. A government was established, as the Italians and French withdrew.

In 1925, after a period of instability, Ahmet Zogu seized power. In 1928 he declared Albania a kingdom and crowned himself King Zog I. However, Italy invaded Albania in 1939, and Zog was forced into exile. Italy occupied Albania during WWII (1939–45), but Communist-led guerrillas under Enver Hoxha resisted Italian and German forces. With the defeat of the Italians and Germans in WWII, Hoxha established a new government based on communist principles.

Under Communist Rule

The constitution of 1946 declared Albania a people's republic. Over the following decades, Albania became more and more isolated from both the West and the other Communist countries. Albania allied itself first with the former USSR, and then with China. As the 1980s began, Albania was locked in a bitter internal conflict. Officials who favored increased relations with the West were executed or purged from the government. During this time, Albania was known as the most rigidly Communist country in Europe.

On 11 April 1985, Enver Hoxha died. He had ruled Albania with an iron fist for four decades. After his death, Albania took steps to end its isolation. In 1987, it established diplomatic relations with Canada, Spain, Bolivia, and the Federal Republic of Germany. However, Albania was still ruled by the Communists.

Democracy and Free Market

By 1990, internal unrest led to mass protests and calls for the government's resignation. After multiparty elections in 1991, a coalition government was formed between Albania's Communist (renamed Socialist) Party and the new Democratic Party. New general elections on 22 March 1992 gave the Democratic Party a majority of seats (92 of 140). Dr. Sali Berisha, a cardiologist, was elected president.

President Berisha pushed hard for radical reforms to create a market economy and democratic institutions. Government policies were directed at bringing Albania back into the international mainstream after half a century of isolation. By the end of 1993, barriers to foreign trade had been removed and relations with other nations had been strengthened.

13 GOVERNMENT

Albania is in the process of drafting a new constitution. Albania's government is still based on the 29 April 1991 Law on Constitutional Provisions. This law was enacted to provide a transition from a communist form of government to a democratic one. It established the principle of separation of powers, the protection of private property and human rights, a multi-party parliament, and a president of the republic with broad powers. Delays in drafting a new constitution caused a severe political crisis in the summer of 1993. The overwhelming defeat of a draft constitution in December 1994 continues to cloud Albania's future.

As of 1987, Albania was divided into 26 districts (rrethe), subdivided into 65 cities and towns, and 438 united villages.

14 POLITICAL PARTIES

In the elections held on 22 March 1992, some 18 parties participated: leading parties were the Democratic Party; the Socialist Party (the new name of the Communist Party); the Social Democratic Party; the Unity for Human Rights (Greek Minority) Party; and the Republican Party.

15 JUDICIAL SYSTEM

The judicial system includes district courts, a court of appeals, and a Court of Cassation. The district courts are trial level courts from which appeal can be taken to the court of appeals and then to the Court of Cassation. There is also a Constitutional Court that has authority over how the constitution is interpreted.

16 ARMED FORCES

As of 1993, the estimated strength of the Albanian armed forces was 42,000. This number includes 27,000 in the army, 2,000 in the navy, and 11,000 in the air force.

17 ECONOMY

With the end of Communist rule in 1992, farmland was returned to private ownership. But despite significant progress, living standards in Albania are among the lowest in Europe. When socialist-style central planning was abandoned, there was no alternate system to take its place. New economic systems are still being developed and the economy continues to falter.

Photo credit: AP/Wide World Photos

A five month old baby is held by his mother as they sit at the Kavaja Children's Hospital in Kavaja, Albania. Doctors at the hospital are trying to save the child, who suffers from malnutrition.

18 INCOME

Albania's gross national product (GDP) was $2.5 billion at current prices, or about $340 per person.

19 INDUSTRY

Production of major items in 1991 included cement, residual fuel oil, gasoline, kerosene, phosphate fertilizers, and cigarettes. Industrial production fell 44% in 1992 and 10% in 1993. The return of business to private ownership is proceeding slowly.

20 LABOR

Since communism was abandoned in favor of a free market economy in 1991, a temporary disruption of workers and resources has taken place, resulting in an estimated unemployment rate of 40% in 1992.

In 1991, workers were granted the legal right to create independent trade unions. All citizens have the right to organize and bargain collectively.

21 AGRICULTURE

In the late 1980s, about 55% of the working population was involved in agriculture (compared with 85% before World War II). After the government abandoned socialist-style central planning, the economy collapsed. Agricultural production recovered in 1992 due to the return of cooperative farms to private ownership.

Wheat is the principal crop. Corn, oats, sorghum, and potatoes are also important. Greater emphasis is being placed on the production of cash crops, including cotton, tobacco, rice, sugar beets, vegetables, sunflowers, and fruits and nuts.

22 DOMESTICATED ANIMALS

The major problem of Albanian animal husbandry has been a shortage of feed. In 1992, Albania had 1 million sheep; 5 million chickens and other poultry; 800,000 goats; 500,000 cattle; 170,000 hogs; and 100,000 horses.

23 FISHING

Fishing is an important occupation along the Adriatic coast. Annual fish production was estimated at 12,000 tons in 1991.

24 FORESTRY

In 1991, forests covered 1.05 million hectares (2.59 million acres), or about 38% of the total land area. The average annual output of sawn wood had been 200,000 cubic meters during the communist era, but climbed to 382,000 cubic meters in 1991.

25 MINING

In 1991, Albania remained an important mineral producer in spite of aging and inadequate machinery and environmental damage. Albania is the principal chrome-producing country in Europe (and the third largest in the world). Chrome ore production was 500,000 tons in 1991. Copper ore production in the same year was estimated at 6,100 tons, and mine output of nickel was 7,500 tons.

26 FOREIGN TRADE

Albania exports chromium ore, ferro-nickel ore, copper wires, electric power, food products, tobacco products, and handicrafts. Imports included raw materials, machinery, fuel, minerals, metals, and food.

Czechoslovakia took 15% of Albania's exports in 1990. Other major destinations were Germany, Italy, Bulgaria, the former Yugoslavia, Switzerland, and Hungary. The chief sources of Albania's imports

Selected Social Indicators

These statistics are estimates for the period 1988 to 1993. For comparison purposes, data for the United States and averages for low-income countries and high-income countries are also given.

Indicator	Albania	Low-income countries	High-income countries	United States
Per capita gross national product†	**$340**	$380	$23,680	$24,740
Population growth rate	**1.2%**	1.9%	0.6%	1.0%
Population growth rate in urban areas	**2.1%**	3.9%	0.8%	1.3%
Population per square kilometer of land	**116**	78	25	26
Life expectancy in years	**72**	62	77	76
Number of people per physician	**1,076**	>3,300	453	419
Number of pupils per teacher (primary school)	**19**	39	<18	20
Illiteracy rate (15 years and older)	**28%**	41%	<5%	<3%
Energy consumed per capita (kg of oil equivalent)	**455**	364	5,203	7,918

† The gross national product (GNP) is the total dollar value of all goods and services produced by a country in a year. The per capita GNP is calculated by dividing a country's GNP by its population. The World Bank defines low-income countries as those with a per capita GNP of $695 or less. High-income countries have a per capita GNP of $8,626 or more. Less than 14% of the world's 5.5 billion people live in high-income countries, while almost 60% live in low-income countries.   > = greater than   < = less than

Sources: World Bank, *Social Indicators of Development 1995,* Baltimore: Johns Hopkins University Press, 1995. Central Intelligence Agency, *World Fact Book,* Washington, D.C.: Government Printing Office, 1994.

were Germany (18%), Italy, Czechoslovakia, Bulgaria, China, and Austria.

27 ENERGY AND POWER

Albania has both thermal and hydroelectric power stations to generate electricity, but hydroelectric power is the more important of the two. Hydroelectric sources accounted for over 90% of the total production in 1991.

Petroleum production has become significant. Oil refineries are located at Ballësh, Fier, and Cërrik. In 1991, Albania also produced 170 million cubic meters of natural gas.

28 SOCIAL DEVELOPMENT

The Act on State Social Insurance provided benefits for disability, old age, survivors, and retirement. An old age pension is granted when the insured reaches a certain age, depending upon class of work and length of service.

Albania's constitution prohibits discrimination based on sex, and women make up roughly half the labor force.

29 HEALTH

In 1990, 92% of the population had access to health care. Total health expenditures for 1990 were $84 million. In 1992, average life expectancy was estimated at 72 years, compared to 38 years at the end of World War II.

30 HOUSING

At the time of the last census in 1986, 72% of Albania's housing units had a water supply, 67% had a bath or shower, 40% had central heating, and 60% had toilet facilities. The total housing stock in 1991 numbered 756,000 units.

31 EDUCATION

Albania's government claims that complete literacy has been achieved. However, Western estimates put the literacy rate at 72%. The basic compulsory school program extends for eight years (ages 7 to 15). Institutions of higher learning include the Institute of Sciences, Enver Hoxha University of Tiranë (formerly Tiranë State University), and the University of Shkodër.

32 MEDIA

In 1990, there were 6,000 telephones. Radiotelevizioni Shqiptar operates 14 radio stations. There were 9 television stations in 1991. In the same year, there were about 285,000 television sets and 577,000 radios.

As of 1992, there were four daily newspapers published in Tiranë. The two major ones were *Zëri i Popullit,* the Workers Party publication, with an estimated daily circulation of 105,000 and *Bashkimi Kombetar,* the Democratic Front's newspaper, with a circulation of 30,000.

33 TOURISM AND RECREATION

Formerly, Albania was the most inaccessible country in Eastern Europe. Since the advent of democracy, Albania has slowly become accessible to the outside world. Tourists are escorted by guides from Alb-turist, the official tourist agency. In 1990, 30,000 foreign tourists visited Albania.

The most popular sports are soccer, gymnastics, volleyball, and basketball.

34 FAMOUS ALBANIANS

Much Albanian popular lore is based on the exploits of the national hero Gjergj Kastrioti (known as Scanderbeg, 1405–68), who led his people against the Turks. Ahmet Bey Zogu (1895–1961) ascended the throne in 1928 as Zog I and fled the country in 1939. Enver Hoxha (1908–85) was postwar Albania's first premier.

Naim Erashëri (1846–1900) is Albania's national poet. Gjergj Fishta (1871–1940), a Franciscan friar who was active in the nationalist movement, wrote a long epic poem, *Lahuta e Malcís (The Lute of the Mountains),* which is regarded as a masterpiece of Albanian literature.

35 BIBLIOGRAPHY

Bland, William B. *Albania.* Santa Barbara, Calif.: Clio, 1988.

Doder, Dusko. "Albania Opens the Door." *National Geographic,* July 1992, 66–94.

Hall, Derek R. *Albania and the Albanians.* New York: St. Martin's Press, 1994.

Logoreci, Anton. *The Albanians: Europe's Forgotten Survivors.* Boulder, Colo.: Westview, 1978.

Pollo, Stefanay, and Arben Puto. *The History of Albania.* London: Routledge & Kegan Paul, 1981.

ALGERIA

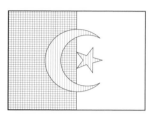

Democratic and Popular Republic of Algeria

Al-Jumhuriyah al-Jaza'iriyah ad-Dimuqratiyah ash-Sha'biyah

CAPITAL: Algiers (Alger).

FLAG: The national flag consists of two equal vertical stripes, one green and one white, with a red crescent enclosing a five-pointed red star in the center.

ANTHEM: *Kassaman (We Pledge).*

MONETARY UNIT: The Algerian dinar (DA) is a paper currency of 100 centimes. There are coins of 1, 2, 5, 10, and 50 centimes and 1, 5 and 10 dinars, and notes of 10, 20, 50, 100, and 200 dinars. DA1 = $0.0385 (or $1 = DA25.945).

WEIGHTS AND MEASURES: The metric system is the legal standard.

HOLIDAYS: New Year's Day, 1 January; Labor Day, 1 May; Overthrow of Ben Bella, 19 June; Independence Day, 5 July; Revolution Day, 1 November. Muslim religious holidays include 'Id al-Fitr, 'Id al-'Adha', 1st of Muharram (Muslim New Year), and Milad an-Nabi. Christians observe their own religious holidays.

TIME: GMT.

1 LOCATION AND SIZE

Situated in northwestern Africa along the Mediterranean Sea, Algeria is the second-largest country on the continent. Comparatively, it is slightly less than 3.5 times the size of Texas, with a total area of 2,381,740 square kilometers (919,595 square miles). Land boundary and claims disputes with Libya and Tunisia were unresolved as of late 1994.

Algeria's capital city, Algiers, is located on the northern boundary of the country along the Mediterranean Sea.

2 TOPOGRAPHY

The parallel mountain ranges of the Tell, or Maritime Atlas, and the Saharan Atlas divide Algeria into three basic zones running generally east–west: the Mediterranean zone or Tell; the High Plateaus, including the regions of Great and Small Kabilia; and the Sahara Desert, accounting for at least 80% of Algeria's total land area. The highest point is Mount Tahat (2,918 meters/9,573 feet), in the Ahaggar Range of the Sahara.

Only the main rivers of the Tell have water all year round, and even then the summer flow is small. None of the rivers is navigable. Northwestern Algeria is a seismologically active area. Earthquakes on 10 October 1980 in a rural area southwest of Algiers left over 2,500 persons dead and almost 100,000 homeless.

3 CLIMATE

Northern Algeria lies within the temperate zone, and its climate is similar to that of other Mediterranean countries, although the variety of the land provides sharp contrasts in temperature. The coastal region has a pleasant climate, with winter temperatures averaging from 10° to 12°C (50° to 54°F) and average summer temperatures ranging from 24° to 26°C (75° to 79°F). Farther inland, the climate changes. Winters average 4° to 6°C (39° to 43°F), with considerable frost and occasional snow on the mountains; summers average 26° to 28°C (79° to 82°F). In the Sahara Desert, temperatures range from −10° to 34°C (14° to 93°F), with extreme highs of 49°C (120°F). There are daily variations of more than 44 degrees Celsius (80 degrees Fahrenheit). Winds are frequent and violent and rainfall is irregular and unevenly distributed.

4 PLANTS AND ANIMALS

Native trees of northern Algeria include the olive and the cork oak. The mountain regions contain large forests of evergreens and some deciduous trees. The forests are inhabited by boars and jackals. They are about all that remain of the many wild animals that were once common. Fig, eucalyptus, agave, and various palm trees grow in the warmer areas.

Vegetation in the Sahara is thin and widely scattered. Animal life is varied but scarce. Camels are used extensively. Other mammals are jackals and rabbits. The desert also abounds with poisonous and nonpoisonous snakes, scorpions, and numerous insects.

5 ENVIRONMENT

Algeria's main environmental problem is the spreading of the desert into the fertile northern section of the country. To slow desertification, the government in 1975 began to erect a "green wall" of trees and vegetation, 1,500 kilometers (930 miles) long and 20 kilometers (12 miles) wide, along the northern fringes of the Sahara. This project costs about $100 million each year.

Other environmental problems include water shortages and pollution. The small amount of water available in Algeria is threatened by regular droughts. The problem is further complicated by lack of sewage control and pollution from the oil industry.

Of the 97 species of mammals, 12 are endangered. Fifteen species of birds are also threatened. One hundred and forty-five of the 3,139 plant species in Africa were endangered as of 1994.

6 POPULATION

The 1987 census listed the population of Algeria at 23,038,942, while the estimated population in 1994 was 27,989,792. The projected population for the year 2000 is 32,693,000. The population is concentrated in the cultivated areas of the north (over 90% in the northern eighth of the country) and thinly distributed in the plateau and desert regions. In 1992, greater Algiers had about 3,033,000 people.

7 MIGRATION

In 1962, some 180,000 Algerian refugees returned from Tunisia and Morocco. After independence was declared that July, about 650,000 French Algerians and more than 200,000 harkis (Algerian Muslims who fought on the French side during the

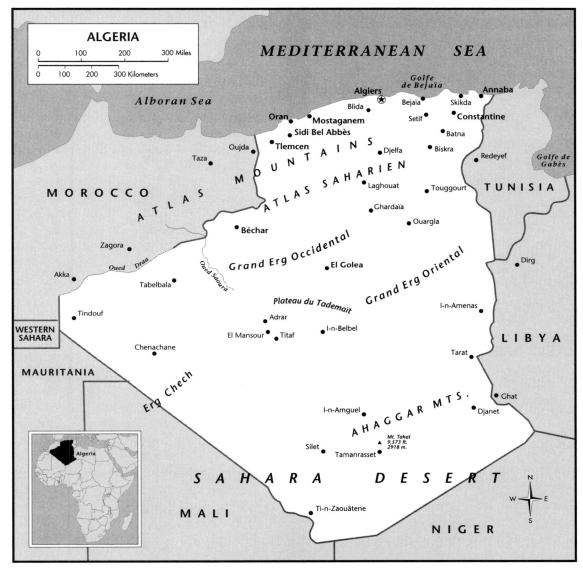

ALGERIA

0	100	200	300 Miles
0	100	200	300 Kilometers

MEDITERRANEAN SEA

Alboran Sea

Golfe de Bejaïa

Algiers ✪
Blida
Oran
Mostaganem
Sidi Bel Abbès
Bejaïa
Skikda
Annaba
Constantine
Setif
Batna

Oujda
Tlemcen
Taza
Djelfa
Biskra
Redeyef
Golfe de Gabès

ATLAS MOUNTAINS

ATLAS SAHARIEN

Laghouat
Touggourt
TUNISIA

Ghardaïa

Ouargla

Béchar

Zagora

Oued Draa
Akka

Oued Saoura

Grand Erg Occidental

El Golea

Grand Erg Oriental

Dirg

Tabelbala

Plateau du Tademaït

I-n-Amenas

Tindouf

WESTERN
SAHARA

Adrar
El Mansour
Titaf
I-n-Belbel

LIBYA

Chenachane

Tarat

MAURITANIA

Erg Chech

Ghat

I-n-Amguel

AHAGGAR MTS.

Djanet

Silet

Mt. Tahat
9,573 ft.
2918 m.

Tamanrasset

SAHARA DESERT

N
W E
S

MALI

Ti-n-Zaouâtene

NIGER

Inset: Algeria location in Africa

MOROCCO

LOCATION: 18°57′ to 37°5′N; 8°44′w to 12°E. **BOUNDARY LENGTHS:** Mediterranean coastline, 1,104 kilometers (686 miles); Tunisia, 958 kilometers (595 miles); Libya, 982 kilometers (610 miles); Niger, 956 kilometers (594 miles); Mali, 1,376 kilometers (855 miles); Mauritania, 463 kilometers (288 miles); Morocco, 1,637 kilometers (1,017 miles). **TERRITORIAL SEA LIMIT:** 12 miles.

war of independence and chose to retain French citizenship) moved to France. As a result of war in the Western Sahara, about 150,000 Sahrawi refugees fled to Algeria. There were 165,000 at the end of 1992, when Algeria was also harboring 50,000 people from Mali and Niger who had sought refuge in southern Algeria.

A vast majority of Algerians follow the Muslim faith in mosques such as this.

8 ETHNIC GROUPS

Apart from about 1 million Europeans, who immigrated or were descended from immigrants who had come since 1830, and about 140,000 Jews, the population before independence was made up almost entirely of Muslims.

9 LANGUAGES

The sole official and majority language is Arabic, with many variations and dialects, but many Algerians also speak French. "Arabization" has been encouraged by the government.

10 RELIGIONS

About 99% of the population adheres to the Muslim religion, or Islam. In 1993 there were 27,000 Roman Catholics and small Protestant and Jewish communities.

11 TRANSPORTATION

In 1991, Algeria's nationally owned railroad had about 4,146 kilometers (2,576 miles) of track. The system consists of a main east–west line linked with the railways of Tunisia and Morocco. It also links with lines serving the mining regions of Béchar (formerly Colomb Béchar); the High Plateaus; the date-producing areas of Biskra, Touggourt, and Tebessa; and the main port cities.

In 1991, there were 80,000 kilometers (49,712 miles) of roads, of which about 75% were paved, used by 760,000 passenger cars and 510,000 commercial vehicles. The French colonial government built a good road system, partly for military purposes, which after independence was not well maintained. However, new roads have been built linking the Sahara oil fields with the coast. Algeria's portion of the trans-Saharan highway, formally known as the Road of African Unity, stretches about 420 kilometers (260 miles) from Hassi Marroket to the Niger border south of Tamanrasset. It was completed in 1985.

Algiers is the principal seaport. Algeria's merchant fleet numbered 67 ships totaling 858,000 gross registered tons as of 1 January 1992.

An extensive air service uses 124 airports and airstrips. The main international airport is about 20 kilometers (12 miles) from Algiers. Air Algérie, the national airline, provides international service, and carried 3,551,100 people in 1992.

12 HISTORY

Before the period of recorded history, the North African coastal area now known as Algeria was inhabited by Berber tribal groups, from whom many present-day Algerians are descended. Phoenician sailors established coastal settlements. After the 8th century BC, the territory was controlled by Carthage, the largest Phoenician settlement. Roman dominance dates from the fall of Carthage in 146 BC. Completely annexed in AD 40, the region (known as Numidia) became a center of Roman culture. Christianity flourished, as did agriculture and commerce. Despite the prosperity of the Roman cities and the cereal-growing countryside, there were frequent Berber revolts. The Roman influence gradually declined, especially after the Vandal invasion of 430–31. The Byzantine Empire conquered eastern Numidia in the 6th century.

After the Arab conquest began in 637, the area was known as Al-Maghrib al-Awsat, or the Middle West. Arabs from the east attacked in the 11th century. The Almoravid dynasty from Morocco also took possession of part of the region during this period. They were followed by Almohads a century later. Although these and other dynasties and individuals united the territory and consolidated it with Morocco and Spain, local rulers retained considerable power.

Photo credit: Gordon Barbery

A stone head found in a Roman ruin. The region that is now Algeria was an important center of Roman culture.

Spain conquered part of the coast in the early 16th century, and Algerians asked the aid of 'Aruj, known as Barbarossa, a Turkish pirate. He expelled the Spaniards from some of their coastal footholds, made himself sultan, and conquered additional territory. Spain held a small area around Oran until 1708 and controlled it again from 1732 to 1791.

Algiers became increasingly independent and, joining with other states along the coast, thrived on piracy. At this time, it had diplomatic and trade relations with many European countries, including France. But with the defeat (though not suppression) of the pirates by US and European fleets during 1815–16, and with the growing European interest in acquiring overseas colonies, Algiers was seen as a possible addition to either the British or the French empire. In 1830, the French took over the principal ports, gained control of the northern regions, and set up a system of fortified posts. Thereafter, revolts often broke out, notably the guerrilla war from 1830 to 1847, led by the legendary hero, Abd al-Qader, and the Kabyle rebellion in 1871. Other sections, however, remained independent of France until the first decade of the 20th century.

Al-Jazair, as it was called in Arabic, became, in French, Algérie, a name that France applied to the territory for the first time in 1839. In 1848, northern Algeria was proclaimed a part of France and was organized into three provinces. Following the Franco-Prussian War of 1870–71, large numbers of French colonizers settled the most fertile lands, as did other Europeans at the invitation of France. Muslims had no political rights except for limited participation in local financial decisions.

Following World War I, France took the first steps toward making all Algeria an integral part of France. In 1919, voting rights were given to a few Muslims, based on education and military service qualifications. (French citizenship had previously been open to Muslims who renounced their religious status.)

During World War II, in exchange for loyalty to France, many Muslims hoped

Abd al–Qader, a political leader and marabout (a member of a Muslim religious order believed to have supernatural powers), led the Muslim resistance against the French during the 1840s.

for increased rights, and moderates believed that France might be persuaded to grant Algeria a separate status while retaining close diplomatic, economic, and defense ties. In 1957, all Muslims became French subjects, but about 9 million Muslims and 500,000 Europeans voted in separate elections for a joint assembly.

Meanwhile, younger nationalists had formed what would become known as the National Liberation Front (Front de Libération Nationale—FLN), and a guerrilla war was launched on 1 November

1954. The FLN's National Liberation Army (Armée de Libération Nationale—ALN) carried out acts of terrorism and sabotage throughout Algeria and gained increasing mass support. Eventually, France was forced to maintain at least 450,000 troops in Algeria. During more than seven years of civil war, well over 100,000 Muslim guerrillas and civilians and 10,000 French soldiers lost their lives.

The war in Algeria toppled several French governments before causing the downfall of the Fourth Republic in May 1958. General Charles de Gaulle was then brought to power by French rightists and military groups in Algeria. To their surprise, however, he pursued a policy of preparing for Algerian independence. He offered self-determination to Algeria in September 1958. Independence was formally proclaimed on 3 July 1962, despite a program of counterterrorism by the French Secret Army Organization operating in Algeria.

With independence achieved, a seven-man Political Bureau, set up as the policy-making body of the FLN, took over control of the country on 5 August 1962. Ahmed Ben Bella became the first premier, and Ferhat Abbas was chosen speaker of the Assembly. The Assembly adopted a constitution, which was endorsed in September 1963.

Elected president in October, Ben Bella began to nationalize foreign-owned land and industry. Opposition to his authoritarian leadership led to an outbreak of armed revolts in the Kabilia and Biskra areas in July 1964 and to open attacks by leading political figures. On 19 June 1965, the Ben Bella government was overthrown in a bloodless takeover directed by Colonel Houari Boumedienne, first deputy premier and defense minister. The 1963 constitution was suspended, and a revolutionary council headed by Boumedienne took power.

The new government shifted to a more gradual approach to national development, with deliberate economic planning and an emphasis on financial stability. During the 1970s, the council nationalized the oil industry and initiated farm reforms. Boumedienne was officially elected president in December 1976 but died two years later.

The FLN Central Committee, with strong army backing, chose Colonel Chadli Bendjedid as the party's leader, and he became president on 7 February 1979. After a period of transition, the Bendjedid government moved toward more moderate policies, expanding powers for the provinces and state enterprises and attempting to breathe new life into the FLN and government agencies.

Serious internal trouble developed in 1988 when young Algerians rioted over high prices, unemployment, and the dictatorship of an aging and corrupt revolutionary government. Shocked by the 500 deaths in the streets, Bendjedid moved to liberalize his government. New political parties were allowed to form outside the FLN. In addition, the prime minister and cabinet were made responsible to the National Assembly.

Burdened by heavy debts and low oil prices, Bendjedid was forced to follow tight economic policies and to abandon socialism for the free market—actions which further inflamed his opposition, now led by the Islamic Salvation Front (FIS). In 1989, the FIS won 55% of urban election seats while the FLN maintained power in the countryside. Elections to the National Assembly, postponed six months, were held in December 1991 under relatively free conditions. FIS candidates won 188 out of 231 contested seats, needing only 28 more places in a second vote to control the 430-member Assembly. The FLN won only 16 seats.

The army, disappointed with the election results, arrested FIS leaders and postponed the second stage vote indefinitely. Bendjedid resigned under pressure from the army and Mohammed Boudiaf, a hero of the revolution, returned from exile to lead the High State Council which the army established. A harsh crackdown on Islamists began. The FIS was banned and its local councils were closed. As acts of terrorism continued by both sides in 1992 and 1993, the regime declared a state of emergency, set up special security courts, and arrested more than 5,000 persons. Boudiaf was assassinated in June 1992 to be replaced by Ali Kafi with Redha Malek as Prime Minister in August 1993. In January 1994, Defense Minister Liamine Zeroual was named President and the five-man presidential council was abolished.

During this period, Islamic militants carried out threats against intellectuals and foreigners (30 killed by April 1994).

Security forces responded with overwhelming force and harsh treatment and reportedly employed death squads against Muslim militants. An average of 11 persons a day were being killed in early 1994. Many observers fear a prolonged civil war in Algeria.

13 GOVERNMENT

The constitution of 1976, as subsequently amended, provides for a strong executive branch headed by a president who is nominated as the sole candidate by the FLN (National Liberation Front) congress and elected for a five-year term. The president appoints the prime minister and cabinet ministers. Until 1992, the highly centralized government was guided in policy matters by the Political Bureau of the FLN's Central Committee. Since 1992, the army has exercised real power behind the appointed High State Council and, in 1994, the president.

The legislative body is the National Assembly, whose 430 deputies are elected to five-year terms.

14 POLITICAL PARTIES

In September 1989 the government approved a multiparty system. By December 1990, over 30 legal political parties existed, including Islamic Salvation Front (FIS), National Liberation Front (FLN), and Socialist Forces Front (FFS).

15 JUDICIAL SYSTEM

The judicial system now includes civil, military, and antiterrorist courts. Within each wilayat (district) is a court for civil and some criminal cases. At the head of

Photo: Gordon Barbery, San Francisco, CA.

A view of the main marketplace of an Algerian city.

the system is the Supreme Court. A special Court of State Security tries all cases involving political offenses.

Algeria's present legal codes, adopted in 1963, are based on the laws of Islam and of other Northern African and Socialist states, as well as on French laws.

16 ARMED FORCES

Six months' military service is compulsory for males. Algeria's armed forces in 1993 totaled 139,000 members. The army had 120,000 officers and men, plus reserves of up to 150,000. Weaponry included 960 main battle tanks. The navy had 7,000 men. Vessels included 2 submarines, 3 frigates, 3 corvettes (both frigates and cor-

vettes are types of warships), and 11 missile patrol craft. The air force had 12,000 men, about 242 combat aircraft, and 58 combat helicopters.

17 ECONOMY

Although almost 25% of Algerians make their living directly from the soil, agriculture produced less than 15% of Algeria's gross domestic product (GDP) in 1990. Saharan oil and natural gas have been important export items since 1959, and they now dominate Algeria's economy, accounting for over 95% of total export value and over 25% of gross domestic product.

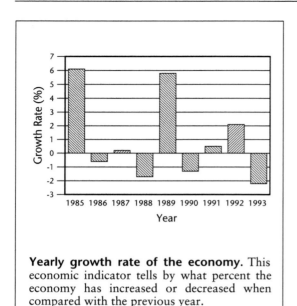

Yearly growth rate of the economy. This economic indicator tells by what percent the economy has increased or decreased when compared with the previous year.

[18] INCOME

In 1992 Algeria's gross national product (GNP) was $48,326 million at current prices, or $1,780 per person.

[19] INDUSTRY

Industries, which are concentrated around Algiers and Oran, include carpet mills, cement factories, chemical plants, automobile assembly plants, food-processing plants, oil refineries, soap factories, and textile plants. Other major industries produce bricks and tiles, rolled steel, farm machinery, electrical supplies, machine tools, phosphates, sulfuric acid, paper and cartons, matches, and tobacco products.

In 1989, industrial production (in tons) included cement, 6,519,000; pig iron, 1,478,000; crude steel, 1,041,000; and phosphate fertilizers, 193,000. Liquid petroleum gas (LPG) production totaled 4.4 million tons in 1992.

[20] LABOR

The minimum age for employment is 16 years. Work inspectors, who report to the Ministry of Labor, are responsible for enforcing the minimum employment age by making inspection visits to work sites. However, many children under the age of 16 are forced into poverty by informal types of employment, such as street vending. Young workers are allowed to work the same hours as regular adult workers.

[21] AGRICULTURE

Although almost 25% of the population is engaged in agriculture (including subsistence farming), only 3% of Algeria's land is cultivated. The soil is poor and subject to erosion. In addition, the water supply is generally irregular and insufficient. About one-quarter of northern Algeria is completely unproductive. Agriculture contributed 15% to gross domestic product in 1992, up from 10.7% in 1985.

Estimated agricultural output in 1992 included 1,750,000 tons of wheat, 1,370,000 tons of barley, 900,000 tons of potatoes, 500,000 tons of tomatoes, 300,000 tons of citrus fruits, 260,000 tons of grapes, and 210,000 tons of wine.

[22] DOMESTICATED ANIMALS

About half of the livestock is owned by only 5% of the herdsmen. In 1992, there were an estimated 18,600,000 sheep, 2,500,000 goats, 1,420,000 head of cattle,

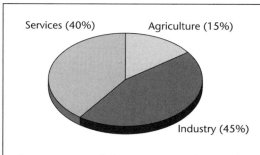

Services (40%)   Agriculture (15%)

Industry (45%)

Components of the economy. This pie chart shows how much of the country's economy is devoted to agriculture (includes forestry, hunting, and fishing), industry, or services.

340,000 donkeys, 130,000 camels, 107,000 mules, and 84,000 horses. There were also 76 million chickens. Algeria has a serious shortage of milk, meat, and cheese and must therefore rely on imports.

23 FISHING

Fishing is fairly extensive along the coast, but the industry is relatively undeveloped. Sardines, bogue, mackerel, anchovies, and shellfish are caught. The 1991 catch was estimated at 80,115 tons.

24 FORESTRY

Less than 2% of the land is forested. The mountain ranges contain dense forests of evergreens (evergreen oak, Aleppo pine, and cedar) and deciduous trees (trees that shed their leaves seasonally), whereas the warmer regions contain large numbers of fruit and palm trees. Algeria is an important producer of cork. Other forestry products are firewood, charcoal, and wood for industrial use. Roundwood pro-

duction was estimated at 2,221,000 cubic meters in 1991.

25 MINING

Algeria's phosphate deposits at Djebel Onk, in the northeast, are among the largest in the world, covering about 800 square miles (2,100 square kilometers) with an output of 1,090,000 tons in 1991. Other mineral production in 1991 included zinc ore, 2,610 tons; bentonite, 25,803 tons; and lead concentrates, 900 tons. Silver, mercury, kaolin, barites, sulfur, fuller's earth, and salt are also mined.

26 FOREIGN TRADE

Crude oil and natural gas account for nearly all of Algeria's export value. Industrial equipment and semifinished goods and foodstuffs dominate the country's imports. In 1986, because of a severe drop in oil prices, exports declined and Algeria experienced a trade deficit for the first time since 1978. It was the largest ever. With continued government control over the level of imports, Algeria was able to register trade surpluses in the following years. The majority of Algerian exports go to Italy, France, the US, Germany, and Spain.

27 ENERGY AND POWER

Natural gas and petroleum dominate the economy. In 1992, their exports were valued at $8.2 billion, or 97% of total exports.

Installed electrical generating capacity in 1991 totaled 5,369,000 kilowatts. Power production was 17,345 million

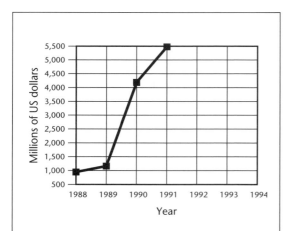

5,500
5,000
4,500
4,000
3,500
3,000
2,500
2,000
1,500
1,000
500

Millions of US dollars

1988 1989 1990 1991 1992 1993 1994

Year

Yearly balance of trade measured in millions of US dollars. The balance of trade is the difference between what a country sells to other countries (its exports) and what it buys (its imports). If a country imports more than it exports, it has a negative balance of trade (a trade deficit). If exports exceed imports, there is a positive balance of trade (a trade surplus).

kilowatt hours, of which only 1.7% was hydroelectric.

28 SOCIAL DEVELOPMENT

Since the early 1960s, the government has repeatedly proposed a family code, based on Islamic principles, that would treat any woman as a legal minor for life, under the authority of her father, husband, or other male head of the family. In part because of opposition by the National Union of Algerian Women, the proposed code was withdrawn by the Council of Ministers after it had been submitted to the National Assembly in early 1982. A compromise code was passed in 1984 that did not fully address the objections of women's groups.

29 HEALTH

The principal health problems have been tuberculosis, malaria, trachoma, and malnutrition. By 1990, the incidence of tuberculosis was 53 in 100,000. In 1992, the average life expectancy was 66 years, with a death rate of 7 per 1,000 people. Infant mortality in 1992 was 60 per 1,000 live births, with 901,000 births that same year. Free medical care was introduced in 1974 under a Social Security system, which reimburses 80% of private consultations and prescription drugs.

30 HOUSING

The need for adequate housing is a serious problem for Algeria. The average number of persons per dwelling was 6.9 in 1987, compared to 5.9 in 1966.

31 EDUCATION

Education is officially compulsory for children between the ages of 6 and 15. Adult literacy stood at 57.8% in 1990 (males, 69.8% and females, 45.5%). In 1991–1992 there were a total of 48,953 teachers and 831,798 students in schools. In 1991 there were 10 universities along with 5 centers, 7 colleges, and 5 institutes for higher learning. The University of Algiers (founded in 1909) and other regional universities enrolled about 300,000 students in 1988.

32 MEDIA

On 30 September 1964, the Algerian Press Service (established in 1961) was given a monopoly over the distribution of news items within Algeria. Until then, foreign press agencies were permitted to distribute

Selected Social Indicators

These statistics are estimates for the period 1988 to 1993. For comparison purposes, data for the United States and averages for low-income countries and high-income countries are also given.

Indicator	Algeria	Low-income countries	High-income countries	United States
Per capita gross national product†	**$1,780**	$380	$23,680	$24,740
Population growth rate	**2.4%**	1.9%	0.6%	1.0%
Population growth rate in urban areas	**3.9%**	3.9%	0.8%	1.3%
Population per square kilometer of land	**11**	78	25	26
Life expectancy in years	**66**	62	77	76
Number of people per physician	**2,322**	>3,300	453	419
Number of pupils per teacher (primary school)	**27**	39	<18	20
Illiteracy rate (15 years and older)	**43%**	41%	<5%	<3%
Energy consumed per capita (kg of oil equivalent)	**955**	364	5,203	7,918

† The gross national product (GNP) is the total dollar value of all goods and services produced by a country in a year. The per capita GNP is calculated by dividing a country's GNP by its population. The World Bank defines low-income countries as those with a per capita GNP of $695 or less. High-income countries have a per capita GNP of $8,626 or more. Less than 14% of the world's 5.5 billion people live in high-income countries, while almost 60% live in low-income countries.

n.a. = data not available   > = greater than   < = less than

Sources: World Bank, *Social Indicators of Development 1995,* Baltimore: Johns Hopkins University Press, 1995. Central Intelligence Agency, *World Fact Book,* Washington, D.C.: Government Printing Office, 1994.

information directly to their Algerian clients. Six daily newspapers (all with FLN orientation) were in circulation in 1991, the largest being Al-Mujahid, with a circulation of 280,000. In 1990 there were 48 periodicals.

In 1991, Algeria had Arabic and French radio networks. There were a total of 26 AM stations. In addition, 18 television stations were operated by the national television network. There were some 6 million radios and 1.9 million television sets in use. The total number of telephones numbered 1,050,951.

33 TOURISM AND RECREATION

Among popular tourist attractions are the Casbah and Court of the Great Mosque in Algiers, as well as the excellent Mediterranean beaches, Atlas Mountains resorts, and tours of the Sahara Desert. The government has encouraged tourism as an increasingly important source of income. In 1991, there were 1,193,210 visitor arrivals, 43% from Africa and 13% from Europe.

The most popular Algerian sport is soccer, which is played throughout the country by professionals and amateurs alike. Tennis is widely played as well.

34 FAMOUS ALGERIANS

The most famous Algerian of ancient times was St. Augustine (Aurelius Augustinus, 354–430), a Church father who was born in eastern Numidia.

Abd al-Qader (1807–83) was an Algerian political leader and marabout (a person thought to have supernatural powers) who led the Muslim resistance against French imperialism in central and western Algeria during the second quarter of the 19th century. Other important nationalist leaders include Messali Hadj (1898?–1974), who organized several political movements, and Ferhat Abbas (1900–86), who led the first provisional government and was elected first speaker of the National Assembly in 1962. Ahmed Ben Bella (b. 1916) was a founder of the FLN and the first premier of independent Algeria.

The renowned French Algerian novelist, playwright, and essayist Albert Camus (1913–60) won the Nobel Prize for literature in 1957. Frantz Fanon (b. Martinique, 1925–61), a psychiatrist, writer, and revolutionary, was a leading critic of colonialism.

35 BIBLIOGRAPHY

Brill, M. *Algeria*. Chicago: Children's Press, 1990.

Entelis, John P. *Algeria*. Boulder, Colo.: Westview, 1985.

Fanon, Frantz. *The Wretched of the Earth*. New York: Grove Press, 1966 (orig. 1961).

Heggoy, Alf A., and Robert R. Crout. *Historical Dictionary of Algeria*. Metuchen, N.J.: Scarecrow, 1981.

Ruedy, John (John Douglas). *Modern Algeria: the Origins and Development of a Nation*. Bloomington: Indiana University Press, 1992.

ANDORRA

Principality of Andorra

Principat d'Andorra

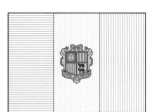

CAPITAL: Andorra la Vella.

FLAG: The national flag is a tricolor of blue, yellow, and red vertical stripes. On the state flag (shown here) the yellow stripe bears the coat of arms.

ANTHEM: The *Himne Andorra* begins "El gran Carlemany mon pare" ("Great Charlemagne my father").

MONETARY UNIT: Andorra has no currency of its own; both the Spanish peseta (P) and the French franc (Fr) are used. P1 = $0.0073 (or $1 = P137.38); Fr1 = $0.1751 (or $1 = Fr5.71).

WEIGHTS AND MEASURES: The metric system and some old local standards are used.

HOLIDAYS: New Year's Day, 1 January; National Festival, 8 September; Christmas, 25 December. Movable religious holidays include Good Friday and Easter Monday.

TIME: 1 PM = noon GMT.

1 LOCATION AND SIZE

Landlocked Andorra lies on the southern slopes of the Pyrenees, with a total boundary length of 125 kilometers (77.7 miles). It is slightly more than 2.5 times the size of Washington, D.C., with a total area of 450 square kilometers (174 square miles).

Andorra's capital city, Andorra la Vella, is located in the southwestern part of the country.

2 TOPOGRAPHY

Most of the country is rough and mountainous. The highest point is Coma Pedrosa (2,946 meters/9,665 feet).

3 CLIMATE

Because of its high elevation, Andorra has severe winters. The northern valleys are completely snowed up for several months. Most rain falls in April and October. Summers are warm or mild, depending on the altitude. There are wide variations between the maximum day and night temperatures.

4 PLANTS AND ANIMALS

The plant and animal life is similar to that found in neighboring parts of France and Spain. Chestnut and walnut trees grow in the area around Sant Julía de Lòria. Elsewhere, evergreen oaks are common. Higher regions have pines and firs. At the highest altitudes there are no trees. There are carnations, violets, bellflowers, and daisies, as well as blackberries, wild strawberries, and moss. Bears, wolves, foxes, rabbits, hares, eagles, vultures, wild ducks, and geese may be found in some areas.

Photo credit: Anne Kalosh

An Andorran policewoman directs city traffic.

5 ENVIRONMENT

Andorra was once heavily forested, but the forested area has been decreasing steadily. Overgrazing of mountain meadows by sheep, causing soil erosion, is another environmental problem.

6 POPULATION

The population in 1990 was 54,507, with a density of 117 persons per square kilometers (302 persons per square miles). The population is concentrated in the seven urbanized valleys that form Andorra's political districts. Andorran citizens are outnumbered three-to-one by other ethnic groups, the majority of whom are of Spanish decent. The capital, Andorra la Vella, had a population of 20,437 in 1990.

7 MIGRATION

Immigration consists mainly of Spanish, Portuguese, and French people who intend to work in Andorra. Living in Andorra in 1990 were 27,066 Spanish and 4,130 French immigrants, who together made up 57% of the resident population.

8 ETHNIC GROUPS

Andorrans, who made up 29% of the population in 1990, are of Catalan descent. The remainder of the population is mostly Spanish (53.6%) and French (6.5%).

9 LANGUAGES

The official language is Catalan. French and Spanish are also spoken.

10 RELIGIONS

Over 92% of all Andorrans are Roman Catholic. There are also small populations of Protestants (0.5%) and Jews (0.4%).

11 TRANSPORTATION

A north-south highway links Andorra la Vella with the Spanish and French borders. There are over 100 kilometers (60 miles) of surfaced roads and, as of 1992, 41,321 motor vehicles. Among several cable cars, the most important operates between Encamp and Engolasters Lake. Most merchandise is transported by vehicles from neighboring countries.

Andorra does not have railways or commercial airports. The nearest international airports are at Barcelona, Spain, and at Toulouse, France.

12 HISTORY

According to one tradition, Charlemagne gave the region the name Andorra for its supposed likeness to the biblical town of Endor. Tradition also asserts that Charlemagne granted the Andorran people a charter in return for their help in fighting the Moors, and that Charlemagne's son Louis I, king of France, confirmed the charter.

It is generally agreed that Charles the Bald, the son of Louis, appointed the count of Urgel overlord of Andorra and gave him the right to collect the imperial tribute. The bishop of Urgel, however, also claimed Andorra as part of the endowment of his cathedral. In 1226, the lords of the countship of Foix, in present-day south-central France, by marriage became heirs to the counts of Urgel. The quarrels between the Spanish bishop and the French counts over rights in Andorra led in 1278 to their adoption of a pareage, a feudal institution recognizing equal rights of two lords to a seigniorage.

Joint rule continued until 1793, when the French revolutionary government renounced its claim to Andorra, despite the wish of the Andorrans to enjoy French protection and avoid being under only Spanish influence. Napoleon restored joint rule in 1806 after the Andorrans asked him to do so. French rule of Andorra later passed from the kings to the president of France.

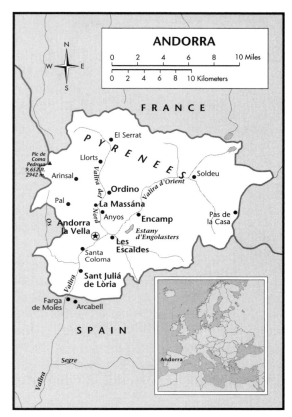

LOCATION: 42°25′ to 42°40′N; 1°25′E. **BOUNDARY LENGTHS:** France, 60 kilometers (37.3 miles); Spain, 65 kilometers (40.4 miles).

Long an impoverished land having little contact with any nations other than adjoining France and Spain, Andorra after World War II achieved prosperity through tourism. It formally became a parliamentary democracy in May 1993.

Its new constitution retained the French and Spanish co-princes, although with reduced powers. Civil rights were greatly expanded including the legalization of political parties and trade unions. Andorra was admitted to the UN on 28 July 1993.

13 GOVERNMENT

The governmental system of Andorra is unique. Authority is shared equally by the president of France and the (Spanish) bishop of Urgel as co-princes. Legislation is enacted by the General Council, consisting of 28 members.

The current President of the Council is Oscar Ribas Reig (the first elected head of government of Andorra), who was elected in December 1993.

14 POLITICAL PARTIES

Prior to 1993, political parties were illegal in Andorra. In the general election of December 1993, five parties won seats in the 28-seat General Council: the National Democratic Grouping (AND); the Liberal Union (UL); the New Democracy (ND); the National Andorran Coalition (CNA), and the National Democratic Initiative (IDN).

15 JUDICIAL SYSTEM

A Superior Council of Justice oversees and administers the judicial system. Appeals from lower courts are decided by a separate Supreme Court. Other details of the new court system have not yet been worked out. The current system provides a hearing for civil and criminal cases, with different appeals systems for each. Sentenced criminals have the choice of French or Spanish jails.

16 ARMED FORCES

France and Spain are pledged to defend Andorra, which has no defense force.

17 ECONOMY

The Andorran economy is primarily based on trade and tourism, with the traffic between France and Spain providing most of the revenue. Andorra is also a tax haven because there are no direct taxes, and there is an active trade in consumer goods because they are duty-free in Andorra.

18 INCOME

In 1992, Andorra's gross national product was $760 million at current prices, or $14,000 per person.

19 INDUSTRY

Andorran industry produces cigars, cigarettes, textiles, leather, building materials, and furniture. There are also distilleries for the production of anisette, vermouth, liqueurs, and brandy. Several firms manufacture woolen goods.

20 LABOR

Commerce employs about 24% of the working population (estimated at around 20,000 in the early 1990s); restaurants and hotels, 19%; manufacturing, 11%; construction, 12%; public administration, 10%; business services, 5%; agriculture, 1%, and other sectors, 18%. Trade unions are not permitted.

21 AGRICULTURE

In spite of Andorra's mountainous landscape, agriculture was the mainstay of the economy until the growth of tourism. Tobacco, the most distinctive Andorran crop, is grown on the best lands. Other farm products include food grains, potatoes, and garden vegetables.

22 DOMESTICATED ANIMALS

For many centuries sheep raising was the basis of Andorra's economy. Livestock includes an estimated 9,000 sheep, 1,100 cattle, and 200 horses. Meat production has increased in recent years, but imports account for about 90% of total meat consumption.

23 FISHING

The streams are full of trout and other freshwater fish, but Andorra imports most fish for domestic consumption from Spain.

24 FORESTRY

Less than one-fourth of the total area is forested. Wood needed for building purposes is cut in rotation from a different district each year.

25 MINING

In addition to iron, small amounts of lead are still mined, as well as alum and building stones.

26 FOREIGN TRADE

Owing to the large traffic in smuggled goods across Andorra's borders, official statistics do not reflect the true volume of transactions. Of recorded trade, close to half is with France and one-third with Spain. The majority of imports consists of consumer goods sold to visitors.

27 ENERGY AND POWER

Hydroelectric power provides about 40% of Andorra's electric power needs. Energy production totaled 140 million kilowatt hours in 1991.

Photo credit: Anne Kalosh

A view of an Andorran city tucked between the mountains.

28 SOCIAL DEVELOPMENT

There is a social welfare system, expanded in 1968 to cover the entire population. Women have only enjoyed full suffrage (the right to vote) since 1970.

29 HEALTH

In 1981, there were 42 doctors and 113 hospital beds. Life expectancy was estimated at 77 years in 1992.

30 HOUSING

Most Andorran houses are made of stone. Because the flat land is used for farm crops, the rural houses are frequently built against the mountainsides.

31 EDUCATION

Education is provided by both French- and Spanish-language schools. A total of 9,024 students attended the 18 schools in Andorra in 1991. In the 1990/91 academic year, 1,861 students were enrolled at pre-schools, 5,584 at primary schools and 1,579 at secondary, technical and special schools. About 50% of Andorran children attend French primary schools, and the rest attend Spanish or Andorran schools.

High school graduates who continue their education attend schools in France or Spain. Just about the entire adult population is literate.

32 MEDIA

In 1990, there were 17,700 telephones. Radio programming, formerly broadcast over French- and Spanish-owned stations, is now run by Andorrans. Television transmission is provided by agreements with Spanish and French networks. In 1991, there were an estimated 10,000 radios and 7,000 television sets.

Andorra's main newspaper, the weekly *Poble Andorra,* had a circulation of 3,000 in 1992. Other newspapers are the dailies *Diari D'Anderra, Independent,* and *Informacions Diari,* and the weeklies *Cerreu Andorra* and *Informacions.* French and Spanish newspapers are also widely read.

33 TOURISM AND RECREATION

Tourism has brought considerable prosperity to Andorra and now constitutes the principal source of income. Visitors, mostly from France and Spain, come to Andorra each summer to attend the fairs and festivals, to buy consumer items at lower prices than are obtainable in the neighboring countries, and to enjoy the pleasant weather and beautiful scenery. There is skiing at Pas de la Casa and Soldeu in winter.

Romanesque churches and old houses of interest are located in Ordino, Encamp, Sant Julía de Lória, Les Escaldes, Santa Coloma, and other villages. Pilgrims come from France and Spain to pay homage on 8 September, the festival day of Andorra's patroness.

There is an International Music Festival each June and July, and an International Jazz Festival at Escaldes-Engordany in July.

An estimated 12 million tourists visit Andorra each year. Over 250 hotels (a majority located in Andorra la Vella and Les Escaldes) cater to their needs.

34 FAMOUS ANDORRANS

There are no internationally famous Andorrans.

35 BIBLIOGRAPHY

Deane, Shirley. *The Road to Andorra.* New York: Morrow, 1961.

Morgan, Bryan. *Andorra, the Country in Between.* Nottingham: Palmer, 1964.

Taylor, Barry. *Andorra.* Santa Barbara, Calif.: Clio Press, 1993.

ANGOLA

Republic of Angola
República de Angola

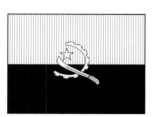

CAPITAL: Luanda.

FLAG: The upper half is red, the lower half black; in the center, a five-pointed yellow star and half a yellow cogwheel are crossed by a yellow machete.

ANTHEM: *Angola Avanti.*

MONETARY UNIT: The Angolan escudo (AE) was the national currency until 1977, when the kwanza (Kw) of 100 lwei replaced it. There are coins of 50 lwei and 1, 2, 5, 10, and 20 kwanza, and notes of 20, 50, 100, 500, and 1,000 kwanza. Kw1 = $0.0334 (or $1 = Kw29.918).

WEIGHTS AND MEASURES: The metric system is used.

HOLIDAYS: New Year's Day, 1 January; Anniversary of Outbreak of Anti-Portuguese Struggle, 4 February; Victory Day, 27 March; Youth Day, 14 April; Workers' Day, 1 May; Armed Forces Day, 1 August; National Heroes' Day, 17 September; Independence Day, 11 November; Pioneers' Day, 1 December; Anniversary of the Foundation of the MPLA, 10 December; Family Day, 25 December.

TIME: 1 PM = noon GMT.

1 LOCATION AND SIZE

Angola is located on the west coast of Africa, south of the equator. Angola is slightly less than twice the size of Texas, with a total area of 1,246,700 square kilometers (481,353 square miles), including the exclave of Cabinda (7,270 square kilometers/2,810 square miles), which is surrounded by Zaire and the Congo. Its total boundary length, including Cabinda's, is 6,798 kilometers (4,224 miles).

2 TOPOGRAPHY

Topographically, Angola consists mainly of broad tablelands above 1,000 meters (3,300 feet) in altitude. A high plateau (planalto) in the center and south ranges up to 2,400 meters (7,900 feet). The highest point in Angola is Mt. Moco, at 2,620 meters (8,596 feet).

3 CLIMATE

Angola's climate varies considerably from the coast to the central plateau and even between the north coast and the south coast. There are two seasons: a dry, cool season from June to late September, and a rainy, hot season from October to April or May. The average temperature is 20°C (68°F). However, temperatures are warmer along the coast and cooler on the central plateau.

4 PLANTS AND ANIMALS

Thick forests cover the wet regions, and in the drier areas there is thinner plains vegetation. Animals include the lion, impala, hyena, hippopotamus, rhinoceros, and elephant. There are thousands of types of birds and a wide variety of insects.

5 ENVIRONMENT

The existing environmental problems in Angola have been increased by a 30-year war. The main problems are land abuse, loss of forests, and impure water. The productivity of the land is threatened by erosion and drought. The cutting of tropical rain forests for the commercial value of the wood contributes to the destruction of the land. Of the 275 species of mammals in Angola, 14 are endangered including the African elephant, black rhinoceros, cheetah, chimpanzee, and gorilla.

6 POPULATION

Angola's population was estimated at 9,390,720 in 1994. A total population of 13,074,000 was projected for the year 2000. Luanda, the capital, had 1,642,000 people in 1990.

7 MIGRATION

According to the UN High Commissioner for Refugees, at the end of 1992 there were 10,800 Zairian and 200 South African refugees in Angola. About 198,000 Angolan refugees were residing in Zaire, and 101,800 in Zambia.

8 ETHNIC GROUPS

The overwhelming majority (more than 95%) of the population is Bantu. A few thousand people in southern and eastern Angola belong to the Khoisan group (Bushmen). The mestiço (or mixed-heritage) population is about 200,000, and there are about 10,000 whites, mostly of Portuguese descent.

9 LANGUAGES

Portuguese remains the official language, although African languages (and their dialects) are used at the local level.

10 RELIGIONS

In 1994, Roman Catholics were believed to be as much as 55% of the population, and Protestants anywhere from 15% to 20%. Perhaps half the population follows African traditional beliefs as well.

11 TRANSPORTATION

In 1991 there were 73,828 kilometers (45,877 miles) of roads, of which 8,577 kilometers (5,330 miles) were paved. There were 120,000 passenger cars and about 40,000 commercial vehicles.

The rail network had a total extension in 1991 of about 2,879 kilometers (1,789 miles) of 1.067 meter-gauge and 310 kilometers (193 miles) of 0.600 meter-gauge track. There is an international airport at Luanda.

12 HISTORY

Originally inhabited by people of the Khoisan group (Bushmen), Angola was occupied by various Bantu peoples from farther north and east between 1300 and 1600.

The Portuguese arrived on the coast in the late 15th century. The first European to reach Angola was the Portuguese explorer Diogo Cao, who landed at the mouth of the Congo River in 1483. Luanda, the current capital, was founded as a trading settlement in 1575. The slave trade assumed great importance during

ANGOLA

LOCATION: Angola proper: 5°49′ to 18°3′s; 11°40′ to 24°5′E. Cabinda: 4°21′ to 5°46′s; 12°2′ to 13°5′E. **BOUNDARY LENGTHS:** Zaire, 2,285 kilometers (1,420 miles); Zambia, 1,086 kilometers (675 miles); Namibia (South West Africa), 1,376 kilometers (855 miles); Atlantic coastline, 1,434 kilometers (891 miles). Cabinda: Zaire, 225 kilometers (140 miles); Congo, 201 kilometers (125 miles). **TERRITORIAL SEA LIMIT:** 20 miles.

the 17th century, when slaves were carried to Portuguese plantations in Brazil. From the late 16th through the mid-19th century, Angola may have provided the New World with as many as two to three million slaves. Slavery was formally abolished in 1836, although under Portuguese rule forced labor was common until the early 1950s.

European domination spread and, in 1951, Angola was made an overseas province of Portugal. Increasing numbers of Portuguese settlers came to Angola, and by 1960 there were about 160,000 Europeans in the country.

Organized armed resistance to Portuguese rule began on 4 February 1961, when urban partisans of the Popular Movement for the Liberation of Angola (MPLA) attacked the police headquarters in Luanda. The National Front for the Liberation of Angola (FNLA), headed by Holden Roberto, set up a revolutionary government-in-exile in Zaire on 3 April 1962. A third movement, the National Union for the Total Independence of Angola (UNITA), came into being as the consequence of a split in the government-in-exile. This group was headed by Jonas Savimbi.

The three movements were divided by political beliefs, ethnic make-up, and personal rivalries. All three movements fought the Portuguese. On 11 November 1975 the Portuguese decided to end their African empire and granted complete independence to Angola. An agreement between the Portuguese and the three movements established a coalition govern-ment headed by the leaders of all three parties. As independence day approached, however, the coalition government fell apart. Mediation attempts by other African countries failed, and the three groups fought among themselves for control of the government. The MPLA was a Marxist-oriented party that received military as well as financial assistance from the USSR and Cuba. The FLNA and UNITA parties had a pro-western orientation, and were aided by South Africa and the United States.

On 11 February 1976, the Organization of African Unity formally recognized the MPLA government as the legitimate government of Angola. With the help of Cuban troops, the MPLA was able to gain control of most of the country. However, the losing parties continued to war against the MPLA government for the next 16 years. During this period, thousands of blacks were killed, most whites left the country, and the economy was totally ruined.

Finally, in April 1991, there was a UN-supervised ceasefire. All parties agreed to hold national elections on 29 and 30 September 1992. The run-up to the election went smoothly. Eighteen parties ran candidates in the legislative election. There were 11 presidential candidates.

The resulting elections were won by the MPLA. However, UNITA leader Savimbi, upset by his unexpected defeat, charged fraud and threatened to take up arms again. Fighting broke out in Luanda in October and more than 1,000 people were killed. UNITA gained control of about

75% of Angola. The UN tried to arrange a ceasefire but UNITA refused to cooperate. This led the UN to condemn UNITA. However, pressure for peace continued and on 20 November 1994 the Angolan government signed a peace treaty with UNITA. The peace agreement called for new elections once the county returned to normalcy.

13 GOVERNMENT

The president of the republic is the president of the MPLA–Workers' Party. The president may rule by decree, exercising legislative functions delegated to him by the People's Assembly. A transitional government was set up in December 1992. It is dominated by the MPLA. UNITA has six cabinet posts and four other parties are represented.

14 POLITICAL PARTIES

The three leading political organizations at the time of independence were the Popular Movement for the Liberation of Angola (Movimento Popular de Libertação de Angola—MPLA), founded in 1956; the National Front for the Liberation of Angola (Frente Nacional de Libertação de Angola—FNLA), founded in 1962; and the National Union for the Total Independence of Angola (União Nacional para a Independência Total de Angola—UNITA), founded in 1966.

15 JUDICIAL SYSTEM

The judicial system currently consists of municipal and provincial courts at the trial level and a Supreme Court at the appellate level. Provincial court judges are nomi-

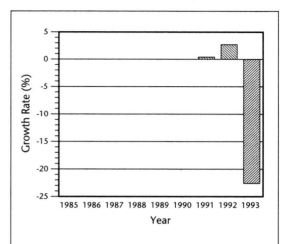

Yearly growth rate of the economy. This economic indicator tells by what percent the economy has increased or decreased when compared with the previous year.

nated by the Supreme Court. The judge of the provincial court, along with two laymen, acts as a jury.

16 ARMED FORCES

National defense is the responsibility of the Armed Popular Forces for the Liberation of Angola (Forças Amadas Populares de Libertação de Angola—FAPLA).

17 ECONOMY

Angola is a potentially rich country of abundant natural resources, a surplus-producing agricultural sector and a sizable manufacturing potential. This promise has remained unfulfilled due to the effects of the 20-year-long civil war.

Cassava is the staple food crop. Petroleum production and diamond mining lead Angola's mineral industry. Angola

Photo credit: Corel Corporation.

A view of the Atlantic coast at Benguela, Angola.

also has significant deposits of high-grade iron ore, copper, manganese, phosphates, and uranium.

18 INCOME

In 1992 Angola's gross domestic product (GDP) was $760 million. The per person national product was calculated at $600.

19 INDUSTRY

As a consequence of the civil war, Angola's industrial sector is operating at a fraction of pre-war levels. Angola's hydroelectric power potential is considerable and is a key to Angola's industrial future.

20 LABOR

The minimum legal age for employment is 14. The Labor Ministry maintains employment centers where prospective employees register.

21 AGRICULTURE

In 1991, even though an abundance of fertile land was available, less than 3% was cultivated. Marketed cash crops in 1992 included coffee, cotton, and sisal. The principal food crops are cassava, corn, and sweet potatoes.

22 DOMESTICATED ANIMALS

What little there was of the livestock industry was virtually destroyed in the civil war. Estimated livestock in 1992 included cattle, 3,200,000 head; goats, 1,550,000; hogs, 810,000; and sheep, 250,000. There were 6 million chickens. Livestock products included an estimated 57,000 tons of beef and veal and 148,000 tons of milk in 1992.

23 FISHING

Fresh fish, fish meal, dried fish, and fish oil are produced for the domestic market and for export. In 1991, the Angolan catch was only 75,062 tons (down from 106,941 tons in 1990).

24 FORESTRY

In 1991, it was estimated that 42% of the country was covered by forests and woodland. Angola's large timber resources include the great Maiombe tropical rain forest north of Cabinda. In addition, eucalyptus, pine, and cypress plantations cover 140,000 hectares (346,000 acres). In

1991, roundwood production was estimated at 6,593,000 cubic meters.

25 MINING

Angola is very rich in mineral resources, especially crude oil, diamonds, iron ore, magnetite, copper, phosphates, gypsum, uranium, gold, asphalt, and feldspar. Diamond production, consisting mainly of gem stones, totaled 960,558 carats in 1991. Large iron ore deposits have been discovered in many areas.

26 FOREIGN TRADE

Angola is a major exporter of crude oil and diamonds. Principal imports include food and food products, civil engineering equipment, motor vehicles and parts, metal products, and medicines and pharmaceuticals. In 1985, Angola's principal trading partners were the United States, Spain, the United Kingdom, and Brazil. Imports came primarily from Portugal, France, and Brazil.

27 ENERGY AND POWER

Total electric power production in 1991 was 1,840 million kilowatt hours, of which 74% was hydroelectric. Crude oil, in the production of which Angola ranks fifth in Africa, has been Angola's chief export since 1973. It is also the leading source of government revenue. Total natural gas reserves were estimated at 50 billion cubic meters.

28 SOCIAL DEVELOPMENT

Until recently, social services for most Africans were almost entirely the responsibility of the various tribal groups. The Roman Catholic Church also played an important part in welfare, health, and educational programs. The MPLA has established a number of self-help organizations.

29 HEALTH

Only an estimated 30% of the population received even rudimentary (basic) medical attention in 1992. In 1990, there were 389 doctors, 8 pharmacists, and 6 dentists. In 1992, average life expectancy was estimated at only 47 years.

30 HOUSING

The rapid growth of Angola's industrial centers has caused the rapid growth of urban slums. Demolition of shantytowns around Luanda is a principal aim of the government. According to the latest available figures, the total housing stock numbered 1,750,000 units with 5.1 people per dwelling.

31 EDUCATION

In 1990 the adult literacy rate was estimated as 42%. Education for children between the ages of 7 and 15 years is compulsory and free. Primary education is for four years and secondary for seven years. Angolan primary schools had 990,155 pupils and 31,062 teachers in 1990. The secondary schools had 186,499 pupils. The University Agostinho Neto in Luanda was established in 1963.

32 MEDIA

All media were nationalized in 1992. Daily newspapers in 1986 were *Jornal de Angola*, with a circulation of 41,000;

Selected Social Indicators

These statistics are estimates for the period 1988 to 1993. For comparison purposes, data for the United States and averages for low-income countries and high-income countries are also given.

Indicator	Angola	Low-income countries	High-income countries	United States
Per capita gross national product†	$600	$380	$23,680	$24,740
Population growth rate	3.7%	1.9%	0.6%	1.0%
Population growth rate in urban areas	6.3%	3.9%	0.8%	1.3%
Population per square kilometer of land	8	78	25	26
Life expectancy in years	47	62	77	76
Number of people per physician	16,152	>3,300	453	419
Number of pupils per teacher (primary school)	32	39	<18	20
Illiteracy rate (15 years and older)	58%	41%	<5%	<3%
Energy consumed per capita (kg of oil equivalent)	96	364	5,203	7,918

† The gross national product (GNP) is the total dollar value of all goods and services produced by a country in a year. The per capita GNP is calculated by dividing a country's GNP by its population. The World Bank defines low-income countries as those with a per capita GNP of $695 or less. High-income countries have a per capita GNP of $8,626 or more. Less than 14% of the world's 5.5 billion people live in high-income countries, while almost 60% live in low-income countries.   > = greater than   < = less than

Sources: World Bank, *Social Indicators of Development 1995,* Baltimore: Johns Hopkins University Press, 1995. Central Intelligence Agency, *World Fact Book,* Washington, D.C.: Government Printing Office, 1994.

Provincia de Angola, 35,000; and *ABC Diario de Angola,* 8,500. All are published in Portuguese. There were about 270,000 radio sets and 21,000 television sets.

33 TOURISM AND RECREATION

Tourism was an important activity until 1972, when an increase in warfare led to a sharp drop in the number of tourists and tourist revenues. Since the mid-1980s, the government has severely restricted the number of foreigners allowed into the country.

34 FAMOUS ANGOLANS

António Agostinho Neto (1922–79), a poet and physician who served as the president of MPLA (1962–79) and president of Angola (1975–79), was Angola's dominant political figure. Jonas Malheiro Savimbi (b.1934), the son of a pastor, founded UNITA in 1966.

35 BIBLIOGRAPHY

Black, Richard. *Angola.* Santa Barbara, Calif.: Clio Press, 1992.
Broadhead, Susan H. (Susan Herlin). *Historical Dictionary of Angola.* 2nd ed. Metuchen, N.J.: Scarecrow Press, 1992.
Laurè, J. *Angola.* Chicago: Children's Press, 1990.

ANTIGUA AND BARBUDA

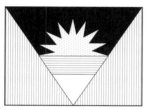

CAPITAL: St. John's.

FLAG: Centered on a red background is a downward-pointing triangle divided horizontally into three bands of black, light blue, and white, the black stripe bearing a symbol of the rising sun in yellow.

ANTHEM: Begins "Fair Antigua and Barbuda, I salute thee."

MONETARY UNIT: The East Caribbean dollar (EC$) is a paper currency of 100 cents, pegged to the US dollar. There are coins of 1, 2, 5, 10, 25 cents and 1 dollar, and notes of 5, 10, 20, and 100 dollars. EC$1 = US$0.3704 (or US$1 = EC$2.70).

WEIGHTS AND MEASURES: Imperial measures are used, but the metric system is being introduced.

HOLIDAYS: New Year's Day, 1 January; Labor Day, 1st Monday in May; CARICOM Day, 3 July; State Day, 1 November; Christmas, 25 December; Boxing Day, 26 December. Movable holidays include Good Friday, Easter Monday, and Whitmonday.

TIME: 8 AM = noon GMT.

1 LOCATION AND SIZE

The state of Antigua and Barbuda is part of the Leeward Islands chain in the eastern Caribbean. The total land area, which includes the uninhabited island of Redonda, is 440 square kilometers (170 square miles), slightly less than 2.5 times the size of Washington, D.C. Redonda is located about 50 kilometers (30 miles) west-southwest of Antigua. The capital city, St. John's, is located on the north-western edge of the island of Antigua.

2 TOPOGRAPHY

Partly volcanic and partly coral in origin, Antigua has deeply indented shores lined by reefs and shoals. Boggy Peak (405 meters/1,329 feet), in southwestern Antigua, is the nation's highest point. Barbuda is a coral island with a large harbor on its west side. Redonda is a low-lying rocky islet.

3 CLIMATE

Temperatures average 24°C (75°F) in January and 29°C (84°F) in July. Rainfall averages 117 centimeters (46 inches) per year.

4 PLANTS AND ANIMALS

Palmetto and seaside mangrove are native trees, and red cedar, white cedar, mahogany, whitewood, and acacia forests have been planted. Barbuda has many deer, wild pigs, guinea fowl, pigeons, and wild ducks.

5 ENVIRONMENT

The water supply, already limited, is threatened by industrial pollution. Energy demands and agricultural development have reduced the nation's forests.

6 POPULATION

The population in May 1991 was 65,962. The overall population density was 147 persons per square kilometer (386 persons per square mile). St. John's, the capital, has an estimated population of 36,000.

7 MIGRATION

The UK has been the traditional destination of Antiguan emigrants, but in recent years it has been replaced by St. Martin, Barbados, the US Virgin Islands, and the US mainland.

8 ETHNIC GROUPS

Antiguans are almost entirely of African descent. There are small numbers of persons of European, Arab, and Asian Indian ancestry.

9 LANGUAGES

English is the official language. An English patois (dialect) is in common use.

10 RELIGIONS

The Church of England claims almost 45% of the population, and other Protestant groups, including Baptist, Methodist, Pentecostal, Seventh-day Adventist, Moravian, and Nazarene, some 42%. Roman Catholics are in the minority at 8.7%.

11 TRANSPORTATION

There are about 240 kilometers (149 miles) of highways. Total motor vehicle registration was 17,000 in 1992. The railway consists of 78 kilometers (48 miles) of narrow-gauge track. The merchant fleet in 1991 consisted of 105 ships with a cargo capacity of 392,000 gross registered tons. Vere Cornwall Bird International Airport, outside St. John's, accommodates the largest jet aircraft.

12 HISTORY

Arawak and Carib Indians inhabited the islands at the time of Christopher Columbus' second voyage in 1493. Antigua formally became a British colony in 1667. In 1674, Sir Christopher Codrington established the first large sugar estate, leasing Barbuda to raise slaves and provide supplies for Antigua. In 1860, Barbuda was annexed to the island of Antigua. The islands were governed under the Federation of the Leeward Islands from 1871 to 1956, and under the Federation of the West Indies from 1958 to 1962.

Antigua achieved full self-government as of 27 February 1967. Antigua and Barbuda became an independent state within the Commonwealth of Nations on 1 November 1981.

13 GOVERNMENT

The British monarch, as head of state, is represented in Antigua and Barbuda by a governor-general. The two-chamber legislature consists of a 17-member House of Representatives, elected for up to five years, and a 17-member Senate, appointed by the governor-general. The prime minister, who must have the support of a majority of the House, is appointed by the governor-general, as is the cabinet.

14 POLITICAL PARTIES

The Antigua Labour Party (ALP) has held power since 1946, except for a period from 1971 to 1976, when the Progressive Labour Movement (PLM) held a parliamentary majority. Other political groups include the Antigua Caribbean Liberation Movement, the United People's Movement, and the National Democratic Party.

15 JUDICIAL SYSTEM

Antigua and Barbuda is under the jurisdiction of the Eastern Caribbean Supreme Court, based in St. Lucia, which also provides a High Court and Court of Appeals. Final appeals may be made to the Queen's Privy council in the United Kingdom. A court of summary jurisdiction on Antigua deals with civil cases.

16 ARMED FORCES

There is a Royal Antigua and Barbuda Defense Force of some 90 men that forms a part of the Eastern Caribbean Regional Security System.

17 ECONOMY

Since the 1960s, tourism has dominated the economy. It now employs 50% of the labor force. Antigua and Barbuda has the largest tourism industry in the Windward and Leeward Islands, with about 480,000 visitors annually. In spite of the growth of tourism, the country hasn't reduced its large foreign debt and trade deficit. In 1992, Antigua and Barbuda registered its first economic growth in three years.

LOCATION: Antigua: 17°9′N; 61°49′W. Barbuda: 17°41′N; 61°48′W. **TOTAL COASTLINE:** 153 kilometers (95 miles). **TERRITORIAL SEA LIMIT:** 12 miles.

18 INCOME

In 1992, Antigua and Barbuda's gross national product (GNP) was US$395 million, or US$6,540 per person.

19 INDUSTRY

Industrial activity has shifted from the processing of local agricultural products to consumer and export industries using imported raw materials. Industrial products include rum, refined petroleum, pottery, paints, garments, furniture, and electrical components.

20 LABOR

The total labor force in 1991 was estimated at 20,500. About 82% of the employed labor force worked in occupations connected with tourism or other services; 7% in industry, and 11% in agriculture, hunting, forestry, and fishing. Unemployment in 1991 officially stood at about 5%.

The minimum working age is 13, and the law is enforced by the Ministry of Labour, which conducts periodic workplace inspections. The Ministry of Labour is unusually effective in enforcing child labor laws, and there have been no reports of minimum age employment violations.

21 AGRICULTURE

Sea-island cotton is a profitable export crop. Vegetables, including beans, carrots, cabbage, cucumbers, plantains, squash, tomatoes, and yams, are grown mostly on small family plots for local markets. Agricultural exports, including mangoes, bananas, coconuts, and pineapples, were estimated at US$1.5 million in 1992. In 1992, an estimated 4,000 tons of sugar were produced from about 8,000 hectares (19,800 acres) harvested.

22 DOMESTICATED ANIMALS

Livestock estimates in 1992 included 16,000 head of cattle, 13,000 sheep, and 12,000 goats. There were some 4,000 hogs in the same year. Most livestock is owned by individual households. Milk production in 1992 was an estimated 6,000 tons.

23 FISHING

Antiguans annually consume more fish per capita (46 kilograms/101.4 pounds) per year live weight than any other nation or territory in the Caribbean. Fish landings in 1991 were 2,300 tons. The lobster catch was 200 tons.

24 FORESTRY

About 11% of the land is forested, mainly by plantings of red cedar, mahogany, white cedar, and acacia. A reforestation program was begun in 1963.

25 MINING

Some limestone and volcanic stone has been quarried for construction purposes, and the manufacture of bricks and tiles from local clay has begun on a small scale. Barbuda produces a small amount of salt.

26 FOREIGN TRADE

In 1991, exports totaled $345.7 million. Primary exports included chemicals, manufacturing goods and materials, food and live animals, machinery and transport equipment. Imports reached $403.1 million, including mineral fuel lubricants and related materials, food, live animals, machinery and transport equipment.

The country exported mostly to the US, UK, Canada, Trinidad and Tobago, and Barbados. Its major import providers were the US, UK, CARICOM, Canada, and the former Yugoslavia.

27 ENERGY AND POWER

Electric power produced in 1991 totaled 95 million kilowatt hours. Gas is now produced and refined locally. Wind power and fast-growing tree species are under study as alternatives to fossil fuels.

28 SOCIAL DEVELOPMENT

A social security fund provides compulsory coverage of persons between the ages of 16 and 60 years. Medical insurance includes maternity benefits. The government operates day-care centers for children under five years of age.

29 HEALTH

Four hospitals care for the sick and aged, as well as 4 health centers and 16 dispensaries. There were 59 physicians in 1991. The average life expectancy in 1992 was 73 years.

30 HOUSING

The Central Housing and Planning Authority rehabilitates houses in the event of disaster, develops new housing tracts, and redevelops deteriorating areas.

31 EDUCATION

Education for children between the ages of 5 and 16 years is compulsory. In 1987–88, there were 43 primary schools and 15 secondary schools. There were 9,097 students enrolled at the primary schools and 4,413 students at the secondary schools.

Photo credit: AP/Wide World Photos

Nine year old Mahasha Johnson carries a water bottle through the streets of St. John's. Antigua was hit by Hurricane Luis in 1995, which knocked out electricity and water supplies to the island's residents.

There currently are two colleges, the University of Health Sciences, and the University of the West Indies School of Continuing Studies.

32 MEDIA

Eight broadcasting stations—four AM, two FM, and two television—were received in 1992 by some 27,000 radios and 23,000 television sets. There are approximately 7,000 telephones. The *Antigua & Barbuda Herald,* with a circulation of about 2,500, is published biweekly.

Selected Social Indicators

These statistics are estimates for the period 1988 to 1993. For comparison purposes, data for the United States and averages for low-income countries and high-income countries are also given.

Indicator	Antigua and Barbuda	Low-income countries	High-income countries	United States
Per capita gross national product†	$6,540	$380	$23,680	$24,740
Population growth rate	0.3%	1.9%	0.6%	1.0%
Population growth rate in urban areas	0.5%	3.9%	0.8%	1.3%
Population per square kilometer of land	147	78	25	26
Life expectancy in years	73	62	77	76
Number of people per physician	n.a.	>3,300	453	419
Number of pupils per teacher (primary school)	n.a.	39	<18	20
Illiteracy rate (15 years and older)	11%	41%	<5%	<3%
Energy consumed per capita (kg of oil equivalent)	2,000	364	5,203	7,918

† The gross national product (GNP) is the total dollar value of all goods and services produced by a country in a year. The per capita GNP is calculated by dividing a country's GNP by its population. The World Bank defines low-income countries as those with a per capita GNP of $695 or less. High-income countries have a per capita GNP of $8,626 or more. Less than 14% of the world's 5.5 billion people live in high-income countries, while almost 60% live in low-income countries.

n.a. = data not available.   > = greater than   < = less than

Sources: World Bank, *Social Indicators of Development 1995,* Baltimore: Johns Hopkins University Press, 1995. Central Intelligence Agency, *World Fact Book,* Washington, D.C.: Government Printing Office, 1994.

33 TOURISM AND RECREATION

Tourism is the main source of income in Antigua and Barbuda. Antigua's abundance of beaches—as many as 365—and its charter yachting and deep-sea fishing facilities have created the largest tourist industry in the Windward and Leeward Islands. The international regatta and Summer Carnival are popular annual events. Cricket is the national pastime. A wide range of hotels and restaurants served 196,571 tourists in 1991, of whom 128,771 were from the Americas and 64,133 from Europe. Receipts from tourism climbed to US$313 million.

34 FAMOUS ANTIGUANS AND BARBUDANS

The first successful colonizer of Antigua was Sir Thomas Warner (d.1649). Vere Cornwall Bird, Sr. (b.1910) has been prime minister since 1981.

35 BIBLIOGRAPHY

Coram, Robert. *Caribbean Time Bomb: The United States' Complicity in the Corruption of Antigua.* New York: Morrow, 1993.

Gooding, Earl. *The West Indies at the Crossroads.* New York: Schenkman, 1981.

ARGENTINA

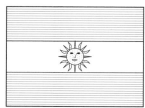

Argentine Republic
República Argentina

CAPITAL: Buenos Aires.

FLAG: The national flag consists of a white horizontal stripe between two light blue horizontal stripes. Centered in the white band is a radiant yellow sun with a human face.

ANTHEM: *Himno Nacional*, beginning "Oíd, mortales, el grito sagrado Libertad" ("Hear, O mortals, the sacred cry of Liberty").

MONETARY UNIT: The peso (A$) is a paper currency of 100 centavos. There are coins of 1, 5, 10, 25 and 50 centavos, and notes of 1, 2, 5, 10, 20, 50, and 100 pesos.

WEIGHTS AND MEASURES: The metric system is the legal standard.

HOLIDAYS: New Year's Day, 1 January; Labor Day, 1 May; Anniversary of the 1810 Revolution, 25 May; Occupation of the Islas Malvinas, 10 June; Flag Day, 20 June; Independence Day, 9 July; Anniversary of San Martín, 17 August; Columbus Day, 12 October; Immaculate Conception, 8 December; Christmas, 25 December. Movable religious holidays include Carnival (two days in February or March) and Good Friday.

TIME: 9 AM = noon GMT.

1 LOCATION AND SIZE

Shaped like a wedge with its point in the south, Argentina is the second-largest country in South America. Argentina is slightly less than three-tenths the size of the United States, with a total area of 2,766,890 square kilometers (1,068,302 square miles). It has a total boundary length of 14,654 kilometers (8,106 miles).

Argentina's capital city, Buenos Aires, is located along the eastern edge of the country on the Atlantic coast.

2 TOPOGRAPHY

Except for the mountainous western area, Argentina is for the most part a lowland country. It is divided into four topographical regions: the Andean region, almost 30% of the country; Patagonia, a desertlike, sparsely populated region which extends westward in a series of plateaus; the subtropical plain of the north, in the area between the Andean piedmont and the Paraná River; and the pampas, the most characteristic feature of Argentine topography. Lush, well-watered level plains, they spread in a semicircle from the Buenos Aires area to the foothills of the Andes, to the Chaco, and to Patagonia. They form the heartland of Argentina, the source of its greatest wealth, and the home of 80% of its people.

The Paraná, Uruguay, Paraguay, and Alto Paraná (located in Brazil) rivers all flow into the Río de la Plata. The highest peak in Argentina is Mt. Aconcagua

Photo credit: Susan D. Rock.

A view of Perito Moreno Glacier in Argentina's Glacier National Park.

(6,960 meters/22,835 feet), also the highest mountain in South America. There is a region of snow-fed lakes in the foothills of the Andes in western Patagonia.

3 CLIMATE

Argentina's climate is generally temperate, but there are many variations due to the great range in altitude and the vast extent of the country. The highest temperature, 49°C (120°F), was recorded in the extreme north, and the lowest, –16°C (3°F), in the southern tip of the country. Rainfall at Buenos Aires averages 94 centimeters (37 inches) annually, and the mean annual temperature is 16°C (61°F).

Throughout Argentina, January is the warmest month and June and July are the coldest. The pampas, despite their immensity, have an almost uniform climate, with much sunshine and adequate precipitation. The coldest winters occur not in Tierra del Fuego, which is warmed by ocean currents, but in Santa Cruz Province, where the July average is 0°C (32°F).

4 PLANTS AND ANIMALS

More than 10% of the world's plant varieties are found in Argentina. The magnificent grasslands have figured prominently in the development of Argentina's world-famous cattle industry. Evergreen beeches and Paraná pine are common. From yerba maté comes the national drink immortalized in folk literature, while the shade-providing ombú is a national symbol.

Many tropical animals thrive in the forests and marshes of northern Argentina. Among them are the capybara, coypu, puma, and various wildcats. In the grasslands and deserts are the guanaco, rhea, and many types of rodents. The armadillo, otter, weasel, opossum, various types of fox, and hog-nosed skunk are common. The ostrich, crested screamer, tinamou, and ovenbird are a few of the many species of birds. Pejerrey, corvina, palameta, pacu, and zurubi abound in the rivers.

5 ENVIRONMENT

As of 1994, the major environmental issues in Argentina are pollution and the loss of agricultural lands. The soil is threatened by erosion and deforestation. Air pollution is a problem due to chemical agents from industrial sources. The water supply is threatened by uncontrolled dumping of pesticides, hydrocarbons, and heavy metals.

Endangered species in Argentina include the Argentinian pampas deer and the jaguar. As of 1994, 23 species of mammals are considered endangered, as well as 53 bird species, and 159 of the nation's 9,000 plant species.

6 POPULATION

Argentina's census population was 32,615,528 in 1991. The projected population for the year 2000 was 36,238,000. Average population density was 12 persons per square kilometer (30 persons per

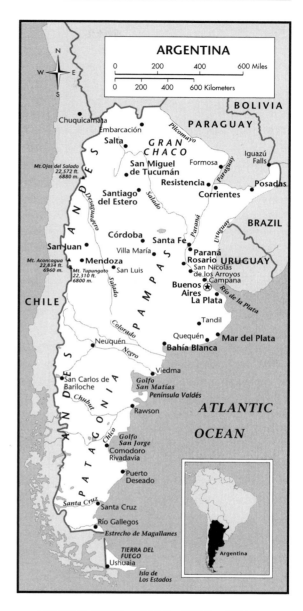

LOCATION: 21°47′ to 55°16′s; 53°38′ to 73°35′w.
BOUNDARY LENGTHS: Bolivia, 832 kilometers (517 miles); Paraguay, 1,880 kilometers (1,168 miles); Brazil, 1,224 kilometers (761 miles); Uruguay, 579 kilometers (360 miles); Atlantic coastline, 4,989 kilometers (3,100 miles); Chile, 5,150 kilometers (3,200 miles). **TERRITORIAL SEA LIMIT:** 200 miles.

square mile) in 1991. More than one-third of all Argentines live in or around Buenos Aires. The population of Buenos Aires as of the 1991 census was 2,965,403.

7 MIGRATION

There is significant immigration from Paraguay, Bolivia, Chile, Uruguay, and Brazil. Some 300,000 illegal aliens were granted amnesty in 1992. In 1992, Argentina's refugee population was estimated at 11,500.

Of much greater importance to Argentina has been the migration of workers from rural areas to the cities, draining rural populations so badly that agriculture and livestock raising, the base of Argentina's wealth, suffered severely. In addition, the inability of the economy to absorb all of the new urban masses led to long-term economic and social problems.

8 ETHNIC GROUPS

Argentina's population is overwhelmingly European in origin (principally from Spain and Italy). There is little mixture of native peoples. An estimated 97% of the people are of European descent, and some 3% are Amerindian or of mixed lineage. The pure Amerindian population has been increasing slightly through immigration from Bolivia and Paraguay.

9 LANGUAGES

The national language of Argentina is Spanish. Argentine Spanish differs in many ways from Castilian, showing the effects of the vast influx of foreigners into Buenos Aires, as well as of Spaniards from Andalucía, Galicia, and the Basque provinces. Italians and French have added their touch to the language as well.

English has become increasingly popular as a second language, especially in cities and in the business and professional community. There are pockets of Italian and German immigrants speaking their native languages. Some Amerindian languages are still spoken.

10 RELIGIONS

In 1993, an estimated 92% of the population was Roman Catholic and 2% Protestant. The remainder belonged to other religions or indicated no preference.

Argentina retains national patronage over the Roman Catholic Church. The Pope's decrees must be proclaimed by the president and sometimes must be incorporated into an act of the Congress.

The 215,000 Jews (as of 1990) constitute the third-largest Jewish concentration in the Americas.

11 TRANSPORTATION

Argentina has the largest railway system in South America, with 34,172 kilometers (21,234 miles) of track as of 1991. The number of passengers carried dropped from 445 million in 1976 to 300 million in 1991. The subway system in Buenos Aires consists of five lines totaling 36 kilometers (22 miles). The number of passengers in 1985 was 182.8 million.

By 1991, the nation had 208,350 kilometers (129,469 miles) of roads. The road system is still far from adequate, especially in view of Argentina's rapidly increasing

Photo credit: Susan D. Rock.

Avenida 9 de Julio in Buenos Aires is the world's widest street.

automotive industry. In 1992, the total number of registered vehicles reached 5,970,775 (including 4,417,882 passenger cars).

The main river system of Argentina consists of the Río de la Plata and its tributaries, the Paraná, Uruguay, Paraguay, and Alto Paraná (located in Brazil) rivers. There is a total of 10,950 kilometers (6,800 miles) of navigable waterways, offering vast possibilities for efficient water transportation. The La Plata ports (Buenos Aires and La Plata) account for more than half of all maritime cargo.

The port of Buenos Aires handles about four-fifths of the country's imports and exports, and it is the focus of river traffic on the La Plata system. Other major ports are Rosario, Quequén, Bahía Blanca, Campana, and San Nicolás.

Buenos Aires is the most important air terminal in South America. Ezeiza Airport, about 40 kilometers (25 miles) from Buenos Aires, is one of the largest in the world and serviced 2,609,000 passengers in 1991. Argentina has a total of 137 airports, 10 of which handle international traffic. The government line is Aerolíneas Argentinas.

12 HISTORY

Before the Spaniards arrived in 1515, about 20 Amerindian groups totaling some 300,000 people lived in the region now called Argentina. Spanish colonists from Chile, Peru, and Paraguay created the first permanent settlements in Argentina, including Buenos Aires in 1580.

In 1776, Spain created the Viceroyalty of Río de la Plata from its territories in southeastern South America, with Buenos Aires as its main port and capital. During the colonial period, there was little interest in Argentina. The region had no mineral wealth, and Spaniards overlooked the fertile soil and temperate climate of the region.

In May 1810, Buenos Aires held an open town meeting (cabildo abierto), deposed the viceroy, and set up an independent government to rule the Viceroyalty. Argentina formally declared its independence on 9 July 1816. A long period of disorder followed until 1862 when Bartolomé Mitre finally unified the nation with Buenos Aires at its center. A period of rapid economic development followed, and the fertile pampas began to shift from livestock to agricultural production. During this time, the country came under the control of a powerful team of wealthy landowners and the military. Although social reforms were enacted in the 1920s, an economic crisis caused by the world depression led to a military takeover in 1930.

For the next thirteen years, Argentina was ruled by the old military-landowner alliance, which brought economic recovery, political corruption, and a worsening of social tensions. Argentina's careful neutrality in World War II masked strong Fascist sympathies, further dividing the nation.

Another military takeover in 1943 launched a new era in Argentine politics. With Argentina's war-related industrial expansion, a large blue-collar workforce had been created. This new power base supported Colonel Juan Domingo Perón in his successful 1946 bid for the presidency. His supporters also won majorities in both houses of Congress.

Perón then began sweeping political, economic, and social changes. Perón combined industrialism, nationalism, and dictatorship. His strong personal appeal was enhanced by the charm of his wife Eva ("Evita"), who captivated the masses with her work on behalf of the poor. Perón also sought to act as a protector of weaker Latin American nations against US and British "imperialists."

After reelection in 1951, Perón became more dictatorial and unpredictable, especially after the death of Evita a year later. Finally, a disillusioned military group took over in September 1955. Perón went into exile in Spain. For the next twenty years, Argentina felt the shadow of Perón, who held veto powers from exile in Spain. Under the military's watchful eye, a succession of governments attempted unsuccessfully to create a new political order.

Perón returned to Argentina in June 1973, and ran for the presidency. He won 61.9% of the vote in a special election in September. His running mate was his third wife, María Estela ("Isabel") Martínez de Perón. However, there was no magic left in the elderly Perón, and the economy continued to decline. When Perón died in July 1974, his widow, Isabel, succeeded to the presidency.

Isabel had none of Evita's appeal, and her administration plunged Argentina more deeply into chaos. In March 1976, she was arrested in a bloodless takeover, and a military group took over.

For seven years, the military attempted to "purify" Argentina by removing all traces of leftism, Perónism, and trade unionism. During this period, the military killed over 5,000 people and jailed and tortured many others. It was also during this time that between 6,000 and 15,000 anti-government activists "disappeared." Major economic reforms included the turning of banking and industry over to private ownership. However, the military was never able to solve the problem of inflation, which remained in triple digits for most of this period.

Troubled by economic woes, the government attempted to gain the support of the people by asserting Argentina's rights to the Falkland Islands. The Falkland Islands lie about 550 kilometers (340 miles) due east of Río Gallegos and were claimed by the United Kingdom. In April 1982, Argentina invaded the Falkland Islands, claiming possession of them. In the war with the UK that followed, Argentina's armed forces were defeated, and were forced to surrender in June.

In elections for a civilian president held in October 1983, the surprise winner was a human-rights activist, Dr. Raúl Alfonsín. Alfonsín called for a new inquiry into the fate of between 6,000 and 15,000 persons who had "disappeared" during 1975–79 and ordered the prosecution of members of the former government. Several were convicted. However, the human rights trials of leading military officers angered the military, and in 1987 Alfonsín was forced to ease his prosecutions.

The Alfonsín administration also acted to halt runaway inflation with the "Austral Plan" of mid-1985. This plan froze wages and prices and created a new unit of currency, the austral, to replace the peso. The initial success of the plan was weakened by renewed inflation and wage demands.

With the failure of the Alfonsín administration to stabilize the economy or bring military leaders to justice, Argentines sought change from an old source: the Perónists. In May 1989, Carlos Saul Menem, running under the Perónist banner, was elected with 47% of the popular vote.

Abandoning his party's traditional support of state enterprises, Menem has cut government spending and reduced the role of government in the Argentine economy. In spite of strong resistance, at times, from his own party, he has had enough success with the economy to speak of continuing in office past his constitutional term limit in 1995.

13 GOVERNMENT

Argentina is a federation of 22 provinces, the federal capital of Buenos Aires, and the territories of Tierra del Fuego, a claim to part of Antarctica, and the Isla de los Estados.

There is a separation of powers among the executive, legislative, and judicial branches, but the president is powerful within this arrangement. The president can draw up and introduce his own bills in Congress and appoint cabinet members and other officials without the consent of the Senate. The president also possesses broad powers to declare a state of siege and suspend the constitution.

The president is commander-in-chief of the army, navy, and air force. The president and vice-president are elected by an electoral college for six-year terms. They must be Roman Catholics, and either they or their parents must be native-born citizens. Voting is compulsory for all citizens 18 to 70 years of age.

The constitution calls for a National Congress consisting of a 46-member Senate and a 254-member Chamber of Deputies.

14 POLITICAL PARTIES

Due to the frequency of military takeovers, parties have often been banned. Still, several parties were formed in the 1980s and continue to be active in the 1990s.

Traditionally, the alignment of Argentine political parties has been along socioeconomic and religious lines. The landowners, the high clergy, and the more conservative lower class supporters have formed an alliance that defends the Church and the status quo. On the other side have been the advocates of change: merchants and professionals who resent the preeminence of the aristocracy and who tend also to be anticlerical. This second group has supported separation of church and state and decentralization. However, in modern times, new parties have emerged to represent the working class, small farmers, and intellectuals.

15 JUDICIAL SYSTEM

The Supreme Court supervises and regulates all other federal courts. Other federal courts include nine appeals courts; single-judge district courts, at least one for each province; and one-judge territorial courts. Provincial courts include supreme courts, appeals courts, courts of first instance, and minor courts.

16 ARMED FORCES

From 1930 through 1983, 14 of Argentina's 18 presidents were military officers. The military remained one of the most powerful political forces in Argentina until it suffered the humiliating defeat in the Falklands War in 1982.

The Argentine armed forces are being reduced and reorganized, and numbered 65,000 in 1993. The other services are the navy (which has air and marine units) of 20,000, a national police force of 17,000, a coast guard of 13,000, and an air force of 10,000.

The navy has 4 submarines, 1 aircraft carrier, 7 frigates, and 6 missile-equipped destroyers. The air force had an estimated 10,000 personnel and 174 combat aircraft. Defense spending has fallen from an estimated $4 billion to $700 million in the last decade.

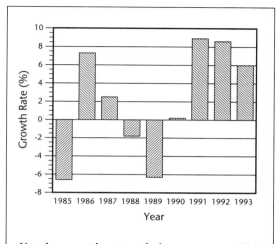

Yearly growth rate of the economy. This economic indicator tells by what percent the economy has increased or decreased when compared with the previous year.

17 ECONOMY

Argentina has one of the most highly developed economies and richest natural resource bases in Latin America, but political instability has kept the economy from realizing its full potential. The country has almost overcome its dependence on imported machinery and finished products, and there is a great demand for parts and raw materials that are assembled or finished within the country.

The inflation rate for 1983 was 434%, the highest in the world. It rose without interruption until it reached 1,200% in mid-1985. At that time, the government introduced the Austral Plan—a bold attempt to halt inflation by freezing wages and prices, adopting a new currency, and resolving not to finance public spending by printing more money. By the end of 1986, the inflation rate had been cut to 82%. By early 1987, however, it had begun to surge again.

In 1991, President Carlos Menem introduced an original stabilization and reform program which has so far been successful.

18 INCOME

In 1992, Argentina's gross national product (GNP) was $200.28 million at current prices, or $7,220 per person.

19 INDUSTRY

Argentina's principal industrial enterprises are heavily concentrated in and around the city of Buenos Aires. The plants are close to both the many raw materials imported by ship and the vast productive area of the pampas. The major industries in Buenos Aires are meat packing, food processing, machinery manufacturing and assembly, flour milling, tanning and leather goods manufacturing, oil refining, oilseed milling, and textile, chemical, pharmaceutical, and cement manufacturing.

Packing and processing of food products is the oldest and most important industry in Argentina. The textile industry was also developed quite early, making use of wool from the vast herds of sheep and the cotton from Chaco Province in the northeast. In addition to these traditional products, a variety of synthetic fibers are now produced.

Portland cement is the country's leading construction material, with 5.55 million tons produced in 1986. The output of crude steel totaled 3.24 million tons in

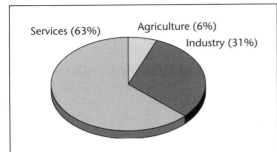

Services (63%)   Agriculture (6%)
                   Industry (31%)

Components of the economy. This pie chart shows how much of the country's economy is devoted to agriculture (includes forestry, hunting, and fishing), industry, or services.

cial occasions; a minimum paid vacation of 14 days annually; and an annual bonus equal to one-twelfth of an employee's yearly pay.

The law prohibits young children under the age of 14 from working, except in family businesses. Young people aged 14 to 18 may work, although there are restrictions on the hours, safety and health conditions, and types of work.

21 AGRICULTURE

Agriculture in Argentina focuses on the production of food grains, oil grains and seeds, sugar, fruit, wine, tea, tobacco, and cotton. Argentina is one of the greatest food-producing and food-exporting countries of the world, with an estimated 27,200,000 hectares (67,210,000 acres) of cropland. The principal agricultural region consists of the humid pampas, one of the world's greatest reaches of fertile land.

Wheat is the leading crop. Argentina normally accounts for about 64% of all wheat produced in South America and is the world's fourth-leading wheat exporter, following the US, France, and Australia. The area sown in 1991/92 was estimated at 4.5 million hectares (11.1 million acres), with production at 9 million tons. Argentina is also the third-largest corn-growing country of Latin America, following Brazil and Mexico.

In 1991, grape production was 2 million tons. Argentina is one of the world's leading producers of wine, accounting for an estimated 1.15 million tons in 1992, or 4% of the world's total production.

1986. Argentina also produces electric appliances, communications equipment—including radios and television sets—motors, watches, and numerous other items.

20 LABOR

In 1990, the economically active population of Argentina was estimated at 12,305,000. According to the most recent estimates, the labor force was divided as follows: 21% in industry, 53% in services, and 13% in agriculture.

Organized labor has probably had a greater effect on the modern history of Argentina than any other group. Long-time dictator Juan Perón used the labor movement as his chief vehicle in achieving and holding dictatorial power. In 1991, 28% of laborers were unionized.

Argentine law specifies that all workers are entitled to a minimum wage (about $98 per month); family allowances for child care, educational expenses, and spe-

22 DOMESTICATED ANIMALS

Argentina is one of the world's leading producers of cattle and sheep. Total meat production was 3.54 million tons in 1992, of which 2.6 million tons consisted of beef. Argentine pastures cover an estimated 142.1 million hectares (351.1 million acres).

The dairy industry has shown steady development. In 1992, the following quantities were produced: milk, 6,700,000 tons; cheese, 280,000 tons; and butter, 42,000 tons. Egg production was 327,600 tons in 1992. In 1992, the number of poultry reached 58 million.

In sheep raising, Argentina ranks thirteenth in the world, with an estimated 23.7 million animals in 1992. Wool output was 128,000 tons in 1992. In 1992, production of mutton and lamb was 85,000 tons.

In 1992, Argentina had 3.3 million horses, a figure among the top five in the world. Argentine horses, especially favored as polo ponies and racehorses, have won many international prizes. Other livestock in 1992 included 4.7 million pigs and 3.3 million goats.

23 FISHING

In a country that is among the world's leaders in meat production, fishing has not been able to develop as an industry of any significance. The most favored saltwater fish are the pejerrey, a kind of mackerel; the dorado, resembling salmon but of a golden color; and the zurubí, an immense yellow and black spotted catfish. There is a limited whaling industry.

Photo credit: Susan D. Rock.

Iguazu Falls is a popular tourist site on Argentina's border with Paraguay and Brazil.

24 FORESTRY

Argentina's forests, estimated at some 59.1 million hectares (146 million acres), or about 21% of the total area, are among its greatest underused natural resources. A major reason for the industry's lack of development is the great distance of most forests from the markets and the high cost of transportation. Woods currently harvested include softwoods, such as the elm and willow; white quebracho, used as a fuel and in the refining of coal; and red quebracho, from which tannin is extracted; as well as cedar, oak, pine, cypress, and larch. Production of round-wood was 10.8 million cubic meters in 1991.

The most important tree is the red quebracho, which contains 21% tannin, the extract used for tanning. Argentina possesses four-fifths of the world's supply of this wood.

25 MINING

The mountainous northwest, especially the province of Jujuy (which borders Bolivia), is rich in a variety of minerals. Output of iron ore peaked at 1.04 million tons in 1988, but by 1991 had declined to 980,000 tons. In 1991, the nation's production of important metal concentrates included zinc, lead, tin, copper, silver, and gold.

Asphaltite, fluorspar, copper, mica, manganese, gold, silver, and antimony are found mainly in the northwest. In 1991, Argentina produced 250,000 tons of boron, ranking 4th in the world after the US, Turkey, and Russia.

26 FOREIGN TRADE

Exports reached $12.6 billion in 1993, while imports totaled $14.88 billion. Argentina has removed practically all non-tariff barriers to trade. The creation of North American Free Trade Association (NAFTA) is viewed as an extremely positive development. The government has remained fully committed to seeing the creation of MERCOSUR (a common market incorporating Argentina, Brazil, Uruguay, and Paraguay). It was completed on January 1, 1995.

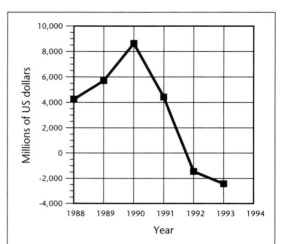

Yearly balance of trade measured in millions of US dollars. The balance of trade is the difference between what a country sells to other countries (its exports) and what it buys (its imports). If a country imports more than it exports, it has a negative balance of trade (a trade deficit). If exports exceed imports, there is a positive balance of trade (a trade surplus).

During the first part of 1994, exports to the US grew by 36.7%, to MERCOSUR countries by 9.8%, and to the European Union by 5%. Imports showed a growing share of commercial goods mainly from the US.

27 ENERGY AND POWER

Despite a shortage of energy resources, production of electric power has steadily increased since 1958. In 1991, about 40% of generating capacity was hydroelectric.

Argentina was the first country in Latin America to install nuclear-powered electric generating plants. Nuclear energy accounted for 14% of total electricity pro-

Selected Social Indicators

These statistics are estimates for the period 1988 to 1993. For comparison purposes, data for the United States and averages for low-income countries and high-income countries are also given.

Indicator	Argentina	Low-income countries	High-income countries	United States
Per capita gross national product†	$7,220	$380	$23,680	$24,740
Population growth rate	1.4%	1.9%	0.6%	1.0%
Population growth rate in urban areas	1.8%	3.9%	0.8%	1.3%
Population per square kilometer of land	12	78	25	26
Life expectancy in years	72	62	77	76
Number of people per physician	368	>3,300	453	419
Number of pupils per teacher (primary school)	20	39	<18	20
Illiteracy rate (15 years and older)	5%	41%	<5%	<3%
Energy consumed per capita (kg of oil equivalent)	1,351	364	5,203	7,918

† The gross national product (GNP) is the total dollar value of all goods and services produced by a country in a year. The per capita GNP is calculated by dividing a country's GNP by its population. The World Bank defines low-income countries as those with a per capita GNP of $695 or less. High-income countries have a per capita GNP of $8,626 or more. Less than 14% of the world's 5.5 billion people live in high-income countries, while almost 60% live in low-income countries.

> = greater than   < = less than

Sources: World Bank, *Social Indicators of Development 1995*, Baltimore: Johns Hopkins University Press, 1995. Central Intelligence Agency, *World Fact Book*, Washington, D.C.: Government Printing Office, 1994.

duction in 1991. Argentina is rich in uranium. Production of uranium concentrate was 60 tons in 1991.

Oil production was 27.9 million tons in 1992. Proven reserves as of 1 January 1992 were estimated at 1.57 billion barrels. The natural gas industry has expanded rapidly. Production in 1992 was 23.3 billion cubic meters. In that year, known reserves were estimated at 579.05 billion cubic meters. There is a network of over 9,900 kilometers (6,150 miles) of gas pipelines. Coal production was reported at 291,546 tons in 1991.

28 SOCIAL DEVELOPMENT

In his early years in office, long-time leader Juan Perón took aggressive steps to enact far-reaching social legislation, although his social policies broke down in many ways after 1953. In the 1940s, new provisions established salary increases, paid holidays, sick leave, job tenure, and many other benefits. Perón's wife Eva joined him in extending legislation to working women and to the poorer classes, called the "shirtless ones" (descamisados). By 1945, a National Social Security Institute administered social insurance programs and a pension system. In the early 1950s, these measures continued and were also extended to the rural sector. Most of the social legislation enacted during the Perón years has remained in effect.

Although guaranteed equality under the Constitution, women are fighting for equal advancement and pay in the labor force.

29 HEALTH

In the field of health care, Argentina compares favorably with other Latin American countries. Nutritional requirements are comfortably met.

Health and medical services for workers are provided by union clinics, and employers are usually required to provide free medical and pharmaceutical care for injured workers. It is estimated that 71% of the population has access to health services. In 1992, life expectancy averaged 72 years (75 years for females and 68 years for males).

30 HOUSING

Housing in Argentina reflects the Italian and Spanish ethnic backgrounds of the population. Concrete, mortar, and brick are generally favored as the principal construction materials. Wood is generally considered less durable and feared as a fire hazard. The total number of dwellings in 1992 was 9.22 million. As of 1993, there was a housing shortage of roughly 2.5 million houses in Argentina.

31 EDUCATION

Argentina has one of the highest literacy rates in Latin America, estimated at 95%. Education is free and compulsory for all children at the primary level. Secondary education lasts for four to six years depending on the type of course.

In 1991, there were 21,703 primary schools with 275,162 teachers and 4,874,306 students enrolled.

Argentina has 46 officially accredited universities with a total of 570,000 students (1988). The largest is the University of Buenos Aires with an enrollment of 187,000 in 1988.

32 MEDIA

In 1992, there were 171 AM radio stations and 231 TV stations. The number of radios was estimated at 22.3 million in 1991, and there were 7.2 million television sets. In 1991, there were 3,921,629 telephones, over half of which were in Buenos Aires and nearby areas.

Buenos Aires is one of the principal editorial centers of the Spanish-speaking world, with more than 50 publishing houses in the 1980s. Two of the great dailies of Buenos Aires, *La Nación* and *La Prensa*, have international reputations, and *La Prensa* is probably the most famous newspaper in Latin America.

33 TOURISM AND RECREATION

In 1991, 2,870,346 foreign tourists visited Argentina, 34% from Uruguay, 20% from Chile, and 10% from Brazil. Receipts from tourism totaled US$2.3 billion. As of 1990, there were 108,812 hotel rooms with 264,804 beds.

Photo credit: Susan D. Rock.

Ushuaia is the southernmost city in the world.

Mar del Plata, on the South Atlantic, about 400 kilometers (250 miles) from Buenos Aires, is the most popular ocean resort. San Carlos de Bariloche, at the entrance to Nahuel Huapi National Park in the Andean lake region of western Patagonia, has become famous as a summer and winter resort, with some of the best skiing in the Southern Hemisphere. The Iguazú Falls, in the province of Misiones, on the border with Paraguay and Brazil, is a major tourist attraction.

The most popular sport is football (soccer). In 1978, the year Argentina hosted the World Cup competition, the Argentine national team won the championship. Tennis, rugby, basketball, and golf are also played.

34 FAMOUS ARGENTINES

The most famous Argentine is José de San Martín (1778–1850), known as the Protector of the South, who was principally responsible for freeing southern South America from Spanish rule.

The most famous Argentine political figures of modern times have been Juan Domingo Perón Sosa (1895–1974) and his second wife, Eva Duarte de Perón (1919–52), known as "Evita." Perón's third wife, María Estela ("Isabel") Martínez de Perón, was vice-president during 1973–74 and, after her husband's death, president from 1974 to 1976.

The leading contemporary writer of Argentina is Jorge Luis Borges (1899–1986), best known for his essays and collections of tales such as *Historia universal de la infamia*.

The most famous Argentine scientist, Bernardo Alberto Houssay (1887–1971), was awarded the 1947 Nobel Prize in medicine for his work on diabetes.

35 BIBLIOGRAPHY

Argentina in Pictures. Minneapolis: Lerner, 1988.

Biggins, Alan. *Argentina*. Oxford, England, and Santa Barbara, Calif.: Clio Press, 1991.

Hintz, M. *Argentina*. Chicago: Children's Press, 1985.

Nagel, Rob, and Anne Commire. "José de San Martín." In *World Leaders, People Who Shaped the World*. Volume III: North and South America. Detroit: U*X*L, 1994.

Nagel, Rob and Anne Commire. "Juan Domingo Perûn." In *World Leaders, People Who Shaped the World*. Volume III: North and South America. Detroit: U*X*L, 1994.

ARMENIA

Republic of Armenia

Hayastani Hanrapetut 'Yun

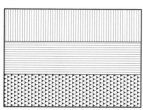

CAPITAL: Yerevan.

FLAG: Three horizontal bands of red (top), blue and gold.

ANTHEM: *Mer Hayrenik.*

MONETARY UNIT: The dram (introduced 22 November 1993) is a paper currency in denominations of 10, 25, 50, 100, 200, and 500 drams. The dram (D) is intended to replace the Armenian ruble and the Russian ruble (R). Currently 1 dram = 200 Armenian rubles or R84. D1 =$0.07 (or $1 = D14.3)

WEIGHTS AND MEASURES: The metric system is in force.

HOLIDAYS: New Year, 1–2 January; Christmas, 6 January; Easter, 1–4 April; Day of Remembrance of the Victims of the Genocide, 24 April; Peace Day, 9 May; Anniversary of Declaration of First Armenian Republic (1918), 28 May; Public Holiday, 21 September; Day of Remembrance of the Victims of the Earthquake, 7 December, New Year, 31 December.

TIME: 4 PM = noon GMT.

1 LOCATION AND SIZE

Armenia is a landlocked nation located in southeastern Europe. Comparatively, the area occupied by Armenia is slightly larger than the state of Maryland with a total area of 29,800 square kilometers (11,506 square miles). Armenia has a total boundary length of 1,254 kilometers (779 miles). The capital city, Yerevan, is located near its southeast boundary.

2 TOPOGRAPHY

Armenia is located in what geographers call the Aral Caspian Lowland. The country has broad sandy deserts and low grassy plateaus. The topography features the high Armenian Plateau, with mountains (many peaks are above 10,000 feet), fast flowing rivers, and the Aras River Valley.

3 CLIMATE

The mean temperature is 25°C (77°F) in August and −3°C (27°F) in January. The capital city receives 33 centimeters of rain annually (13 inches), though more rainfall occurs in the mountains.

4 PLANTS AND ANIMALS

The region is home to European bison, snow leopards, cheetahs, and porcupines.

5 ENVIRONMENT

In 1994, Armenia's chief environmental problems were the result of natural disasters, pollution, and warfare. Radiation from the meltdown of the nuclear reactor facility at Chernobyl in the former Soviet Union also polluted the environment in Armenia.

6 POPULATION

The population of Armenia was estimated at 3,415,566 in mid-1992. A population of 3,608,000 was estimated for the year 2000. Yerevan, the capital, had an estimated population of 1,202,000 at the beginning of 1990.

7 MIGRATION

There are Armenian communities in Turkey, Iran, Azerbaijan, Russia, Georgia, Lebanon, Syria, and the US. It is estimated that than 500,000 people fled Armenia between 1991 and 1994.

8 ETHNIC GROUPS

Armenians comprise 93% of the population. Another 2.6% are Azerbaijanis, 1.7% are Kurds, and 1.6% are Russians.

9 LANGUAGES

Armenian belongs to an independent branch of the Indo-European linguistic family. There are two main dialects: East Armenian, the official language of the country, and West, or Turkish, Armenian.

10 RELIGIONS

In 1992, 94% of the population was Armenian Orthodox, with smaller representations of Russian Orthodox and Roman Catholic.

11 TRANSPORTATION

As of 1990, there were 840 kilometers (522 miles) of 1 meter-gauge railroad. The highway system includes 10,500 kilometers (6,525 miles) of surfaced roads. Four-lane highways connect the major cities.

The airport at Yerevan receives scheduled flights from Moscow, Paris, New York, and Sofia. Cargo shipments to landlocked Armenia are routed through ports in Georgia and Turkey.

12 HISTORY

Armenia existed as an independent kingdom long before the birth of Christ. In the first century BC, Armenian rule extended into what is now Syria and Iraq. Defeated by the Roman general Pompey in 67 BC, Armenia came under the dominance of the Roman Empire. Armenia adopted Christianity at the beginning of the fourth century AD.

Although there were periods of relative independence (notably from 809 to 1045), over the centuries Armenia came under the control of several empires, including the Roman, Byzantine, Persian, Arab, and Ottoman. In 1639, Armenia was divided between the Ottoman and Persian empires. In 1828, Russia seized what had been Persian Armenia.

With the collapse of the Russian and Ottoman empires, Armenia declared its independence on 28 May 1918. The August 1920 Treaty of Sevres gave international recognition to Armenian independence, but shortly afterwards both Turkey and Soviet Russia invaded.

The Soviet Republic of Armenia was declared on 29 November 1920. During the 1920s, the Soviet government separated the Armenian region of Nagorno-Karabakh from the rest of Soviet Armenia by a few miles of territory in Soviet Azerbaijan. Nagorno-Karabakh had the status of an "autonomous republic" within the Soviet Republic of Azerbaijan.

When Armenia decided to seek independence from the Soviet Union on 23 August 1990, Armenia and Azerbaijan began fighting over who would control Nagorno-Karabakh. The Armenians think of Nagorno-Karabakh as the cradle of their race, and their traditional last sanctuary when their country has been invaded. Fighting between mostly Christian Armenia and mostly Muslim Azerbaijan continued until May 1994 when a cease fire was announced. At that time, Armenian forces had captured the entire Nagorno-Karabakh region plus a significant portion of Azerbaijan itself. Despite Armenian military success, the war has resulted in a prolonged economic crisis for the new republic.

13 GOVERNMENT

Armenia still operates under its Soviet-era constitution. Free elections to the Supreme Soviet (since renamed the National Assembly) were held in 1990. Armenia is divided into over two dozen administrative regions.

14 POLITICAL PARTIES

The president, Levon Ter-Petrossyan, belongs to the Armenian Pan-National Movement (APNM). There are seven opposition parties represented in parliament. Most of them are ultra-nationalist, calling for recognition of the Nagorno-Karabakh Republic.

LOCATION: 40°0′N to 45°0′E **BOUNDARY LENGTHS:** Total boundary lengths, 1,254 kilometers (780 miles); Azerbaijan (east), 566 kilometers (352 miles); Azerbaijan (south), 221 kilometers (137 miles); Georgia, 164 kilometers (102 miles); Iran, 35 kilometers (22 miles); Turkey, 268 kilometers (167 miles).

15 JUDICIAL SYSTEM

The court system consists of district courts, a Supreme Court, and military tribunals. Criminal procedures include the right to an attorney, a public trial, and the right to appeal. There is currently no bail and no trial by jury.

Photo credit: AP/Wide World Photos

An Armenian boy dances on the roof of a car in downtown Yerevan after a referendum on Armenian independence. The vote was overwhelmingly for independence.

16 ARMED FORCES

The armed forces may number 50,000 regular soldiers and 30,000 militiamen, reinforced with 23,000 Russian soldiers in four divisions.

17 ECONOMY

The Armenian economy is mainly agricultural. In December 1988, a severe earthquake seriously damaged the Armenian economy, which has also been severely disrupted by the break-up of the former Soviet Union. Armenia's economic out-

look is bleak due to ethnic strife and high dependance on foreign resources.

18 INCOME

In 1992, the gross national product (GNP) was $2,719 million at current prices, or $660 per person.

19 INDUSTRY

The main industries are mechanical engineering, chemicals, textiles, and food processing. Since the collapse of the former Soviet Union, industrial production has been severely disrupted by political instability and shortages of power. A severe earthquake in December 1988 destroyed about one-tenth of the industrial capacity of the country. Much of the industrial sector has not been repaired.

20 LABOR

In 1990, of the total labor force of 1,630,000, 42% was involved in industry and construction, 18% in forestry and agriculture, and 40% in other sectors.

21 AGRICULTURE

Before the collapse of the Soviet Union, about 16% of Armenia's land was cultivated. Major crops include vegetables and melons, potatoes, wheat, grapes, and tobacco.

22 DOMESTICATED ANIMALS

Over one-fifth of the total land area is permanent pastureland. In 1992, the livestock population included: sheep, 980,000; cattle, 550,000; pigs, 200,000; and chickens, 9,000. In 1992, some 56,000 tons of meat were produced. In 1992, 300,000 tons of milk, 22,000 tons of eggs, and 2,000 tons of wool were also produced.

23 FISHING

Fishing is limited to the Arpa River and Sevana Lich. Commercial fishing is not a significant part of the economy.

24 FORESTRY

Soviet mismanagement, an earthquake in 1988, wars with Azerbaijan, and fuel shortages have hurt the timber industry. Available timber is used for firewood during the harsh winters.

25 MINING

Mineral resources in Armenia are mostly in the southern region, near Azerbaijan and Iran, where there are several copper and molybdenum mines. Perlite is mined southeast of Yerevan, and a gold mine is located near Zod.

26 FOREIGN TRADE

In 1988, inter-republic trade represented 82% of Armenia's imports and 98% of its exports. Oil from Russia accounts for two-thirds of Armenia's imports.

27 ENERGY AND POWER

Electricity production in 1992 totaled 6,800 million kilowatt hours. The December 1988 earthquake disrupted the Yerevan nuclear power plant, which had supplied 40% of Armenia's power needs, creating almost total dependence on imported oil and natural gas for power.

28 SOCIAL DEVELOPMENT

Women in Armenia largely occupy traditional roles defined by their families. A 1992 employment law does formally prohibit discrimination based on sex.

29 HEALTH

Life expectancy in 1991 averaged 73 years (75 years for females and 68 years for males). The country spent a total of $506 million on health care in 1990.

30 HOUSING

In 1990, Armenia had 15 square meters of housing space per person. As of 1 January 1991, there were 142,000 households on waiting lists for housing in urban areas, or 34.6% of all households. The 1988 earthquake is estimated to have destroyed up to 10% of the housing in Armenia.

31 EDUCATION

Adult literacy was estimated at 98.8% in 1990 (males, 99.4%, and females, 98.1%). Education is compulsory and free at the primary and secondary levels. There are two universities in Yerevan. In 1990, a total of 68,400 students were enrolled in all higher level institutions.

32 MEDIA

There are approximately 260,000 telephones, or 8 per 100 persons. Armenian and Russian radio and television stations broadcast throughout the country. In 1989, there were 85 newspapers in Armenia, of which 79 were published in the Armenian language. These had a combined 1989 circulation of 1.5 million.

Selected Social Indicators

These statistics are estimates for the period 1988 to 1993. For comparison purposes, data for the United States and averages for low-income countries and high-income countries are also given.

Indicator	Armenia	Low-income countries	High-income countries	United States
Per capita gross national product†	$660	$380	$23,680	$24,740
Population growth rate	1.5%	1.9%	0.6%	1.0%
Population growth rate in urban areas	1.9%	3.9%	0.8%	1.3%
Population per square kilometer of land	123	78	25	26
Life expectancy in years	73	62	77	76
Number of people per physician	261	>3,300	453	419
Number of pupils per teacher (primary school)	n.a.	39	<18	20
Illiteracy rate (15 years and older)	<2%	41%	<5%	<3%
Energy consumed per capita (kg of oil equivalent)	897	364	5,203	7,918

† The gross national product (GNP) is the total dollar value of all goods and services produced by a country in a year. The per capita GNP is calculated by dividing a country's GNP by its population. The World Bank defines low-income countries as those with a per capita GNP of $695 or less. High-income countries have a per capita GNP of $8,626 or more. Less than 14% of the world's 5.5 billion people live in high-income countries, while almost 60% live in low-income countries.   n.a. = data not available   > = greater than   < = less than
Sources: World Bank, *Social Indicators of Development 1995,* Baltimore: Johns Hopkins University Press, 1995. Central Intelligence Agency, *World Fact Book,* Washington, D.C.: Government Printing Office, 1994.

33 TOURISM AND RECREATION

Circumstances in recent years—including the 1988 earthquake and ethnic conflict over the Nagarno-Karabakh region—have been unfavorable for tourism.

34 FAMOUS ARMENIANS

Levon Ter-Petrossyan has been president of Armenia since November 1991. Gregory Nare Katzi, who lived in the 10th century, was Armenia's first great poet.

Nineteenth-century novelists include Hakob Maliq-Hakobian, whose pen name is "Raffi," and the playwright Gabriel Sundukian.

35 BIBLIOGRAPHY

Bournoutian, George A. *A History of the Armenian People.* Costa Mesa, Calif.: Mazda Publishers, 1993.

Nersessian, Vrej. *Armenia.* Oxford, England, and Santa Barbara, Calif.: Clio, 1993.

Walker, Christopher J. *Armenia: the Survival of a Nation,* Rev. 2nd ed. New York: St. Martin's Press, 1990.

AUSTRALIA

Commonwealth of Australia

CAPITAL: Canberra.

FLAG: The flag has three main features: the red, white, and blue Union Jack in the upper left quarter, indicating Australia's membership in the Commonwealth of Nations; the white five-star Southern Cross in the right half; and the white seven-pointed federal star below the Union Jack. The flag has a blue ground. Of the five stars of the Southern Cross, four have seven points and one has five points.

ANTHEM: *God Save the Queen* is reserved for regal and state occasions and whenever singing is appropriate; the national tune is *Advance Australia Fair.*

MONETARY UNIT: The Australian dollar (A$) is a paper currency of 100 cents. There are coins of 5, 10, 20, and 50 cents and 1 and 2 dollars, and notes of 5, 10, 20, 50 and 100 dollars. A$1 = US$0.7008 (US$1 = A$1.4269).

WEIGHTS AND MEASURES: Metric weights and measures are used. The Australian proof gallon equals 1.37 US proof gallons.

HOLIDAYS: New Year's Day, 1 January; Australia Day, last Monday in January; Anzac Day, 25 April; Queen's Birthday, 2d Monday in June; Christmas, 25 December; Boxing Day, 26 December. Numerous state holidays are also observed. Movable religious holidays include Good Friday, Easter Saturday, and Easter Monday.

TIME: Western Australia, 8 PM = noon GMT; South Australia and Northern Territory, 9:30 PM; Victoria, New South Wales, Queensland, and Tasmania, 10 PM. Summer time is 1 hour later in all states except Western Australia, Queensland, and the Northern Territory.

1 LOCATION AND SIZE

Lying southeast of Asia, between the Pacific and Indian oceans, Australia is the world's smallest continent. Australia is slightly smaller than the United States, with a total area of 7,686,850 square kilometers (2,967,909 square miles). Australia's capital city, Canberra, is located in the southeastern part of the country.

2 TOPOGRAPHY

The continent of Australia is divided into four general topographic regions: (1) a low, sandy eastern coastal plain; (2) the eastern highlands, extending from Cape York Peninsula in northern Queensland southward to Tasmania; (3) the central plains, consisting mostly of a north-south series of drainage basins; and (4) the western plateau, covered with great deserts and "bigger plains" (regularly spaced sand ridges and rocky wastes). The highest point is Mt. Kosciusko, 2,228 meters (7,310 feet); the lowest point is Lake Eyre, 12 meters (39 feet) below sea level.

The most important river system in the country is formed by the Murray, Darling, and Murrumbidgee rivers in the southeast. The Murray River, Australia's largest, flows some 2,600 kilometers (1,600 miles) west and southwest to empty into the sea below Adelaide, South Australia. The Great Barrier Reef, the longest coral reef in the world, extends for about 2,010 kilometers (1,250 miles) off the east coast of Queensland.

3 CLIMATE

Although it has many different climatic conditions, Australia is generally warm and dry, with no extreme cold and little frost. July mean temperatures average 9°C (48°F) in Melbourne in the southeast and 25°C (77°F) in Darwin in the north. January mean temperatures average 20°C (68°F) in Melbourne and 30°C (86°F) in Darwin.

Except for a few areas, rainfall is insufficient. Mean annual rainfall is 42 centimeters (17 inches), much less than the world mean of 66 centimeters (26 inches). Droughts and floods occur frequently over large areas.

4 PLANTS AND ANIMALS

There are some 500 species of eucalyptus and 600 species of acacia (wattle). Other outstanding trees are the baobab, blackwood, red cedar, coachwood, jarrah, Queensland maple, silky oak, and walnut. Native trees shed bark instead of leaves. There are numerous types of wildflowers, including boronia, Christmas bush, desert pea, and kangaroo paw. There are 470 varieties of orchids.

About 400 kinds of mammals, 200 kinds of lizards, and 700 kinds of birds are native to Australia. Apart from marsupials (mammals who raise their young in pouches, including bandicoots, kangaroos, koalas, opossums, Tasmanian devils, tree kangaroos, and wallabies), the most unusual animals are the dingo, echidna, flying fox (fruit bat), platypus, and wombat. Birds include the anhinga, bellbird, bowerbird, cassowary, emu, galah, kookaburra (laughing jackass), lyrebird, fairy penguin, and rosella.

5 ENVIRONMENT

Water being a scarce resource in Australia, problems of water quality and availability are a constant concern. As of 1994, the country had only 82.3 cubic miles of water supply. Gas emissions from the burning of fossil fuel affect the ozone layer and constitute a health hazard as well. Australia ranks seventh in the world as a producer of carbon dioxide emissions from industry.

Of the 102 mammals native to southern Australia, 28% are extinct and 40% are endangered. The Whale Protection Act of 1981 prohibits killing, capturing, injuring, or interfering with a whale, dolphin, or porpoise by Australian vessels and aircraft and their crews. As of 1993, 38 species of mammals, 39 species of birds, and 2,133 species of plants were threatened.

6 POPULATION

The estimated population in mid-1992 was 17,528,982. The populations of the six states and two mainland territories in 1992 were estimated as follows: New

AUSTRALIA

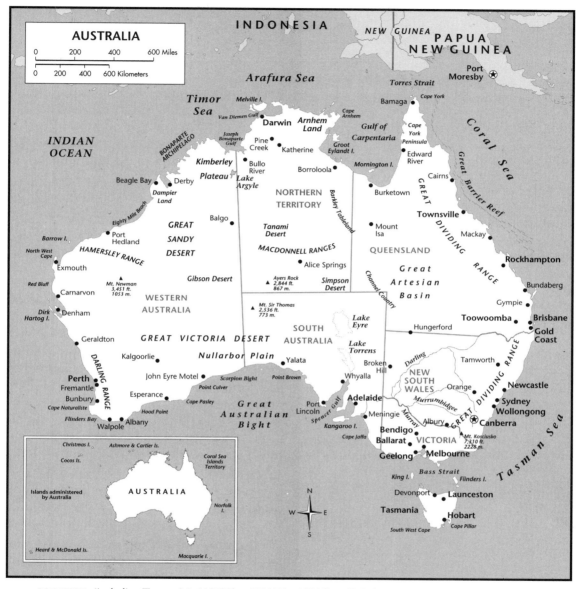

LOCATION: (including Tasmania): 113°09′ to 153°39′E; 10°41′ to 43°39′S. **TERRITORIAL SEA LIMIT:** 3 miles.

South Wales, 5,974,146; Victoria, 4,458,895; Queensland, 3,037,405; South Australia, 1,459,622; Western Australia, 1,662,777; Tasmania, 471,118; Australian Capital Territory (a specially designated area within New South Wales that surrounds Canberra), 296,376; and Northern Territory, 168,643. Population growth between 1987 and 1992 averaged 1.4%. A population of 19,595,000 was projected by the UN for the year 2000.

Population density in 1992 was two persons per square kilometer (5.9 per square mile). The population is unevenly distributed. One-third of Australia is virtually uninhabited. Another third is sparsely populated. Most of the people live in the southeast section and in other coastal areas.

7 MIGRATION

From World War II to 1991, over 460,000 refugees settled in Australia. These included more than 130,000 Indochinese. Interstate migration favors Queensland, which gained 282,300 more people from the rest of Australia than it lost between 1982–92. Victoria lost a total of 125,300 people through interstate migration in this period.

8 ETHNIC GROUPS

Most Australians are of British or Irish ancestry. In 1991, nearly four-fifths were Australian-born. Persons born in the UK and Ireland formed another 7% of the population. European-born persons made up 13.9% of the population in 1991, while the Asian-born population grew to 4.1% in 1991.

After the coming of the Europeans, the aboriginal, or native, population declined drastically, from about 300,000 to about 60,000 by the early 1920s. By the 1950s, however, the decline was reversed. In the 1991 census 265,492 people identified themselves as being of aboriginal or Torres Strait Islander origin. Many of them live in tribal conditions on government reservations. Aboriginals were not given full citizenship rights until 1963, and they continue to suffer from discrimination and a lower living standard than European Australians generally.

Beginning in the 1960s, the government abandoned its policy of "assimilation" of the aboriginals, recognizing the uniqueness of aboriginal culture and the right of the aboriginals to determine their own patterns of development.

9 LANGUAGES

More than 99% of the population speaks English. There are no class variations of speech, and few if any local dialects. Many different dialects are spoken by the aboriginal tribes. There is no written aboriginal language, but markings on "letter sticks," sometimes carried by messengers from one tribe to another, are readily understood by tribal chiefs. In rural areas, 42% of the aboriginal and Torres Strait Islander people speak an aboriginal language at home.

10 RELIGIONS

Constitutionally, there can be no state religion or state aid to any religion. As of 1992, 25.9% of Australians were Anglicans, 24.3% other Protestants, 27.5% Roman Catholics, and 2.7% Eastern Orthodox. About 12.7% of Australians indicated in 1992 that they had no religion. As of 1992, there were an estimated 88,000 Jews.

A street in Chinatown, Sydney, Australia. Australia is one of the world's most culturally diverse nations.

11 TRANSPORTATION

As of 1991, government-operated railways totaled about 40,478 kilometers (25,153 miles). There are also some private railways, mainly for the iron ore industry in Western Australia. Australian railway systems do not interconnect well, and rail travel between principal cities involves changing trains.

Highways provide access to many districts not served by railroads. As of 1991, there were 837,872 kilometers (520,674 miles) of roads, about 30% of which were paved. Motor vehicles in 1992 totaled about 9,954,000, including 7,913,000 passenger cars, and 2,041,000 commercial trucks, buses, and taxis.

In addition to the fine natural harbors of Sydney and Hobart, many other harbors have been artificially developed. In 1991, there were some 70 commercially significant ports.

The Australian overseas airline, Qantas, carries more than 3 million passengers per year to and from Australia, nearly 40% of the total carried by all airlines serving Australia. There are international airports at Adelaide, Brisbane, Cairns, Darwin, Hobart, Melbourne, Perth, Sydney, and Townsville. Some 30.9 million passengers were carried on domestic and overseas flights via the major airports.

12 HISTORY

Human beings may have inhabited what is now Australia as long as 100,000 years ago. The aboriginals—the first inhabitants—migrated to Australia from Southeast Asia at least 40,000 years before the first Europeans arrived on the island continent. The aboriginals developed a rich, complex culture and numbered about 300,000 by the 18th century. However, with the onset of European settlement, conflict and disease reduced their numbers significantly.

The first recorded explorations of the continent by Europeans took place early in the 17th century. It was then that Dutch, Portuguese, and Spanish explorers sailed along the coast and discovered what is now Tasmania. However, none took formal possession of the land until 1770, when Capt. James Cook claimed possession in the name of Great Britain.

The first settlement was a British penal colony at Port Jackson (now Sydney), founded in 1788. As the number of free settlers grew, the country developed, the interior was penetrated, and six colonies were created: New South Wales in 1786, Van Diemen's Land in 1825 (renamed Tasmania in 1856), Western Australia in 1829, South Australia in 1834, Victoria in 1851, and Queensland in 1859.

Sheep raising and wheat growing were introduced and soon became the backbone of the economy. The discovery of gold in Victoria (1851) attracted thousands of prospectors, and in a few years the population had quadrupled.

Until the end of the 19th century, Australia's six self-governing colonies remained separate. However, the obvious advantages of common defense and irrigation, and many other joint functions, led to the federation of the states into the Commonwealth of Australia in 1901. The Northern Territory, which belonged to South Australia, became a separate part of the Commonwealth in 1911. In the same year, territory was acquired from New South Wales for a new capital located at Canberra.

Australian forces fought along with the British in Europe during World War I. In World War II, the Australian forces supported the UK in the Middle East between 1940 and 1942 and, after the Japanese attack on Pearl Harbor, played a major role in the war in the Pacific. In the decades following World War II, Australia supported the US military presence in Asia. Australian troops served in Vietnam between 1965 and 1971. However, in 1972, the government began the process of dissociating Australia from US and UK policies and strengthening ties with non-Communist Asian nations. In addition, diplomatic relations with the People's Republic of China were established.

13 GOVERNMENT

Australia is divided into six states and two territories. The government consists of the British sovereign, represented by a governor-general, and the Australian Parliament. Officially, executive power belongs to the governor-general and an executive council. In practice, however, it is normally exercised by a cabinet chosen and presided over by a prime minister, representing the political party or coalition with a majority in the House of Representatives.

Legislative power is exercised by the Parliament, which is composed of a 76-member Senate, representing the states and territories, and a 148-member House of Representatives, representing electoral districts. Twelve senators are elected from each state and two senators each from the Northern Territory and Capital Territory. House membership is not quite double that of the Senate, with a minimum of five representatives for each state. There are two members from the Australian Capital Territory and one from the Northern Territory. Parliament must meet at least once a year.

Voting is universal for all persons 18 years of age and older. Voting is compulsory in national and state parliamentary elections.

14 POLITICAL PARTIES

The Labour Party is a trade-union party, officially socialist in policy and outlook. The Liberal party represents business interests, while the National Party (formerly the Country Party) is allied with farmers. Smaller parties include the Democratic Labour Party, the Communist Party, the Australian Democrats Party, and the Green Party.

15 JUDICIAL SYSTEM

The High Court of Australia consists of a Chief Justice and six Associate Justices appointed by the governor general. It is the supreme authority on interpreting the Australian constitution and has the authority to decide whether state and federal legislation is constitutional. Special cases may be referred to a 25-member federal court which deals with commercial law, copyright law, taxation, and trade practices. There is also a family court.

States and territories have their own court systems. Cases receive their first hearing in local or circuit courts, magistrates' courts, children's courts, or higher state courts.

16 ARMED FORCES

The all-volunteer Australian armed forces numbered 67,900 in 1993. The army had an official strength of 30,300; the navy, 15,300; the air force, 22,300; and reserve forces, 29,200 for all three services. The active forces include 8,500 women. Military weapons systems included 103 battle tanks, 5 submarines, 3 destroyers, 8 frigates, 157 air force combat aircraft. Australia's defense expenditure in 1992 was $7.5 billion.

17 ECONOMY

Wool, food, and minerals provide raw materials for industry at home and around two-thirds of foreign earnings. Australia grows all needed basic foodstuffs and has large surpluses for export. Australia is the world's largest wool-producing country, as well as one of the world's great wheat exporters, and also exports large quantities of meat and dairy products. The country is also a major world supplier of iron ore, bauxite, lead, zinc, and copper. Coal,

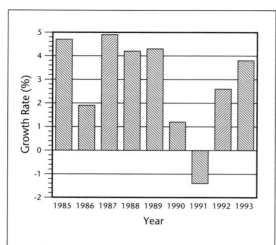

Yearly growth rate of the economy. This economic indicator tells by what percent the economy has increased or decreased when compared with the previous year.

Australia produces most of its own foods, as well as its beverages, building materials, many common chemicals, some domestic electrical appliances, radios, plastics, textiles, and clothing. In addition, most of its needed communications equipment, farm machinery (except tractors), furniture, leather goods, and metal manufactures are domestically produced. Recent years have seen the rapid growth of high-tech industries including aircraft, communications and other electronic equipment, electrical appliances and machinery, pharmaceuticals, and scientific equipment.

20 LABOR

The Australian work force numbers 8,700,000, of whom 41.6% are women. About 20% of the labor force works in wholesale and retail trade; 29.7% in social, personal, and community services; 14.6% in manufacturing; 11% in financial services; 7% in construction; 5.1% in agriculture, fishing, and forestry; and 12.6% in other areas.

Australia is highly unionized. About 40% of all wage and salary earners belong to trade unions. In 1991, 275 trade unions (down from 329 in 1985) had a membership of 2,660,000. The standard workweek is under 40 hours, generally from Monday through Friday. Nearly all Australian workers receive four weeks of annual vacation, many at rates of pay 17.5% above regular pay.

21 AGRICULTURE

Australia is an important producer and exporter of agricultural products and a

beach sand minerals, and nickel have become major industries as well.

18 INCOME

In 1992, Australia's gross national product (GNP) was US$299,323 million at current prices, or US$17,500 per person.

19 INDUSTRY

In proportion to its total population, Australia is one of the world's most highly industrialized countries. The manufacturing sector has undergone significant expansion in recent years and turns out goods ranging from automobiles to chemicals and textiles. The leading industries are food processing, beverages, motor vehicles, metalworking, and paper and paper products.

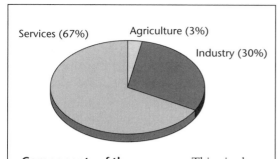

Components of the economy. This pie chart shows how much of the country's economy is devoted to agriculture (includes forestry, hunting, and fishing), industry, or services.

Services (67%) Agriculture (3%) Industry (30%)

Australia's wide climate differences permit the cultivation of a range of fruits, from pineapples in the tropical zone to berry fruits in the cooler areas. In 1990/91, over 18.2 million hectares (45 million acres) were cultivated for orchard fruit (apples, oranges, pears, peaches), and 17.5 million hectares (43.1 million acres) were cultivated for tropical (bananas and pineapples) and other fruit. Australia's wine industry is also growing. In 1990/91 it occupied 59,241 hectares (146,385 acres) and produced 825,792 tons of grapes for winemaking, drying, and other uses.

22 DOMESTICATED ANIMALS

More than 54% of Australia's land is used in stock raising. Wool production, the largest in the world, was an estimated 1,305,346 tons in 1992. Australia's flocks, some 146.8 million in 1992, now account for approximately 13% of the world's sheep but produce about 28% of the world's wool supply. Sheep of the Merino breed, noted for its heavy wool yield, make up about three-quarters of Australian flocks.

In 1992, there were an estimated 2.7 million hogs and 23.6 million head of cattle. Total poultry production in 1992 was 444,000 tons. Egg production is around 200 million dozen per year, mostly for domestic consumption. Australia produces some 25,000 to 30,000 tons of honey per year, half of which is exported. With a value of over $2 billion, Australia led the world in beef exports in 1992, which accounted for 5% of total exports.

major world supplier of grain, sugar, and fruit. Lack of water is the principal limiting factor for agriculture. Droughts, fires, and floods are common hazards. As of 1991, more than 1,831,000 hectares (4,524,400 acres) of land were irrigated.

Production of wheat for grain in 1990/91 was an estimated 13,053,000 tons. Western Australia and New South Wales are the chief wheat-producing states. Australia also produces barley, oats, corn and potatoes.

About 95% of sugar production comes from Queensland. The estimated 1992 sugar cane harvest from 348,000 hectares (860,000 acres) yielded about 29.3 million tons of sugar cane. Although tobacco growing is a relatively small industry, it is important in some areas. In 1992, some 5,000 hectares (12,400 acres) were planted with tobacco, and about 13,000 tons were produced. In 1992, cotton production amounted to 431,000 tons.

23 FISHING

Fishing is relatively unimportant. Even with a low per person fish consumption, Australia must import about half its normal requirements. The 1991 catch of fish, crustaceans, and mollusks totaled 227,300 tons, 98% from marine waters.

24 FORESTRY

In 1991, forestland covered 106 million hectares (261.9 million acres), or about 13.9% of the total area. Native forests consist principally of hardwood and other fine cabinet and veneer timbers. Eucalyptus dominates about 35 million hectares (86.5 million acres). Limited softwood resources had been seriously reduced, but new plantations were established in the 1980s. Softwood plantations supply more than half the timber harvested annually.

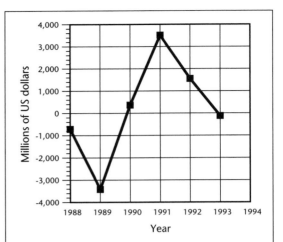

Yearly balance of trade measured in millions of US dollars. The balance of trade is the difference between what a country sells to other countries (its exports) and what it buys (its imports). If a country imports more than it exports, it has a negative balance of trade (a trade deficit). If exports exceed imports, there is a positive balance of trade (a trade surplus).

25 MINING

Australia is the world's leading producer of alumina, bauxite, diamonds, ilmenite, mined lead, monazite, opal, rutile, sapphire, and zircon. It is the second-largest producer of mined zinc. In addition, it is the third leading producer of mined gold and iron ore. Bauxite deposits in northern Queensland are among the world's largest, and the Argyle diamond mine, near the shores of Lake Argyle in Western Australia, is the largest diamond mine in the world.

26 FOREIGN TRADE

Measured by foreign trade volume per capita, Australia is one of the great trading nations of the world, and it continues to show a steady rise in trade volume. Mineral fuels, minerals, wheat, textile fibers, and meat are the main exports. Machinery, computer equipment, office machines, crude oil, and petroleum products are the major import items.

Japan is Australia's chief trading partner, accounting for roughly 25% of its exports. In recent years, Australia's foreign trade has tended to shift from European markets to developing Asian nations, which now buy nearly 35% of Australia's exports, compared with about 10% 20 years ago.

27 ENERGY AND POWER

Because of its relatively small hydroelectric resources and only recently discovered

Selected Social Indicators

These statistics are estimates for the period 1988 to 1993. For comparison purposes, data for the United States and averages for low-income countries and high-income countries are also given.

Indicator	Australia	Low-income countries	High-income countries	United States
Per capita gross national product†	$17,500	$380	$23,680	$24,740
Population growth rate	1.4%	1.9%	0.6%	1.0%
Population growth rate in urban areas	1.3%	3.9%	0.8%	1.3%
Population per square kilometer of land	2	78	25	26
Life expectancy in years	78	62	77	76
Number of people per physician	519	>3,300	453	419
Number of pupils per teacher (primary school)	17	39	<18	20
Illiteracy rate (15 years and older)	<1%	41%	<5%	<3%
Energy consumed per capita (kg of oil equivalent)	5,316	364	5,203	7,918

† The gross national product (GNP) is the total dollar value of all goods and services produced by a country in a year. The per capita GNP is calculated by dividing a country's GNP by its population. The World Bank defines low-income countries as those with a per capita GNP of $695 or less. High-income countries have a per capita GNP of $8,626 or more. Less than 14% of the world's 5.5 billion people live in high-income countries, while almost 60% live in low-income countries.   > = greater than   < = less than

Sources: World Bank, Social Indicators of Development 1995, Baltimore: Johns Hopkins University Press, 1995. Central Intelligence Agency, World Fact Book, Washington, D.C.: Government Printing Office, 1994.

oil, Australia has had to rely on coal-burning steam plants for about three-quarters of its public power requirements. The remainder has been supplied by hydroelectricity, gas turbines, and internal combustion generators. Power generation in 1991 totaled 156,883 million kilowatt hours, of which less than 8% was privately produced.

28 SOCIAL DEVELOPMENT

The Commonwealth Social Services Act of 1947, as amended, provides for invalid and old age pensions and a variety of other benefits. The government provides allowances to families for every child born. Widows' pensions are also provided. The Sex Discrimination Act of 1984 bars discrimination on the basis of sex, marital status, or pregnancy. In 1992, the Parliament passed amendments that strengthened it significantly.

29 HEALTH

Australia is one of the healthiest countries in the world. The common cold and other respiratory infections are the most prevalent forms of illness. Arteriosclerosis is the most common cause of death. The estimated life expectancy in 1992 was 78 years (80 years for females and 74 years for males).

Under Medicare (the national health insurance program introduced in 1984), all Australians have access to free care at public hospitals. The plan also meets three-fourths of the bill for private hospital treatment, while patients pay the rest.

The federal government provides grants to the states and aboriginal organizations for the development of special health services for aboriginals, who are often reluctant to use general community health services. As of 1992, aboriginals and Torres Strait Islanders had unacceptably low levels of health. They have access to the same health care system as any other Australian, but don't take full advantage of it.

30 HOUSING

In 1992, there were 6,339,000 dwellings in Australia. A total of 132,000 new houses and apartments were completed the same year. Central heating, formerly available only in the most modern and expensive homes and apartments, is now generally available in the coldest areas of the country. Most apartments and houses are equipped with hot water, refrigeration, and indoor bath and toilet facilities.

31 EDUCATION

Illiteracy is practically nonexistent except among the aboriginals. Education is compulsory for children from the age of 6 to 15 (16 in Tasmania). Free education is provided in municipal kindergartens and in state primary, secondary, and technical schools. There are also state-regulated private schools. Correspondence courses and educational broadcasts are given for children living in the remote "outback" areas.

The government expenditure on education in the 1989–1990 financial year was 13.2% of the total government spending. In 1992, nearly 2.2 million children attended government schools and 864,000 attended private institutions.

Australia had 39 higher education institutions with 339,000 full-time students in 1992. There is a state university in each capital city and each provincial area; a national post-graduate research institute in Canberra; and a university of technology in Sydney with a branch at Newcastle.

32 MEDIA

The Australian Broadcasting Commission operates a nationwide noncommercial radio and television service. In 1992, there were 258 AM stations and 67 FM stations. Commercial and government-owned networks broadcast over 134 television stations. In 1991, an estimated 22,000,000 radios and 8,330,000 television sets were in use. As of 1991 there were 8,727,163 telephones, about 1 for every 1.9 Australians.

In 1991, there were 68 newspapers. Leading dailies and their estimated circulation figures are the *Herald-Sun* (612,500), the *Daily Telegraph-Mirror* (480,000), and the *Morning Herald* (365,900). Major Sunday newspapers include the *Sun-Herald* (562,600) and the *Sunday Telegraph* (562,215) in Sydney,

Photo credit: Susan D. Rock.

The Sydney Opera House with its striking contemporary architecture and seaside location is a well-known Australian landmark.

and the *Sunday Mail* in Brisbane (340,600).

33 TOURISM AND RECREATION

Among Australia's natural tourist attractions are the Great Barrier Reef, a mecca for scuba divers; the varied and unusual plants and animals; and the sparsely habited outback regions, which in some areas may be toured by camel. Other attractions include Ballarat and other historic gold-rush towns near Melbourne.

Among the sports that lure tourists are surfing, sailing, fishing, golf, tennis, cricket, and rugby. Melbourne is famous for its horse racing (Australia's most cele-

brated race is the Melbourne Cup) and for its 120,000-capacity cricket ground, perhaps the biggest in the world. In 1983, *Australia II* captured the America's Cup, dominating world yachting in a series of races against *Liberty,* the US entrant, at Newport, R.I.

In 1991, Australia attracted 2,370,400 foreign visitors, of whom 22% were Europeans, 20% came from New Zealand, and 14% were North American residents. Tourist expenditures totaled US$4.18 billion.

34 FAMOUS AUSTRALIANS

The most highly regarded contemporary Australian writer is Patrick White (b.1912), author of *The Eye of the Storm* and other works of fiction, and winner of the 1973 Nobel Prize for literature. Germaine Greer (b.1939) is a writer on feminism. A prominent Australian-born publisher of newspapers and magazines, in the UK and the US as well as Australia, is Keith Rupert Murdoch (b.1931).

An outstanding bacteriologist was Sir Frank Macfarlane Burnet, O.M. (1899–1985), director of the Melbourne Hospital and cowinner of the 1960 Nobel Prize for medicine. Sir John Carew Eccles (b.1903) shared the 1963 Nobel Prize for medicine. John Warcup Cornforth (b.1917) shared the 1975 Nobel Prize for chemistry for his work on organic molecules.

Film stars have included Australian-born Errol Flynn (1909–50), Paul Hogan (b.1940), and US-born Mel Gibson (b.1956). Popular singers include Helen Reddy (b.1941) and Olivia Newton-John (b.UK, 1948).

In recent decades, the tennis world was dominated by such Australian players as Frank Sedgman (b.1927), Lewis Hoad (b.1934), Rod (George) Laver (b.1938), John David Newcombe (b.1944), and Evonne Goolagong Cawley (b.1951).

Record-breaking long-distance runners include John Landy (b.1930) and Herb Elliott (b.1938). Jon Konrads (b.1942) and his sister Ilsa (b.1944) have held many world swimming records, as did Dawn Fraser (b.1937), the first woman to swim 100 meters in less than a minute.

The principal modern Australian statesman is Sir Robert Gordon Menzies (1894–1978), who served as prime minister from 1939 to 1941 and again from 1949 to 1966.

35 BIBLIOGRAPHY

Arden, Harvey. "Journey into Dreamtime." *National Geographic,* January 1991, 8–41.

Atkinson, Alan. *The Muddle-headed Republic.* New York: Oxford University Press, 1993.

Australia in Pictures. Minneapolis, Minn.: Lerner, 1993, 1990.

Bassett, Jan. *The Oxford Illustrated Dictionary of Australian History.* New York: Oxford University Press, 1993.

Breeden, Stanley. "The First Australians." *National Geographic,* February 1988, 266–290.

Ellis, Richard. "Australia's Southern Seas." *National Geographic,* March 1987, 286–319.

Kurian, George Thomas. *Facts on File National Profiles. Australia and New Zealand.* New York: Facts on File Publications, 1990.

Lepthien, E. *Australia.* Chicago: Children's Press, 1982.

Vessels, Jane. "The Simpson Outback." *National Geographic,* April 1992, 64–93.

AUSTRIA

Republic of Austria
Republik Österreich

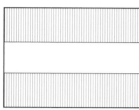

CAPITAL: Vienna (Wien).

FLAG: The flag consists of a white horizontal stripe between two red stripes.

ANTHEM: *Land der Berge, Land am Ströme (Land of Mountains, Land on the River).*

MONETARY UNIT: The schilling (s) is a paper currency of 100 groschen. There are coins of 1, 2, 5, 10, and 50 groschen and 1, 5, 10, 20, 25, 50, 100, 500, 1,000, and 2,000 schillings, and notes of 20, 50, 100, 500, 1,000, and 5,000 schillings. s1 = $0.0851 (or $1 = s11.757).

WEIGHTS AND MEASURES: The metric system is in use.

HOLIDAYS: New Year's Day, 1 January; Epiphany, 6 January; May Day, 1 May; Assumption, 15 August; National Day, 26 October; All Saints' Day, 1 November; Immaculate Conception, 8 December; Christmas, 25 December; St. Stephen's Day, 26 December. Movable religious holidays include Easter Monday, Ascension, Whitmonday, and Corpus Christi. In addition, there are provincial holidays.

TIME: 1 PM = noon GMT.

1 LOCATION AND SIZE

Austria, with an area of 83,850 square kilometers (32,375 square miles), is a landlocked country in Central Europe. It is slightly smaller than the state of Maine and has a total boundary length of 2,496 kilometers (1,551 miles). Austria's capital city, Vienna, is located in the northeastern part of the country.

2 TOPOGRAPHY

Most of western and central Austria is mountainous, and much of the flatter area to the east is hilly. The principal geographic regions are the Eastern Alps; the Alpine and Carpathian foothills; the Pannonian lowlands in the east; the granite and gneiss highlands of the Bohemian Massif; and the Vienna Basin. The highest point of the Austrian Alps is the Grossglockner, 3,797 meters (12,457 feet). The Danube River is the chief waterway.

3 CLIMATE

Climatic conditions depend on location and altitude. Temperatures range from an average of about –2°C (28°F) in January to about 19°C (66°F) in July. Rainfall ranges from more than 200 centimeters (80 inches) annually in the hills bordering the Alps to less than 60 centimeters (24 inches) in the driest region, east of the Neusiedler See.

4 PLANTS AND ANIMALS

Austria is one of Europe's most heavily wooded countries. Deciduous trees (particularly beech, birch, and oak) and conifers (fir) cover the mountains up to about 1,200 meters (4,000 feet). Above that point fir predominates and then gives way to larch and stone pine.

There is a large variety of wildlife. Deer, hare, fox, badger, marten, Alpine chough, grouse, marmot, partridge, and pheasant are plentiful. Birds include purple heron, spoonbill, and avocet.

5 ENVIRONMENT

As of 1994, Austria faces air, water, and land pollution. One major source of the problem is industrial and power facilities which use coal and oil. The Austrian government has placed strict regulations on gas emissions, which helped to reduce sulphur dioxide by two-thirds over an eight-year period beginning in 1980.

The same chemical agents that pollute the air eventually reach the land and water supplies. Austrians continue to fight the problem of acid rain which has damaged 25% of the country's forests. The Danube and Mur rivers have been the special focus of efforts to improve water quality.

Of the country's 85 species of mammals, two are threatened. Thirteen of Austria's 201 bird species are endangered. There are 25 endangered plant species in a total of 2,900 as of 1994.

6 POPULATION

According to the 1991 census, Austria's population was 7,795,786. The population density in 1991 was 93 persons per square kilometer (241 persons per square mile). Around 28% of the population lives in five major cities: Vienna, the capital,

1,539,848; Graz, 237,810; Linz, 203,044; Salzburg, 143,978; and Innsbruck, 118,112.

7 MIGRATION

Between 1945 and 1983, 1,942,782 refugees from more than 30 countries came to Austria. About 590,000 of them became Austrian citizens. As of 1992, there were 273,884 foreign workers in Austria, of whom 133,576 were Yugoslavs and 55,637 Turks. The total number of foreigners was about 413,400 in 1990. At the end of 1992, Austria was harboring 60,900 refugees, including 42,100 from the former Yugoslavia.

Of Austrians living abroad, some 186,900 were residents of Germany in 1991.

8 ETHNIC GROUPS

Austrians are a people of mixed Dinaric, Nordic, Alpine, and East Baltic origin. Aside from resident foreigners, ethnic minorities include about 20,000 Slovenes near the Slovenian border and 25,000 Croatians near the Hungarian border. About 2% of the Burgenland population is Hungarian. There are also some Czechs, Slovaks, Serbians, and Italians.

9 LANGUAGES

The official language is German, and nearly 99% of the inhabitants speak it as their mother tongue. In certain provinces, Austrians speak Bavarian dialects. There are also Croatian-, Slovene-, and Hungarian-speaking minorities, and small groups of Czech, Slovak, and Polish speakers in Vienna.

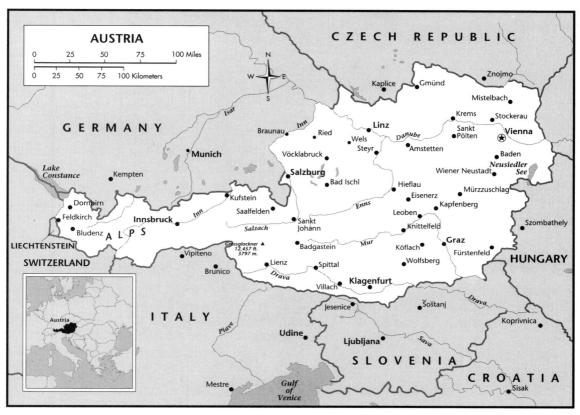

AUSTRIA

| 0 | 25 | 50 | 75 | 100 Miles |
| 0 | 25 | 50 | 75 | 100 Kilometers |

LOCATION: 46°22′ to 49°1′N; 9°22′ to 17°10′E **BOUNDARY LENGTHS:** Germany, 819 kilometers (509 miles); Czech and Slovak Republics, 571 kilometers (355 miles); Hungary, 354 kilometers (220 miles); the former Yugoslavia, 330 kilometers (205 miles); Italy, 430 kilometers (267 miles); Liechtenstein, 35 kilometers (22 miles); Switzerland, 168 kilometers (104 miles).

10 RELIGIONS

Up to 84% of the people are Roman Catholic. Protestants make up 6%, and 2% belong to other religious groups, including Muslims (1%). Austria's Jewish population was more than 200,000 in 1938. By the end of World War II and the Nazi Holocaust, it stood at no more than 4,000.

11 TRANSPORTATION

The Federal Railway Administration controlled 90% of Austria's 6,028 kilometers (3,746 miles) of railways in 1991. In 1991, the public railroads carried 173 million passengers and 64.7 million tons of goods. In 1991, highways totaled 95,412 kilometers (59,289 miles), of which paved roads accounted for 34,612 kilometers (21,508 miles). In 1991, there were 3,100,014 passenger cars and 259,308 trucks.

Austria has 446 kilometers (277 miles) of inland waterways. Most of Austria's overseas trade passes through the Italian port of Trieste. The rest is shipped from German ports.

Of the six major airports in Austria— Schwechat (just outside Vienna), Graz, Innsbruck, Klagenfurt, Linz, and Salzburg—Schwechat is by far the most important. In 1992, Austrian airports performed 4,867 million passenger-kilometers (3,024 million passenger-miles) and 101 million freight ton-kilometers (62.8 million freight ton-miles) of service. In 1991, a total of 52 airlines provided flights for 3,722,567 arriving and 3,722,535 departing passengers.

12 HISTORY

Human settlements have existed in what is now Austria since prehistoric times. In 15–14 BC, the region was conquered by the Romans, who founded several towns that survive today, including Vienna (Vindobona) and Salzburg (Juvavum). After the fall of the Roman Empire, Austria became a province of the French leader Charlemagne's empire from around 800 AD until the tenth century, when it was joined to the Holy Roman Empire as Österreich ("Kingdom of the East").

From the late thirteenth to the early twentieth centuries, the history of Austria was tied to that of the ruling Habsburg family. Great Habsburg rulers included King Charles I of Spain, who ruled over Austria, Spain, the Netherlands, and much of Italy. Holy Roman Emperor Joseph II (r.1765–90), sought to abolish serfdom and introduce religious freedom. Joseph II's rule spanned the careers of the composers Haydn and Mozart. One of the last Habsburg rulers was Franz Josef I. He occupied the Austrian throne for 68 years until his death in 1916. During his reign, Austria attempted to set up a strong central government that would unify all the Habsburg possessions under its leadership. But nationalist tensions persisted, and Austrian dominance was challenged in Italy, Germany, and Hungary.

On 28 June 1914, at Sarajevo, Serbian nationalists assassinated Archduke Francis Ferdinand, a nephew of the emperor and heir to the Austrian throne. Their act set off World War I, in which Austria-Hungary was joined by Germany, Italy, and Turkey. They became known as the Central Powers. However, in 1915, Italy went over to the side of the Allies—France, Russia, the UK, and the US. The Central Powers were defeated, the Austrian empire collapsed, and Austria became a republic.

During the decade after the war, Austria was hit by inflation, food shortages, unemployment, financial scandals, and growing political unrest. As the political climate deteriorated, Austria struggled to remain independent in the face of the growing military threat from Germany. The Nazi party, headed by Adolf Hitler, had taken over Germany and had set a course for world domination.

On 11 March 1938, German troops entered Austria, and two days later Austria was proclaimed a part of the German Reich. In 1939, Austria, now known as Ostmark, entered World War II on the side of Germany.

Germany lost the war and allied troops entered Austria. The country was divided into US, British, French, and Soviet zones

A view of Vienna, Austria from St. Stephen's Cathedral.

of occupation. The occupying powers permitted Austrians to set up a provisional government, but limited its powers.

On 15 May 1955, after more than eight years of negotiations, representatives of Austria and the four powers signed the Austrian State Treaty. This treaty reestablished an independent and democratic Austria. In October, all occupation forces withdrew from the country.

Although Austria is now a neutral nation, it cannot escape its Nazi past. On 8 July 1986, former UN Secretary-General Kurt Waldheim was sworn in as president of Austria. During the presidential campaign, Waldheim was accused of having belonged to Nazi organizations during World War II and of having taken part in war crimes while serving with the German army. Waldheim denied the charges.

After his inauguration, diplomats of many nations made a point of avoiding public contact with the new president. On 27 April 1987, the US Justice Department banned him from entering the US. Because of the controversy, Waldheim declined to run for a second term.

13 GOVERNMENT

Austria is a federal republic with a democratically elected parliament. The president, elected by popular vote for a six-year term, appoints a federal chancellor

(Bundeskanzler), usually the leader of the largest party in parliament. The president is limited to two terms of office.

The parliament, known as the Federal Assembly (Bundesversammlung), consists of the National Council (Nationalrat) and Federal Council (Bundesrat). The Bundesrat has 63 members, elected by the country's provincial legislatures (Landtage). The Nationalrat has 183 members, elected directly in nine election districts for four-year terms. All citizens 19 years of age or older may vote. Voting is compulsory for presidential elections.

14 POLITICAL PARTIES

The Austrian People's Party (Österreichische Volkspartei—ÖVP), also referred to as Austria's Christian Democratic Party, favors free enterprise, competition, and the reduction of class differences. It advocates provincial rights and strongly supports the Catholic Church.

The SPÖ, also known as the Social Democratic Party, advocates moderate reforms through democratic processes. It favors continued nationalization of key industries, economic planning, and widespread social welfare benefits.

The Freedom Party of Austria (Freiheitliche Partei Österreichs—FPÖ), an anti-socialist group, favors individual initiative over collective security. In June 1992, FPÖ dissidents founded the Free Democratic Party.

15 JUDICIAL SYSTEM

As of 1985, Austria had about 200 local courts (Bezirksgerichte) with civil jurisdic-tion. There were also 20 provincial and district courts (Landesgerichte and Kreisgerichte) with civil and criminal jurisdiction and four higher provincial courts (Oberlandesgerichte) with criminal jurisdiction, located in Vienna, Graz, Innsbruck, and Linz.

The Supreme Court (Oberster Gerichtshof), in Vienna, acts as the final appeals court for criminal and civil cases. The Constitutional Court (Verfassungsgerichtshof) has supreme jurisdiction over constitutional and civil rights issues. The Administrative Court (Verwaltungsgerichtshof) ensures the legal functioning of public administration.

Criminal defendants are afforded a presumption of innocence, public trials, and jury trial for major offenses.

16 ARMED FORCES

In 1993, the Austrian armed forces totaled 52,000. The Austrian army had 46,000 members, and the air service 6,000, with 54 combat aircraft. Active reserve strength is 200,000 with 66,000 receiving annual training. Another 960,000 have had military training.

17 ECONOMY

The government plays a large role in the Austrian economy, although private enterprise continues to occupy a central position. Basic industries, including mineral production, heavy industry, rail and water transport, and utilities, were taken over by the government during 1946–47. In 1970, they were reorganized under the Austrian Industrial Administration.

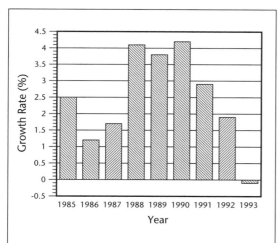

Yearly growth rate of the economy. This economic indicator tells by what percent the economy has increased or decreased when compared with the previous year.

From the 1950s through the early 1970s, the economy was characterized by a high rate of growth and modest price increases. By 1975, Austrian industry, the single most important sector of the economy, had more than quadrupled in value over 1945. But the general economic slowdown that followed the oil price hike of late 1973 affected Austria as it did other European countries.

In 1982, Austria endured its most prolonged recession since World War II, but the following years saw an improvement. Unemployment, generally low in post-World War II Austria, reached 6.8% in 1993. Inflation was moderate, and the cost of living rose 17.7% between 1986 and 1992.

18 INCOME

In 1992, Austria's gross national product (GNP) was $174,767 million, or $23,510 per person.

19 INDUSTRY

Industrial output has increased vastly since the beginning of World War II. Major parts of the electric and electronics, chemical, iron and steel, and machinery industries are government controlled. However, a return to private ownership was being planned for many companies during 1993–94.

In 1992, 3,953,107 tons of crude steel and 3,435,180 tons of rolled steel were produced. A total of 20,026 automobiles, buses, trucks, and tractors; 8,203 motorcycles; 8,149 mopeds; and 105,041 bicycles were manufactured in 1989.

The most important areas of the textile industry are embroidery, spinning, weaving, and knitting.

The chemical industry, which was relatively unimportant before World War II, now ranks third in value of production. In 1992, it produced 182,595 tons of fertilizers, 115,050 tons of rubber and asbestos products, 105,379 tons of paints and coating compounds, 178,035 tons of soaps and scouring agents, and more than $1 billion worth of pharmaceuticals. Petroleum refinery products (in tons) included fuel oil, 1,821,275; diesel oil, 3,242,282; gasoline, 2,458,365; and kerosene, 391,334.

Other leading industries are electrical and electronic machinery and equipment,

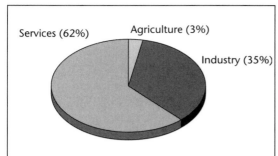

Components of the economy. This pie chart shows how much of the country's economy is devoted to agriculture (includes forestry, hunting, and fishing), industry, or services.

pulp and paper, ceramics, and especially foodstuffs and allied products. Austria has always been famous for its skilled craftspeople, such as glassblowers, goldsmiths, jewelers, lacemakers, potters, stonecutters, and woodcarvers.

20 LABOR

In 1991, there were 3,481,700 employed persons, of whom 1,283,700 were employed in industry. Foreign laborers, mainly from the former Yugoslavia and Turkey, constitute about 5% of the total work force.

In 1992, 58% of the work force was unionized. Most Austrian workers put in 38 hours per week. Every employee is entitled to a paid vacation of 30–36 workdays annually, depending on length of employment. In addition, since 1977 every employee has had the right to one week of paid leave each year to look after a close relative in case of sickness. The minimum legal working age is 15.

21 AGRICULTURE

Although small, the agricultural sector is highly diversified and efficient. Most production is oriented toward local consumption. Farms are almost solely family-owned. Austria today uses less land and manpower and produces more food than it did before World War II.

Chief crops are wheat, rye, oats, barley, potatoes, and sugar beets. Austria supplies almost all its own wheat, oats, rye, fruits, vegetables, sugar, and a number of other items.

22 DOMESTICATED ANIMALS

Dairy and livestock breeding are traditionally the major agricultural activities. Austrian milk, butter, cheese, and meat are excellent, and Austria supplies all its own dairy products and most of its own meats. In 1992, livestock included 3,629,000 hogs, 323,000 sheep, 44,900 horses, and 14 million poultry. Meat and poultry production in 1992 totaled 824,000 tons.

23 FISHING

Fishing is not important commercially, although a sizable portion of the population engages in sport fishing. Commercial catches consist mainly of carp and trout.

24 FORESTRY

About 46% of Austria's total area is forested, mostly in the foothills and mountains. To prevent overcutting, export restrictions have been introduced, and reforestation is widely promoted. Exports of raw timber and cork are supplemented by exports of such forestry products as

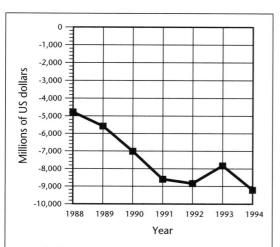

Yearly balance of trade measured in millions of US dollars. The balance of trade is the difference between what a country sells to other countries (its exports) and what it buys (its imports). If a country imports more than it exports, it has a negative balance of trade (a trade deficit). If exports exceed imports, there is a positive balance of trade (a trade surplus).

paper, cardboard boxes, prefabricated houses, toys, matches, and turpentine.

25 MINING

After a period of expansion following World War II, mineral production has generally declined in recent decades. Today, the iron ore production is insufficient for domestic needs. Austria also produces crude magnesite, graphite, talc, gypsum, aluminum, sulfur, crude kaolin, and common salt.

26 FOREIGN TRADE

Austria depends heavily on foreign trade, and the government consistently maintains strong ties with the West while being careful to preserve the country's neutrality.

Principal exports in 1992 were machinery; chemical products; paper and cardboard products; iron and steel; and textiles. Principal imports were transportation equipment; chemical products; mineral fuels and energy; clothing; and food.

In 1992, 39.8% of Austria's exports and 42.9% of its imports were accounted for by Germany. Other important trading partners are Italy, accounting for 8.8% of total exports and 8.6% of total imports; France, 4.4% of both exports and imports; and Switzerland, 5.9% of exports and 4% of imports.

27 ENERGY AND POWER

Austria is one of the foremost producers of hydroelectric power in Europe. In 1991, total power production amounted to 51,484 million kilowatt hours, of which 32,728 million kilowatt hours (64%) were produced by hydroelectric plants and 18,756 million kilowatt hours (36%) by thermal plants. Total domestic consumption during that year was 52,209 million kilowatt hours.

28 SOCIAL DEVELOPMENT

Austria has one of the most advanced and comprehensive systems of social legislation in the world. Health insurance is available to industrial and agricultural workers, federal and professional employees, and members of various other occupational groups. For those without insurance or adequate means, treatment is paid for by public welfare funds.

Selected Social Indicators

These statistics are estimates for the period 1988 to 1993. For comparison purposes, data for the United States and averages for low-income countries and high-income countries are also given.

Indicator	Austria	Low-income countries	High-income countries	United States
Per capita gross national product†	**$23,510**	$380	$23,680	$24,740
Population growth rate	**0.7%**	1.9%	0.6%	1.0%
Population growth rate in urban areas	**0.7%**	3.9%	0.8%	1.3%
Population per square kilometer of land	**93**	78	25	26
Life expectancy in years	**76**	62	77	76
Number of people per physician	**230**	>3,300	453	419
Number of pupils per teacher (primary school)	**11**	39	<18	20
Illiteracy rate (15 years and older)	**<1%**	41%	<5%	<3%
Energy consumed per capita (kg of oil equivalent)	**3,277**	364	5,203	7,918

† The gross national product (GNP) is the total dollar value of all goods and services produced by a country in a year. The per capita GNP is calculated by dividing a country's GNP by its population. The World Bank defines low-income countries as those with a per capita GNP of $695 or less. High-income countries have a per capita GNP of $8,626 or more. Less than 14% of the world's 5.5 billion people live in high-income countries, while almost 60% live in low-income countries.   > = greater than   < = less than

Sources: World Bank, Social Indicators of Development 1995, Baltimore: Johns Hopkins University Press, 1995. Central Intelligence Agency, World Fact Book, Washington, D.C.: Government Printing Office, 1994.

Family allowances are paid monthly, depending on the number of dependent children, with the amount doubled for any child who is severely handicapped. The state provides school lunches for more than 100,000 children annually.

The state also grants a special birth allowance and a payment for newlyweds setting up their first home. Unmarried people establishing a common household may apply for tax relief.

Although women make up an increasing percentage of the work force, they are still underrepresented in business and the professions, and not allowed in the military. A 1975 federal law provides for complete equality between husband and wife in maintaining the household and raising children.

29 HEALTH

Anyone is entitled to use the facilities provided by Austria's health service. The costs are borne by the social insurance plan, or, in cases of hardship, by the social welfare program.

Life expectancy at birth is 76 years (80 years for women and 73 years for men). Mandatory maternity leave (during which employment is prohibited by law) amounts to eight weeks before and eight weeks after birth.

Vienna's medical school and research institutes are world famous. Spas (with thermal springs), health resorts, and sanatoriums are popular among Austrians as well as foreigners.

30 HOUSING

The Housing Improvement Act of 1969 provides for government support for modernization of outdated housing. In 1990, 25% of Austria's housing stock had been built before 1919, and 19% between 1971 and 1980. About 61% of all dwellings had a private bath and central heating.

31 EDUCATION

All schools are coeducational, and education at state schools is free of charge. Financial support is provided for postsecondary schooling.

Primary education lasts for four years after which students can choose between two systems: the extended elementary school or secondary school. This lasts for four years, after which they may either attend a one-year polytechnical course followed by vocational training, or join the upper classes of secondary school, which runs for four years. Those who complete their studies at secondary or higher vocational school are qualified to attend the universities.

There are 12 university-level institutions and six fine arts colleges offering 430 subjects and about 600 possible degrees. In 1991–92, about 216,529 students

Photo credit: Susan D. Rock

This hotel along the River Inn in Innsbruck is an example of traditional Austrian architecture.

enrolled full time in universities and all higher level institutions. The teaching staff numbered 15,201.

32 MEDIA

The Austrian Broadcasting Corporation broadcasts nationally over three radio and two television networks. At the beginning of 1991, there were 2,500,000 licensed television sets and 2,636,000 licensed radios. In 1991, 4,309,564 telephones were in use.

As of 1991, Austria had 34 daily newspapers. Freedom of the press is constitutionally guaranteed, and there is no government censorship.

33 TOURISM AND RECREATION

Austria ranks high among European tourist destinations. It has a year-round tourist season. In winter, tourists come to the famous skiing resorts and attend outstanding musical events in Vienna. In summer, visitors are attracted by scenery, sports, and cultural festivals, notably in Vienna and Salzburg. Of the 4,000 communities in Austria, nearly half are considered tourist centers.

Tourism is a major contributor to the Austrian economy. Of an estimated 19,092,000 foreign tourists in 1991, travelers from Germany accounted for 64.5%, followed by Dutch travelers, representing 9.3%. In the same year, receipts from tourism amounted to US$13.9 billion. There were 315,141 rooms in hotels, inns, and pensions.

34 FAMOUS AUSTRIANS

Monarchs who played a leading role in Austrian and world history include Rudolf I of Habsburg (1218–91), founder of the Habsburg dynasty and Holy Roman emperor from 1273; Joseph II (1741–90), the "benevolent despot" who became Holy Roman emperor in 1765; and Franz Josef (1830–1916), emperor of Austria at the outbreak of World War I.

Adolf Hitler (1889–1945), born in Braunau, was the founder of the Nazi Party and dictator of Germany from 1933 until his death.

Beginning in the 18th century and for 200 years, Vienna was the center of European musical culture. Among its great masters were Franz Joseph Haydn (1732–1809), Wolfgang Amadeus Mozart (1756–91), Franz Schubert (1797–1828), and Arnold Schönberg (1874–1951).

Although born in Czechoslovakia, the poet Rainer Maria Rilke (1875–1926) and the novelist and short-story writer Franz Kafka (1883–1924) are usually identified with Austrian literary life.

Psychoanalysis was founded in Vienna by Sigmund Freud (1856–1939). A renowned geneticist was Gregor Johann Mendel (1822–84).

Austrians have excelled in international Alpine skiing competition. Annemarie Moser-Pröll (b.1953) retired in 1980 after winning a record six women's World Cups. Arnold Schwarzenegger (b.1947) is the most famous bodybuilder in the world.

35 BIBLIOGRAPHY

Bischof, Gunter and Anton Pelinka, eds. *Austria in the New Europe.* New Brunswick, N.J.: Transaction, 1993.

Federal Press Service. *Austria: Facts and Figures.* Vienna: Federal Press Service, 1992.

Greene, C. *Austria.* Chicago: Children's Press, 1986.

Salt, Denys. *Austria.* Santa Barbara, Calif.: ABC-Clio, 1986.

Sweeney, Jim and Josef Weidenholzer, eds. *Austria: a Study in Modern Achievement.* Brookfield, Vt.: Avebury, 1988.

AZERBAIJAN

Azerbaijan Republic

Azerbaijan Respectability

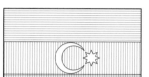

CAPITAL: Baku.

FLAG: Three equal horizontal bands of blue (top), red, and green; a crescent and eight-pointed star in white are centered in the red band.

ANTHEM: *Azerbaijan National Anthem,* composed by Azure Hajibayov.

MONETARY UNIT: Manat, introduced in 1992, remains tied to the Russian ruble; exchange rates are widely fluctuating as of 1994.

WEIGHTS AND MEASURES: The metric system is in force.

HOLIDAYS: Day of Sorrow (commemorating 1990 Soviet invasion of Baku), 20 January; Novrus (Holiday of Spring), 1 March; Independence Day (1918), 28 May; Day of Solidarity of Azerbaijanis, 31 December.

TIME: 4 PM = noon GMT.

1 LOCATION AND SIZE

Azerbaijan is located in southeastern Europe, between Armenia and the Caspian Sea. Comparatively, it is slightly larger than the state of Maine, with a total area of 86,600 square kilometers (33,436 square miles), including the Nakhichevan Autonomous Republic and the Nagorno-Karabakh Autonomous Oblast. Azerbaijan's boundary length totals 2,013 kilometers (1,251 miles). Azerbaijan's capital city, Baku, is located on the Apsheron Peninsula.

2 TOPOGRAPHY

The main features of the land are the large, flat Kura-Aras Lowland (much of it below sea level) and the Great Caucasus Mountains to the north. The Karabakh Upland lies in the west.

3 CLIMATE

The country's climate ranges from subtropical in the eastern and central parts to alpine-like in the mountains. In Baku, the capital, the mean temperature is 27.2°C (81°F) in July and 1.1°C (34°F) in January. Rainfall varies according to the nine climate zones in the country.

4 PLANTS AND ANIMALS

The country's plants and animals are rich and varied. There are 16 nature reserves and more than 28 forest reserves and hunting farms.

5 ENVIRONMENT

UN agencies report severe air and water pollution in Azerbaijan. The combination of industrial, agricultural, and oil-drilling pollution has created an environmental

Photo credit: AP/Wide World Photos

An Azerbaijani mother holds her baby as she is held hostage in Stepanabert, the Nagorno-Karabakh capital, in June, 1993. They were unable to flee when Armenian troops seized the Kelbajar region of western Azerbaijan on April 2, 1993. Taking and exchanging hostages is an ancient tradition in the Caucasus Mountains.

crisis in the Caspian Sea. These sources of pollution have contaminated 100% of the coastal waters in some areas and 45.3% of Azerbaijan's rivers. As of 1994, 14 species of mammals, 36 species of birds, 5 species of fish, 13 kinds of reptiles, and 40 species of insects are threatened with extinction.

6 POPULATION

The population of Azerbaijan was estimated at 7,450,787 in mid-1992. A population of 7,987,000 was projected for the year 2000. The population density was estimated at 84 persons per square kilometer (223 per square mile) in 1992. Baku, the capital, had an estimated population of 1,149,000 at the beginning of 1990.

7 MIGRATION

According to the government, in early 1994 more than a million people in Azerbaijan were refugees uprooted by the war with Armenia.

8 ETHNIC GROUPS

It is estimated that 83% of the population consists of Azerbaijanis, about 5.6% are Russians, and another 5.6% Armenians.

9 LANGUAGES

Azerbaijani (or Azari) is a language related to Turkish and is also spoken in northwestern Iran.

10 RELIGIONS

According to 1991 statistics, 87% of the population was Muslim, 70% of whom are Shiites and the remainder Sunnis. A population of 21,000 Jews was identified in 1990.

11 TRANSPORTATION

Railroads in Azerbaijan extend some 1,200 kilometers (750 miles). Suburban trains carry 150,000 passengers each day. In 1990, the highway system totaled 36,700 kilometers (22,800 miles), of which 31,800 kilometers (19,800 miles) were hard-surfaced. Ships from the Caspian fleet have called at some 125 ports in over 30 countries. There are flights from

Baku's Bina Airport to more than 70 cities of the former Soviet Union.

12 HISTORY

The territory of present-day Azerbaijan has been continuously inhabited since the Paleolithic era. Starting around 1000 BC, it was ruled by groups including the Medians, Persians, and Greeks. In the third and fourth centuries AD, battles between Rome and the Sassanid state in Persia inflicted great damage, leaving Azerbaijan open to raids by Turkic nomadic tribes from the north. New invaders appeared in the seventh and eighth centuries, when Arabs conquered much of the area.

In the 1230s, Azerbaijan was conquered by the famous Mongol warrior Genghis Khan. In the sixteenth and seventeenth centuries, the Safawid state emerged, rebuilding agriculture and commerce destroyed under the Mongols. In the eighteenth century Azerbaijan became the intersection of the Turkish, Persian, and Russian empires, as well as the focus of British and French attempts to block Russian expansion. The northern part of the territory was incorporated into Russia in the first third of the nineteenth century, but the area did not become important until the 1880s, when its plentiful oil gained commercial importance.

After the 1917 revolution in Russia, Communist Bolsheviks overthrew the government in Azerbaijan and declared the country a Soviet state. In the 1920s, the Soviet Union changed the borders between Azerbaijan and its neighbor Armenia and placed the Armenian region of Nagorno-Karabakh within Azerbaijan's borders.

LOCATION: 40°30′N; 47°0′E **BOUNDARY LENGTHS:** Total boundary lengths, 2,013 kilometers (1,251 miles); Armenia (west), 566 kilometers (352 miles); Armenia (south), 221 kilometers (137 miles); Georgia, 322 kilometers (200 miles); Iran (south), 432 kilometers (268 miles); Iran (southeast), 179 kilometers (111 miles).

This move would eventually lead to war between Azerbaijan and Armenia. The Armenians in Nagorno-Karabakh are mostly Christians while the Azerbaijanis are mostly Muslims.

In 1988, the ethnic Armenians living in Azerbaijan's Nagorno-Karabakh region declared their intent to leave Azerbaijan and become part of the Armenian republic. This led to a civil war. Inability to solve the conflict was one of the problems which brought down Mikhail Gorbachev and broke apart the Soviet Union.

Azerbaijan declared itself independent of the Soviet Union on 30 August 1991, and in December of that year, the Armenians of Nagorno-Karabakh voted to secede from Azerbaijan. They were helped by Armenian soldiers. Fighting between Armenia and Azerbaijan escalated in 1992 and continued until May 1994 when a cease fire was announced. At the time of the cease fire, Armenian forces were in control of Nagorno-Karabakh.

13 GOVERNMENT

The nation has been operating under the constitution of 1978, as modified by presidential and parliamentary decree. Effective governmental authority appears to rest with the president and the ministers he appoints. The Soviet-era legislature has been replaced by a 50-member National Council, or parliament, now called the Majlis. The Soviet-era administrative division of the country into 6 cities and 51 regions has been retained.

14 POLITICAL PARTIES

In March 1994, there were 28 political parties registered in Azerbaijan. The most important is probably the New Azerbaijan Party of President Heydar Aliev. The Azerbaijan Popular Front is the main opposition party. Two other opposition parties are the Milli Istiglal (National Independence Party) and the Musavat. There are also separatist parties advocating indepen-

dence for three ethnic groups: the Armenians, the Talysh, and the Lezghins.

15 JUDICIAL SYSTEM

The court system includes district courts and municipal courts that hear cases for the first time, and a Supreme Court which hears appeals. Criminal defendants have the right to an attorney and to an appointed lawyer, the right to a public trial, the right to be present at trial, and the right to confront witnesses.

16 ARMED FORCES

A republic of the former Soviet Union, Azerbaijan still has 62,000 Russian troops, but has formed its own National Defense Army of 5,000. These forces face 30,000–50,000 rebels in Nagorno–Karabakh. Azerbaijan's defense expenditures may be the equivalent of $1.7 billion.

17 ECONOMY

Azerbaijan is one of the oldest oil-producing regions of the world. Remaining oil reserves are estimated at about 1 billion tons, and gas reserves about 6 trillion cubic feet. Azerbaijan has varied industry and agriculture and a well-developed transport network. Like those of other post-Soviet republics, Azerbaijan's economy has been severely affected by the break-up of its traditional trading arrangements within the former USSR, a steep drop in consumer buying power, and the decline in military-related industrial activity. Conflicts over the provinces of Nagorno-Karabakh and Nakhichevan have added to the republic's economic troubles. However, in comparison with

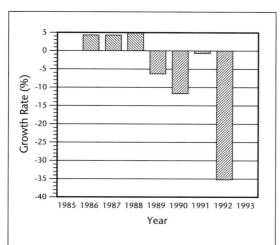

Yearly growth rate of the economy. This economic indicator tells by what percent the economy has increased or decreased when compared with the previous year.

many other post-Soviet republics, Azerbaijan has been relatively successful at controlling its debts and at expanding trade with countries beyond the former Soviet Union. Azerbaijan introduced its own currency, the manat, in August 1992.

18 INCOME

In 1992, Azerbaijan's gross national product (GNP) was $6,290 million at current prices, or $730 per person.

19 INDUSTRY

The oil and gas industry has traditionally been important to the wider industrial sector in Azerbaijan. Total oil refinery output averaged 291,000 barrels per day in 1991. Output of diesel fuel was 3,211,000 tons in 1992, and production of gasoline was 1,035,000 tons. Other important indus-trial areas in the Azerbaijani economy include finished food products, metal goods, machine tools, chemicals and petrochemicals, and some electronics.

20 LABOR

There are nearly 2.8 million people in the Azerbaijani labor force. In 1991, agriculture accounted for 34% of employment; industry, 16%; education and culture, 12%; and other areas, 38%. Strikes are legally permitted and increasing in frequency. There is a nationwide minimum wage, and the legal workweek is 41 hours. The minimum age for employment is 16. Children aged 14 are allowed to work during vacations with permission from their parents and a certificate from a physician. Children aged 15 may work if the workplace's labor union does not object.

21 AGRICULTURE

There are currently 59 agricultural regions in 10 geographic zones. The principal crops are grapes, cotton, and tobacco. Since independence, former state-owned farms have become more productive, and private fruit and vegetable farming is increasing. Of the total crop production of 1991, grapes accounted for 23%; cotton, 19%; tobacco, 13%; fruits and vegetables, 30%; grains, 7%; and other crops, 8%. More than 1.3 million tons of grapes are produced annually. Azerbaijani wines have frequently won awards at international exhibitions.

22 DOMESTICATED ANIMALS

Azerbaijan has some 2.2 million hectares (5.4 million acres) of permanent pasture.

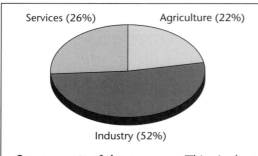

Services (26%) Agriculture (22%)

Industry (52%)

Components of the economy. This pie chart shows how much of the country's economy is devoted to agriculture (includes forestry, hunting, and fishing), industry, or services.

The livestock population in 1992 included 27,000,000 chickens, 5,000,000 sheep, 1,800,000 cattle, 212,000 goats, 100,000 pigs, and 35,000 horses. Meat production in 1992 amounted to 145,000 tons, almost three-fourths of which was beef and mutton. In 1992, about 800,000 tons of cow's milk, 49,400 tons of eggs, 14,400 tons of wool, and 2,500 tons of butter were produced.

23 FISHING

The Caspian Sea is Azerbaijan's principal fishing resource. Commercial fishing centers on caviar and sturgeon.

24 FORESTRY

About 11% of the land area consists of forests and woodlands. Soviet-era policies gave priority to high production and rapid growth at the expense of the environment. The State Committee for Ecology and Use of Natural Resources has recently introduced new regulations to protect forest resources.

25 MINING

Besides its mineral fuel reserves of petroleum and natural gas along the Caspian Sea, Azerbaijan also has iron ore reserves near the disputed Nagorno–Karabakh region, as well as lead, zinc, and copper–molybdenum deposits in the Nakhichivan area. Other mineral commodities in Azerbaijan include alunite and bromine–iodine.

26 FOREIGN TRADE

Processed foods, petroleum, and machinery and metal works together accounted for about 85% of exports to other former Soviet republics in 1992. Imports from former Soviet republics were led by ferrous metallurgy, machinery and processed metals, and chemicals and petroleum. The major trading partners among the former Soviet republics are Russia and Ukraine, as well as Turkmenistan, Kazakhstan, and Georgia.

Trading partners outside of the former Soviet republics include Iran, Turkey, and the UK. Seventy-six percent of exports to these countries are made up of oil and petroleum. Leading imports from these countries are grains, flour, other foodstuffs, and machinery.

27 ENERGY AND POWER

Almost all production now comes from offshore in the Caspian Sea. Proven oil reserves at the end of 1992 totaled about 1.3 billion barrels (200 million tons). Production in 1992 totaled 220,000 barrels per day. Less than one-quarter comes from onshore fields. Estimated natural gas reserves amount to 11 trillion cubic feet

Selected Social Indicators

These statistics are estimates for the period 1988 to 1993. For comparison purposes, data for the United States and averages for low-income countries and high-income countries are also given.

Indicator	Azerbaijan	Low-income countries	High-income countries	United States
Per capita gross national product†	**$730**	$380	$23,680	$24,740
Population growth rate	**1.3%**	1.9%	0.6%	1.0%
Population growth rate in urban areas	**1.8%**	3.9%	0.8%	1.3%
Population per square kilometer of land	**84**	78	25	26
Life expectancy in years	**71**	62	77	76
Number of people per physician	**254**	>3,300	453	419
Number of pupils per teacher (primary school)	**n.a.**	39	<18	20
Illiteracy rate (15 years and older)	**3%**	41%	<5%	<3%
Energy consumed per capita (kg of oil equivalent)	**2,470**	364	5,203	7,918

† The gross national product (GNP) is the total dollar value of all goods and services produced by a country in a year. The per capita GNP is calculated by dividing a country's GNP by its population. The World Bank defines low-income countries as those with a per capita GNP of $695 or less. High-income countries have a per capita GNP of $8,626 or more. Less than 14% of the world's 5.5 billion people live in high-income countries, while almost 60% live in low-income countries.

n.a. = data not available.   > = greater than   < = less than

Sources: World Bank, *Social Indicators of Development 1995,* Baltimore: Johns Hopkins University Press, 1995. Central Intelligence Agency, *World Fact Book,* Washington, D.C.: Government Printing Office, 1994.

(310 billion cubic meters). Production of natural gas in 1992 totaled 280 billion cubic feet (7.8 billion cubic meters).

Electricity production in 1992 totaled 19.8 billion kilowatt hours. Consumption of electricity in 1992 was 19.6 billion kilowatt hours.

28 SOCIAL DEVELOPMENT

The minimum wage was raised several times in 1992, but it still does not provide adequately for a worker and family. A decent living can only be assured by the "safety net" of the extended family struc-ture. Health and safety standards are often ignored in the workplace.

29 HEALTH

Total health expenditures for 1990 reached $785 million. Azerbaijan's infant mortality rate for 1992 was 37 per 1,000 live births. The overall death rate in 1993 was 7 per 1,000 inhabitants.

30 HOUSING

In 1990, Azerbaijan had 12.5 square meters of housing space per person. As of 1 January 1991, 138,000 households (or 15.6%) were on waiting lists for housing in urban areas. In 1989, 31.5% of all privately owned urban housing had running water, 6.7% had sewer lines, 5.7% had bathtubs, and 96.8% had gas.

31 EDUCATION

The educational system is extensive and illiteracy is practically unknown. In 1990, adult literacy rate was estimated at 97.3% (males: 98.9% and females: 95.9%). The usual language of instruction is Azerbaijani, although Russian, Armenian, and Georgian are also offered by some schools.

There are two universities: the Azerbaijan Polytechnic Institute, located in Baku, has an enrollment of 12,000 students; the State University, also located at Baku, was founded in 1919 and has an enrollment of over 15,000 students.

32 MEDIA

There are several radio stations in the capital, broadcasting in a variety of languages, as well as Baku Television, established in 1956. In 1989, there were over 150 newspapers, 133 published in Azerbaijani. Those with the greatest circulation were *Khalg Gazeti*, published six days a week, *Gadzhlyar* (three days a week), and *Azadlyg* (weekly). Over 100 periodicals are published, more than half in Azerbaijani.

33 TOURISM AND RECREATION

The capital city of Baku is one of the prime tourist destinations of the Caucasus region. Its Old Town, with the Shirvanshah palace dating back to the fifteenth century, is especially popular with sightseers. Elsewhere in Azerbaijan, the Gobustan Museum displays prehistoric dwellings and cave paintings, and the village of Surakhani attracts visitors to the Atashgah Fire-Worshipper's Temple. Visitors are also welcome at the carpet-weaving factory in the village of Nardaran.

34 FAMOUS AZERBAIJANIS

Peter the Great conquered what is now Azerbaijan in 1723. The poet Nizami Ganjavi (1141?–1209?) is celebrated for his *Khamsa*, a collection of five epic poems. Muhammed Fizuli (1438–1556) based his poems on traditional folktales, and his poetic versions provide the bases for many twentieth century plays and operas. The composer Uzeyis Hajibayov wrote the first Azerbaijani opera, founded the Azerbaijani Symphonic Orchestra, and composed Azerbaijan's National Anthem.

35 BIBLIOGRAPHY

Aganbegyan, Abel. *Perestrokda Revolution*. New York: Harper & Row, 1990.

Edwards-Jones, Imogen. *The Taming of Eagles: Exploring the New Russia*. London: Weidenfeld & Nicolson, 1993.

Rost, Yuri. *Armenian Tragedy*. New York: St. Martin's, 1990.

Shoemaker, M. Wesley. *Russia, Eurasian States and Eastern Europe 1993*. Washington, D.C.: Stryker-Post, 1993.

Wolfe, Bertram. *Three Who Made a Revolution*. New York: Dial Press, 1948.

BAHAMAS

Commonwealth of the Bahamas

CAPITAL: Nassau.

FLAG: Three horizontal stripes of blue, gold, and blue, with a black triangle at the hoist.

ANTHEM: *March on Bahamaland.*

MONETARY UNIT: The Bahamas dollar (B$) of 100 cents has been in use since May 1966. As of June 1972, the Bahamas dollar ceased to be part of the sterling area and was set on a par with the US dollar. There are coins of 1, 5, 10, 15, 25, and 50 cents, and 1, 2, and 5 dollars, and notes of 50 cents and 1, 3, 5, 10, 20, 50, and 100 dollars. B$1=US$1 (or US$1=B$1).

WEIGHTS AND MEASURES: Imperial weights and measures are in use.

HOLIDAYS: New Year's Day, 1 January; Labor Day, 1st Friday in June; Independence Day, 10 July; Emancipation Day, 1st Monday in August; Discovery Day, 12 October; Christmas Day, 25 December; Boxing Day, 26 December. Movable religious holidays include Good Friday, Easter Monday, and Whitmonday.

TIME: 7 AM = noon GMT.

1 LOCATION AND SIZE

The Commonwealth of the Bahamas occupies a 13,940-square kilometer (5,382-square mile) group of islands between southeast Florida and northern Hispaniola. The area occupied by the Bahamas is slightly larger than the state of Connecticut. There are nearly 700 islands, of which about 30 are inhabited.

The Bahamas' capital city, Nassau, is located on New Providence Island in the center of the island group.

2 TOPOGRAPHY

The islands are for the most part low and flat. The terrain is broken by lakes and mangrove swamps, and the shorelines are marked by coral reefs.

3 CLIMATE

Temperatures average 23°C (73°F) in winter and 27°C (81°F) in summer. Rainfall averages 127 centimeters (50 inches), and there are occasional hurricanes.

4 PLANTS AND ANIMALS

The islands abound in such tropical plants as bougainvillea, jasmine, oleander, orchid, and yellow elder. Native trees include the black olive, casuarina, cascarilla, cork tree, manchineel, pimento, and seven species of palm. Birds include flamingos, hummingbirds, and waterfowl.

5 ENVIRONMENT

Environmental issues include waste disposal, water pollution, and the impact of tourism on the environment. Endangered species include 2 mammals and 4 birds. A rookery on Great Inagua affords protection to some 30,000 flamingos as well as to the roseate spoonbill.

6 POPULATION

The population in 1990 was 255,095. Some two-thirds of the people reside on the island of New Providence, the site of Nassau, the largest city.

7 MIGRATION

Illegal immigrants from Haiti numbered an estimated 30,000–40,000 in 1993. There is inter-island migration, chiefly to New Providence and Grand Bahama islands.

8 ETHNIC GROUPS

Descendants of slaves brought to the Western Hemisphere from Africa make up about 86% of the legal population. About 8% of the population is of mixed origin. The remainder is white, mostly of British origin.

9 LANGUAGES

English is the spoken and official language of the Bahamas. Haitian immigrants speak French or a Creole patois (dialect).

10 RELIGIONS

The population is overwhelmingly Christian, with Baptists comprising 32%. Roman Catholics (19%) and Anglicans (20%) also have sizable memberships.

11 TRANSPORTATION

In 1991 there were about 2,400 kilometers (1,500 miles) of highways. There were 70,000 passenger cars and 15,000 commercial vehicles that year. There are no railways.

On 1 January 1992, the nation had a merchant fleet of 756 ships with a volume capacity of 18.2 million gross registered tons and a deadweight capacity of 30.5 million tons (seventh in the world). Nassau is a major port of call for cruise ships. There are international airports at Nassau and Freeport. In 1990, approximately 1.23 million passengers embarked or disembarked through Freeport International Airport.

12 HISTORY

The first permanent European settlement was established in 1647 by a group of religious refugees from England. They and later settlers imported blacks as slaves during the seventeenth century.

The British established a crown colony on the islands in 1717. After the end of slavery in 1838, the Bahamas served only as a source of sponges and occasionally as a strategic location. During the US Civil War, Confederate blockade runners operated from the islands. After World War I, prohibition rum-runners used the islands as a base. During World War II, the US used them for naval bases.

The Bahamas achieved independence in stages, with full independence granted on 10 July 1973. The country's first prime minister, Lynden O. Pindling, ruled for nearly 20 years, during which the Bahamas benefited from tourism and foreign investment. By the early 1980s, the islands had also become a major center for the drug trade. In August 1992, the Bahamas had its first transfer of political power, when Hubert Ingraham became prime minister.

13 GOVERNMENT

The Bahamas has a republican form of government, formally headed by the British sovereign, who is represented by a governor-general. A prime minister and a cabinet have executive authority. The two-chamber legislature consists of a 16-member Senate appointed by the governor-general and an elected 49-member House of Assembly. The prime minister is the leader of the majority party in the House.

14 POLITICAL PARTIES

The Progressive Liberal Party (PLP) emerged as the Bahamas' majority party in the early 1970s. The Free Progressive Liberal Party, a splinter group formed in 1970, merged with another opposition group, the United Bahamian Party, to form the Free National Movement (FNM). After years of loyal opposition, the FNM took power in 1992, winning 32 seats, compared to 17 for the PLP.

15 JUDICIAL SYSTEM

The highest court is the Court of Appeal, consisting of three judges. Ultimate appeals go to the Privy Council of the UK. Lower courts include three magistrates' courts on New Providence and one on Freeport. Police abuse of suspects has been a serious problem. In 1993, a coroner's court was established to investigate cases in which criminal suspects die while in police custody.

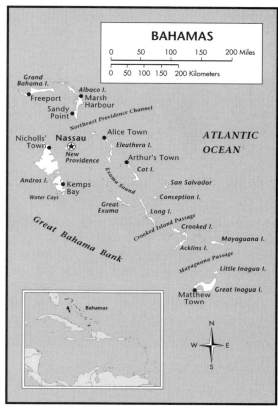

LOCATION: 20°50′ to 27°25′N; 72°37′ to 82°32′W. **TOTAL COASTLINE:** 3,542 kilometers (2,201 miles) **TERRITORIAL SEA LIMIT:** 3 miles.

16 ARMED FORCES

The Royal Bahamas Defense Force of 700 sailors is responsible for external security. Defense expenditures are $65 million (1990).

17 ECONOMY

Tourism, the mainstay of the economy, directly or indirectly involves most of the population. Tourism in the Bahamas is recovering from a decline which began in 1990, due to the US recession and competition from other Caribbean nations.

Photo credit: Susan D. Rock.

Government buildings in Nassau, the capital city of the Bahamas.

18 INCOME

In 1992, Bahamas' gross national product (GNP) was $3,161 million, or $11,420 per person. For the period 1985–92 the average inflation rate was 5.5%, resulting in a real growth rate in gross national product of –1.2% per person.

19 INDUSTRY

In 1983, 2.93 million tons of petroleum products were produced. Cement and rum production are also important, and enterprises producing pharmaceuticals and steel pipe have been developed. Heineken, Europe's largest beer company, con-structed a brewery in Nassau in 1985 with an annual production capacity of 1.2 million cases of beer.

20 LABOR

The total number of workers was estimated at 127,500 in 1991, the overwhelming majority employed in tourism or tourist-related activities. About 30,000 workers (25% of the labor force) were unionized in 1991. Unemployment in 1992 stood at about 20,000, or 14.8%.

In the Bahamas, children under the age of 14 are prohibited from industrial work, work during school hours, or work at night. Other than these rules, there are no laws concerning child labor, and children are free to seek employment in grocery stores, gas stations, and other types of small businesses.

21 AGRICULTURE

Agriculture is carried out on small plots throughout most of the islands. The main crops are vegetables: onions, okra, and tomatoes, the last two raised mainly for export.

22 DOMESTICATED ANIMALS

In 1992, the livestock population included 5,000 head of cattle, 40,000 sheep, 19,000 goats, 20,000 hogs, and 2,000,000 poultry. About 3,000 tons of cow's milk and 420,000 tons of eggs were produced in 1992.

23 FISHING

The 1981 catch amounted to 9,202 tons, over 80% of which was comprised of spiny lobsters (crayfish). In 1991, fisheries exports totaled $51 million.

24 FORESTRY

Caribbean pine and cascarilla bark are the major forestry products, but there is no commercial forestry industry.

25 MINING

Salt (about 1 million tons produced annually) and aragonite, a component in glass-making, are the only commercially important mineral products.

26 FOREIGN TRADE

Total exports, totaling $310.2 million in 1992, included pharmaceuticals, shellfish, salt, cement, rum, aragonite, cascarilla bark, tomatoes, and citrus. Total imports totaled $1,156.4 million, primarily composed of foodstuffs, meat, motor vehicles, oil, animal feed, petroleum products, clothing, machinery, and appliances. Bahamas' major trade partners are the US, Canada, the UK, and Japan.

27 ENERGY AND POWER

Electricity production totaled 965 million kilowatt hours in 1991. In 1986, a US company began drilling for offshore oil in the Great Bahama Bank area.

28 SOCIAL DEVELOPMENT

Workers' compensation and retirement, maternity, survivors', and funeral benefits are provided. Bahamian women are well represented in business, the professions, and government.

29 HEALTH

The government operates the 478-bed Princess Margaret Hospital in Nassau and 4 other hospitals. In 1985, there were 228 physicians and 120 midwives. Average life expectancy in 1992 was 73 years. The country is free from tropical diseases.

30 HOUSING

Overcrowding is a problem on New Providence, and decent low-cost housing is in short supply. The Bahamas Housing Authority was established in 1983 to develop housing for low-income people.

31 EDUCATION

Government expenditure on education (1988) was 20.7% of the total budget. Education is compulsory for children aged 5–14. In 1990, 101 primary schools enrolled 25,452 pupils, and 37 junior/senior high schools enrolled 23,502. Higher education is provided by the College of the Bahamas, with an enrollment of about 2,050 students. Over 90% of Bahamians are reported literate.

32 MEDIA

There are three AM and two FM stations, and one television station. In 1991, there were an estimated 140,000 radios and 56,000 television sets on the islands. In 1990, 132,522 fully digital telephones were in service. Two daily newspapers are published in Nassau: The *Tribune* (circulation 14,000 in 1991) and the *Guardian* (17,000). The daily Freeport *News* has a circulation of 6,000.

Selected Social Indicators

These statistics are estimates for the period 1988 to 1993. For comparison purposes, data for the United States and averages for low-income countries and high-income countries are also given.

Indicator	Bahamas	Low-income countries	High-income countries	United States
Per capita gross national product†	$11,420	$380	$23,680	$24,740
Population growth rate	1.5%	1.9%	0.6%	1.0%
Population growth rate in urban areas	2.2%	3.9%	0.8%	1.3%
Population per square kilometer of land	19	78	25	26
Life expectancy in years	73	62	77	76
Number of people per physician	776	>3,300	453	419
Number of pupils per teacher (primary school)	19	39	<18	20
Illiteracy rate (15 years and older)	10%	41%	<5%	<3%
Energy consumed per capita (kg of oil equivalent)	6,900	364	5,203	7,918

† The gross national product (GNP) is the total dollar value of all goods and services produced by a country in a year. The per capita GNP is calculated by dividing a country's GNP by its population. The World Bank defines low-income countries as those with a per capita GNP of $695 or less. High-income countries have a per capita GNP of $8,626 or more. Less than 14% of the world's 5.5 billion people live in high-income countries, while almost 60% live in low-income countries.

> = greater than   < = less than

Sources: World Bank, *Social Indicators of Development 1995,* Baltimore: Johns Hopkins University Press, 1995. Central Intelligence Agency, *World Fact Book,* Washington, D.C.: Government Printing Office, 1994.

33 TOURISM AND RECREATION

In 1991, 1.43 million tourists visited the islands. Some 1.17 million were from the US, 90,120 from Canada, and 11,204 from Europe. In the same year, tourists spent a total of $1.22 billion in the islands, and there were 13,165 hotel rooms with a 56.3% occupancy rate.

Visitors are attracted to the Bahamas' excellent climate, beaches, and recreational and resort facilities. Water sports (including excellent deep-sea fishing) are the favorite pastimes.

34 FAMOUS BAHAMIANS

Lynden Oscar Pindling (b.1930), a lawyer and leader of the PLP, became the Bahamas' first prime minister following independence in 1973.

35 BIBLIOGRAPHY

Boultbee, Paul G. *The Bahamas.* Oxford, England, and Santa Barbara, Calif.: Clio Press, 1989.

Craton, Michael. *Islanders in the Stream: A History of the Bahamian People.* Athens: University of Georgia Press, 1992.

Keegan, William F. *The People Who Discovered Columbus: The Prehistory of the Bahamas.* Gainesville: University Press of Florida, 1992.

BAHRAIN

State of Bahrain
Dawlat al-Bahrayn

CAPITAL: Manama (Al-Manamah).

FLAG: Red with a white vertical stripe on the hoist, the edge between them being saw-toothed.

ANTHEM: Music without words.

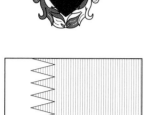

MONETARY UNIT: The Bahrain dinar (BD) is divided into 1,000 fils. There are coins of 5, 10, 25, 50, and 100 fils and notes of 500 fils and 1, 5, 10, and 20 dinars. BD1 = $2.6596 (or $1 = BD0.3760).

WEIGHTS AND MEASURES: The metric system is used; local measures are also used.

HOLIDAYS: New Year's Day, 1 January; National Day, 16 December. Movable Muslim religious holidays include Hijra (Muslim New Year), 'Ashura, Prophet's Birthday, 'Id al-Fitr, and 'Id al-'Adha'.

TIME: 3 PM = noon GMT.

1 LOCATION AND SIZE

The State of Bahrain consists of a group of 33 islands (6 inhabited) in the western Persian Gulf, with a total area of 620 square kilometers (239 square miles), slightly less than 3.5 times the area of Washington, D.C. Bahrain, the main island, is linked by bridges to Al Muharraq and Sitra islands and to Sa'udi Arabia. Other islands include the Hawar group (off the west coast of Qatar), Nabih Salih, Umm an-Na'san, and Jidda. The total coastline is 161 kilometers (100 miles). Bahrain's capital, Manama, is located on the northeastern coast.

2 TOPOGRAPHY

The north coast of Bahrain is irrigated by natural springs and wells. South of this fertile area, the land is barren, with low rolling hills and numerous rocky cliffs.

From the shoreline the surface rises gradually toward the center, where it drops into a basin surrounded by steep cliffs. Here Jabal ad-Dukhan, a steep, rocky hill rises to 137 meters (450 feet) above sea level. Most of the lesser islands are flat and sandy.

3 CLIMATE

Summers in Bahrain are hot and humid, and winters are relatively cool. Daily average temperatures in July range from a minimum of 29°C (84°F) to a maximum of 37°C (99°F). In January, the minimum is 14°C (57°F); the maximum 20°C (68°F). Rainfall averages less than 10 centimeters (4 inches) annually.

4 PLANTS AND ANIMALS

Outside the cultivated areas, desert shrubs, grasses, wild date palms, and wild

Photo credit: AP/Wide World Photos

A young Arab woman, wearing a black abaya and aerobic shoes, arrives at a hotel fitness club in Bahrain. Physical fitness is a sensitive subject in the Arab world, where religion and custom decree that women's bodies and faces be covered.

desert flowers are found. Mammals are limited to the jerboa (desert rat), gazelle, mongoose, and hare. Some 14 species of lizard and 4 types of land snake are also found. Bird life is especially varied and includes larks, song thrushes, swallows, and terns, as well as bulbuls, hoopoes, parakeets, and warblers.

5 ENVIRONMENT

Bahrain's main environmental problems are scarcity of fresh water, expansion of the desert, and pollution from oil production. In 1994, 100% of Bahrain's urban dwellers and 57% of the rural population had pure water. Pollution from oil production was made worse by the Persian Gulf War and the damage to oil-producing facilities in the Gulf area. A wildlife sanctuary established in 1980 is a home for threatened Gulf species. Bahrain has also established captive breeding centers for falcons and for the rare Houbara bustard.

6 POPULATION

In 1991, the population was 508,037. The population projection for the year 2000 is 653,000. Population density was 762 per square kilometer (1,910 per square mile) in 1991. Manama, the capital, had a 1990 estimated population of 133,784.

7 MIGRATION

The proportion of aliens to residents was an estimated 33% (171,872) in 1990. Most are temporary workers from other Arab countries: Iran, Pakistan, India, and the Republic of Korea.

8 ETHNIC GROUPS

In 1990, 67% of the population consisted of native Bahrainis (336,165), of whom the vast majority of northern Arab stock. Iranians form the largest non-native group (perhaps 20% of the total), followed by other Arabs.

9 LANGUAGES

Arabic (the Gulf dialect) is the universal language. English is widely understood.

10 RELIGIONS

In 1993, an estimated 70% of native Bahrainis were Shiite Muslim and about 30% Sunni Muslim. Religious minorities—mostly foreign workers—included Christians and small numbers of Hindus and Baha'is. Islam is the official religion.

11 TRANSPORTATION

In 1991, there were 200 kilometers (124 miles) of bituminous surfaced highways. In 1991, there were 132,180 motor vehicles. Bahrain's main port is Mina Salman. In 1991, Bahrain had a merchant fleet of 9 ships with 188,000 gross registered tons. The international airport near Al-Muharraq can handle large jet aircraft and serves more than two dozen international airlines.

12 HISTORY

Known as Dilmun, Bahrain was a thriving trade center around 2000 BC. The islands were visited by the ships of Alexander the Great in the third century BC. Bahrain accepted Islam in the seventh century AD.

The Portuguese occupied Bahrain from 1522 to 1602. The present ruling family, the Khalifa, who are related to the Sabah family of Kuwait and the Sa'udi royal family, captured Bahrain in 1782. Contact with the British followed in the nineteenth century, concluding in an 1861 treaty of protection. After a plan to federate the nine sheikhdoms of the southern Gulf failed, Bahrain became a sovereign state on 15 August 1971.

Owing to its small size, Bahrain, a founding member of the Gulf Cooperation

LOCATION: 25°47′10″ to 26°17′3″N; 50°22′45″ to 50°40′20″E. **TOTAL COASTLINE:** 161 kilometers (100 miles). **TERRITORIAL SEA LIMIT:** 3 miles.

Council, generally takes its lead in foreign affairs from its Arab neighbors on the Gulf. During the 1980–88 Iran-Iraq War, Bahrain joined most other Arab states in supporting Iraq. However, when Iraq invaded Kuwait in 1990, Bahrain stood with the US and its Middle Eastern allies, contributing military support and facilities to the defeat of Iraq. Bahrain has long assisted the American naval presence in the Persian Gulf. In 1991, the US signed an agreement giving the Department of Defense access to facilities on the island.

13 GOVERNMENT

Bahrain is a constitutional monarchy headed by an emir. A council of ministers, appointed by the emir, acts as a legislature (the constitution provides for a National Assembly, but none has existed since 1975). Bahrain consists of six major towns and five rural communities.

14 POLITICAL PARTIES

Political parties are illegal in Bahrain. Several underground groups, including pro-Iranian militant Islamic groups, have been active and are vigorously opposed by the government.

15 JUDICIAL SYSTEM

The law of Bahrain represents a mixture of Islamic religious law (Shari'a) and government decrees dealing with criminal and commercial matters. In ordinary civil and criminal courts there are open trials, a right to counsel (including legal aid when determined to be necessary), and a right to appeal.

16 ARMED FORCES

The Bahrain army in 1993 had 5,000 officers and men in one combined arms brigade. Bahrain sent troops to Sa'udi Arabia during the 1990–91 Gulf War. Defense expenditures in 1990 were $194 million.

17 ECONOMY

Bahrain's economy has been based on oil for the last five decades. However, its present oil supply is expected to be exhausted by the late 1990s, so the government has developed other areas, such as aluminum production, and increased natural gas production to some 20 million cubic meters per day.

18 INCOME

In 1992, Bahrain's gross national product (GNP) was $3,690 million at current prices. For the period 1985–92, the average inflation rate was 0.2%, resulting in a real growth rate in gross national product of –1.7% per person.

19 INDUSTRY

Petroleum refining, begun modestly in 1942, was Bahrain's first modern industrial enterprise. A total of 89,543 million barrels of petroleum products were produced in 1986. Aluminum production was 450,000 tons in 1993.

20 LABOR

The number of people employed in non-government jobs in 1991 totaled 103,488, of whom nearly 60% were non-Bahrainis. The majority of workers were employed in community, social, and personal services.

The minimum age for employment is 14. Young people between the ages of 14 and 16 may not be employed in hazardous

Photo credit: AP/Wide World Photos

A Bahrainian man in typical Arab dress arrives in his Mercedes for work.

conditions. They are also prohibited from working at night or working more than six hours a day. Child labor in the industrial sector is well monitored. Some young people work in family-operated businesses.

21 AGRICULTURE

Ninety farms produce fruits and vegetables, as well as alfalfa for fodder. In 1992, 10,000 tons of vegetables and 23,000 tons of fruit crops were produced.

22 DOMESTICATED ANIMALS

A few thousand cattle and goats are kept for milk and meat production. In 1992, Bahrain produced 2,950 tons of eggs and met 22% of its poultry demands.

23 FISHING

Local fishing and pearl diving have declined because of industrial pollution. The catch totaled 7,553 tons in 1991.

24 FORESTRY

There are no forests in Bahrain.

25 MINING

The mining industry consists almost entirely of oil and natural gas production. Some cement is also produced.

26 FOREIGN TRADE

Refined oil products account for over 80% of the island's exports, which were valued at $3.76 billion in 1990. Refined aluminum, frozen shrimp, paper goods, air-conditioning units, and flour are other export earners. Imports in 1990 totaled $3.34 billion, with crude oil the principal commodity, followed by machinery, manufactured goods, food, and live animals. The principal markets for Bahrain's exports in 1989 were Sa'udi Arabia, the US, and the United Arab Emirates. The major sources of imports were the UK, the US, and Japan.

27 ENERGY AND POWER

In 1993, an estimated 70% ($2.4 billion) of export revenues came from petroleum exports. Total daily crude petroleum in 1992 was 40,000 barrels. Total recoverable oil reserves in the Bahrain field were estimated at 69.6 million barrels in 1993. Production of natural gas totaled 290 billion cubic feet (8.2 billion cubic meters) in 1992. In 1991, Bahrain had a total electrical power output of 3,495 million kilowatt hours.

28 SOCIAL DEVELOPMENT

Impoverished families receive survival allowances from the government. Since 1976, a social security fund has provided old age, disability, survivor, and accident insurance.

29 HEALTH

In 1990, there were 4 government-operated hospitals. In 1991, Bahrain had 668

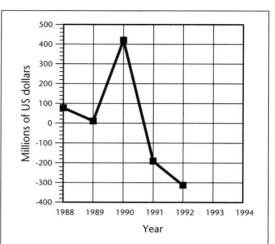

Yearly balance of trade measured in millions of US dollars. The balance of trade is the difference between what a country sells to other countries (its exports) and what it buys (its imports). If a country imports more than it exports, it has a negative balance of trade (a trade deficit). If exports exceed imports, there is a positive balance of trade (a trade surplus).

physicians. Life expectancy in 1992 was 72 years.

30 HOUSING

At the 1981 census, roughly 45% of all homes were traditional dwellings. A major program for low- and middle-income housing, costing $195 million, was inaugurated in 1987 with Sa'udi aid.

31 EDUCATION

In 1990, the literacy rate was estimated by UNESCO at 77.4% (82.7% males and 69.3% females). Primary education lasts for six years, intermediate for three years, and secondary for three years. The Univer-

Selected Social Indicators

These statistics are estimates for the period 1988 to 1993. For comparison purposes, data for the United States and averages for low-income countries and high-income countries are also given.

Indicator	Bahrain	Low-income countries	High-income countries	United States
Per capita gross national product†	**$8,030**	$380	$23,680	$24,740
Population growth rate	**2.8%**	1.9%	0.6%	1.0%
Population growth rate in urban areas	**3.4%**	3.9%	0.8%	1.3%
Population per square kilometer of land	**762**	78	25	26
Life expectancy in years	**72**	62	77	76
Number of people per physician	**799**	>3,300	453	419
Number of pupils per teacher (primary school)	**21**	39	<18	20
Illiteracy rate (15 years and older)	**23%**	41%	<5%	<3%
Energy consumed per capita (kg of oil equivalent)	**11,925**	364	5,203	7,918

† The gross national product (GNP) is the total dollar value of all goods and services produced by a country in a year. The per capita GNP is calculated by dividing a country's GNP by its population. The World Bank defines low-income countries as those with a per capita GNP of $695 or less. High-income countries have a per capita GNP of $8,626 or more. Less than 14% of the world's 5.5 billion people live in high-income countries, while almost 60% live in low-income countries.

> = greater than   < = less than

Sources: World Bank, Social Indicators of Development 1995, Baltimore: Johns Hopkins University Press, 1995. Central Intelligence Agency, World Fact Book, Washington, D.C.: Government Printing Office, 1994.

sity of Bahrain was founded in 1986, and the Arabian Gulf University in 1980.

32 MEDIA

Telephones numbered 141,245 in 1991. The government operates a radio station and a color television station. In 1991, there were 278,000 radios and 215,000 television sets in use.

In 1991, *Akhbar al-Khalij,* a daily paper published in Arabic, had a circulation of 25,000, while the English daily, the *Gulf Daily News,* reached 12,000.

33 TOURISM AND RECREATION

In 1990, Bahrain had 3,222 hotel rooms with a 55.9 percent occupancy rate. In 1991, there were 1.67 million tourist arrivals, mostly from Sa'udi Arabia and other Arab countries, and tourism receipts totaled $162 million. Tourist attractions include Qal-at Al-Bahrain (The Portuguese Fort), the National Museum, and the Heritage Center.

34 FAMOUS BAHRAINIS

Since 1961, the emir has been Sheikh 'Isa bin Salman al-Khalifa (b. 1933).

35 BIBLIOGRAPHY

Fakhro, Munira A. (Munira Ahmed). *Women at Work in the Gulf*. New York: Kegan Paul International, 1990.

Fox, M. *Bahrain*. Chicago: Children's Press, 1992.

Jenner, Michael. *Bahrain, Gulf Heritage in Transition*. New York: Longman, 1984.

BANGLADESH

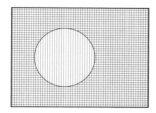

People's Republic of Bangladesh
Gana-Prajatantri Bangladesh

CAPITAL: Dhaka (formerly Dacca).

FLAG: The national flag is a red circle against a dark-green background.

ANTHEM: *Amar Sonar Bangla (My Golden Bengal).*

MONETARY UNIT: The taka (T) of 100 poisha is a paper currency set on a par with the Indian rupee. There are coins of 1, 2, 5, 10, 25, and 50 poisha, and notes of 1, 5, 10, 20, 50, and 100 taka. T1 = $0.0248 (or $1 = T40.250).

WEIGHTS AND MEASURES: Bangladesh adopted the metric system as of 1 July 1982. Customary numerical units include the lakh (equal to 100,000) and the crore (equal to 10 million).

HOLIDAYS: New Year's Day, 1 January; National Mourning Day (Shaheel Day), 21 February; Independence Day, 26 March; May Day, 1 May; Victory Day, 16 December; Christmas, 25 December; Boxing Day, 26 December. Movable religious holidays include Good Friday, Jamat Wida, Shab-i-Bharat, 'Id al-Fitr, 'Id al-'Adha', and Durga Puja.

TIME: 6 PM = noon GMT.

1 LOCATION AND SIZE

Located in South Asia, Bangladesh, before it became an independent state, was the eastern province of Pakistan. It was known as East Bengal and, later, as East Pakistan. Bangladesh is slightly smaller than the state of Wisconsin, with a total area of 144,000 square kilometers (55,599 square miles). It has a total boundary length of 4,826 kilometers (2,999 miles). Bangladesh's capital city, Dhaka, is located near the center of the country.

2 TOPOGRAPHY

Bangladesh is a tropical country, situated mainly on river deltas flowing from the Himalayas. Its rivers include the Brahmaputra (known locally as the Jamuna), the Ganges, the Padma, and the Meghna. Most of the delta area is only a meter or two (a few feet) above sea level. The northwestern section of the country, drained by the Tista (Teesta) River, is somewhat higher and less flat, but the only really hilly regions are in the east. Near the Burmese border is the Keokradang, at 1,230 meters (4,034 feet) the highest peak in Bangladesh.

3 CLIMATE

Bangladesh has a tropical monsoon climate. Annual rainfall is high, averaging from about 119 centimeters (47 inches) up to 145 centimeters (57 inches). There are three distinct seasons. The winter, which lasts from November through February, is cool and dry, with average temperatures for most of the country at about 7°C (45°F). Temperatures rise rapidly in early March, and during the summer season—

Photo credit: AP/Wide World Photos

A Bangladeshi family, holding their livestock, leaves their flooded home for a shelter in the northeastern district of Sylhet.

March through May—average about 32°C (90°F). From June to October, temperatures drop somewhat, seldom exceeding 31°C (88°F). For parts of the year, tropical cyclones, accompanied by high seas and heavy flooding, are common. Storms and floods in 1970, 1974, 1980, and 1983 devastated the country and caused many deaths. In 1993, a cyclone killed over 131,000 people and caused $2.7 billion in damages.

4 PLANTS AND ANIMALS

Bangladesh has the plant and animal life typical of a tropical swamp. The landscape, which for most of the year is lush green, is dotted with palms and flowering trees. The large forest area of the Sunderbans in the southwest is the home of the endangered Bengal tiger. There are also cheetahs, leopards, crocodiles, elephants, spotted deer, monkeys, boars, bears, pheasants, and many varieties of birds and waterfowl.

5 ENVIRONMENT

Overpopulation has severely strained Bangladesh's limited natural resources, and natural disasters have added to the strain on an agricultural system which supports one of the world's most crowded countries. Water supply is a major problem because of population size and lack of purification.

Despite the Wildlife Preservation Act of 1973, wildlife continues to suffer from human activity. In 1994, there were 15 species of mammals, 27 species of birds, and 33 plant species considered to be endangered.

6 POPULATION

Bangladesh is one of the world's most densely populated nations, and controlling population growth is a major government priority. The census population in 1991 was estimated at 109,876,977. A population of 144,265,000 is projected for the year 2000. The population is heavily rural, with the great majority living in more than 85,000 villages. Dhaka, the capital, had a 1991 population of 3,637,892.

7 MIGRATION

Since 1947, there has been a regular interchange of population between India and what is now Bangladesh, with Hindus immigrating to India and Muslims emigrating from India. Before and during the 1971 war for independence, an estimated 8 to 10 million Bengalis fled to India. Most of these refugees returned after the independence of Bangladesh was firmly established.

8 ETHNIC GROUPS

Some 98% of the people are Bengalis (or Banglas). About 12 tribes inhabiting the Chittagong Hill Tracts are ethnically distinct from the Bengalis, with facial features and language closer to the Burmese. There are about 600,000 Biharis, non-Bengali Muslims who emigrated from India to what was then East Pakistan after 1947.

9 LANGUAGES

Bengali (Bangla), part of the Indo-European language family, is the official language of Bangladesh and is spoken by about 98% of the population. Non-Bengali emigrants from India still speak Urdu (and Hindi) today, and this language is widely understood in urban areas. The tribal peoples of the Chittagong Hill Tracts also speak distinct Tibeto-Burmese languages, akin to Burmese and Assamese. English is still used for official and legal purposes and is widely used in business.

10 RELIGIONS

According to the most recent census, 86.6% of the people are believers in Islam, making Bangladesh the world's third-largest Muslim country after Indonesia and Pakistan. Most of these are Sunni Muslims. From 12% to 16% of the population is Hindu, 0.6% Buddhist, and 0.3% Christian.

LOCATION: 20°34′ to 26°38′N; 88°1′ to 92°41′E.
BOUNDARY LENGTHS: India, 2,583 kilometers (1,605 miles); Myanmar, 197 kilometers (122 miles); Bay of Bengal coastline, 574 kilometers (357 miles).
TERRITORIAL SEA LIMIT: 12 miles.

11 TRANSPORTATION

The large number of rivers and the annual flooding hazard make it difficult to build and maintain adequate transportation facilities in Bangladesh. Railways and waterways are the chief means of transportation. The Bangladesh Railway, which operates 2,892 kilometers (1,797 miles) of track, carries over 90 million passengers and 3 million tons of freight yearly.

The country has two deepwater ports: Chittagong and Chalna. There are five main river ports—Dhaka, Nārāyanganj, Chandpur, Barisal, and Khulna—and more than 1,500 smaller ports.

There are 3,840 kilometers (2,386 miles) of paved roads. Because of the difficulties of land travel, the number of motor vehicles remains comparatively small. In 1992, there were an estimated 130,000 motorized vehicles, including 67,000 passenger automobiles, and 63,000 commercial taxis, trucks, and buses. Bangladesh Biman, the national airline, operates international flights from Dhaka airport. In 1992, it carried 1,051,500 domestic and international passengers.

12 HISTORY

The area now known as Bangladesh was home to a flourishing civilization in the fourth century BC. The region, then called Bengal, was eventually conquered by the Hindu Maurya empire that reached its height under Emperor Asoka around 207 BC. From this time onward, the history of Bengal was part of the wider history of the Indian subcontinent.

Islam came to South Asia in the years following AD 800 but did not reach Bengal until Muslim invaders from the west secured a foothold there around AD 1200. In the thirteenth and fourteenth centuries, after waves of Turkish, Persian, and Afghan invaders, the religion began to take a firm hold in the area, which became known for its industries based on the weaving of silk and cotton cloth.

By the middle of the eighteenth century, the British established themselves in Calcutta and expanded quickly into all of what is now Bangladesh. British traders and officials gained control of most of the Indian subcontinent by 1859. In general, Hindus in Bengal prospered under the British. The Muslim aristocracy of eastern Bengal, on the other hand, resisted British rule. However, by the turn of the twentieth century, both communities united in anti-British feeling.

The subcontinent's demand for independence from Britain grew under the leadership of Mahatma Gandhi in the early 1930s. Finally, in 1947, Britain granted independence to the Indian subcontinent. British India was partitioned into a predominately Hindu India and a predominately Muslim Pakistan.

However, the new state of Pakistan was made up of Muslim-majority districts at both the eastern and western ends of formerly British India. These two distinct territories were separated by 1600 kilometers (1000 miles) of predominantly Hindu India. The division cut across long-established lines of trade and communication, divided families, and started a mass movement of millions of refugees caught on the "wrong" side of the partition markers.

In language, culture, and ethnic background, East and West Pakistan were totally different—the main bonds being Islam and a fear of potential Indian (Hindu) expansion. Pakistan's early years as a nation were dominated by unsuccessful attempts to create a nation that would somehow bridge these differences. The differences persisted and demands for a separate state in the east began to mount.

After continued refusal by West Pakistan to grant East Pakistan's requests for independence, civil war broke out in 1971. Swamped with a million refugees from the fighting, India intervened militarily on behalf of those seeking a separate state. India's intervention helped create the independent nation of Bangladesh in 1972. Sheikh Mujibur (Mujib) Rahman, a leader of the fight for autonomy, was released from prison in West Pakistan and became Prime Minister of the new nation.

The civil war was a disaster for Bangladesh, undoing much of the limited progress East Pakistan had made in recovering from the social disruption of the 1947 partition. The nation's new leader faced a task for which his administrative and political experience was not enough. He fought and won a massive victory in the 1973 election, but two years later, he suspended the political process and took power into his own hands.

With this move, public opinion turned against Mujib. On 15 August 1975, a

Photo credit: AP/Wide World Photos

A woman examines the produce in a bustling market in the hill tracts that border India.

group of young military officers seized power. They killed Mujib and many of his family members and imposed martial law. A succession of military takeovers and new governments followed until General Hussain Mohammad Ershad seized power in 1981. Ershad gained support by cracking down on corruption and opening up the economy to foreign trade.

In 1982, Ershad declared Bangladesh an Islamic republic. This move angered the Hindu minority. Ershad remained in power until the end of 1990 when he was forced to resign the presidency.

A temporary government scheduled elections for February 1991. The elections were described as the fairest vote ever held in the country. In the elections the Bangladesh National Party (BNP) won control of the government and continues to lead the country today.

13 GOVERNMENT

The constitution of December 1972 (amended in 1991) established a democratic republic, with an indirectly elected president as official head of state and a prime minister as head of government and chief executive. The prime minister and his government are responsible to a single-chamber legislature—the National Assembly. Bangladesh is divided into 64 districts.

14 POLITICAL PARTIES

The Bangladesh National Party (BNP) is the most powerful party in Bangladesh. The leader of the opposition is Sheikh Hasina Wajid of the Awami League (AL). Other parties in the assembly include the Islamic Jamaat-i-Islami (JI), the Jatiyo Party (JP), and the Bangladesh Communist Party (BCP).

15 JUDICIAL SYSTEM

The judicial system consists of a Low Court and a Supreme Court, both of which hear civil and criminal cases. The Low Court consists of administrative courts (magistrate courts) and session judges. The Supreme Court also has two divisions, a High Court which hears original cases and reviews decisions of the Low Court, and an Appellate Court which hears appeals from the High Court.

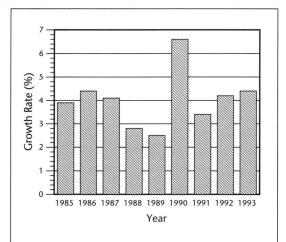

Yearly growth rate of the economy. This economic indicator tells by what percent the economy has increased or decreased when compared with the previous year.

16 ARMED FORCES

In 1993, Bangladesh had an army of 93,000 men, a navy of 7,500, and an air force of 6,500. Paramilitary forces of border guards, armed police, and security guards totaled 55,000. The military budget in 1992 was $339 million.

17 ECONOMY

Bangladesh is a poor country with few natural resources and an economy dominated by agriculture. Over the last several decades, Bangladesh has suffered from the 1971 war with Pakistan, a severe famine in 1971, and a series of weather-related disasters, the most recent of which included a devastating cyclone in April 1991. However, measures taken by the newly elected government in 1991 allowed Bangladesh to weather the combined effects of the 1990–91 Gulf War, domestic political disturbances, and the 1991 cyclone, and to bring inflation to a record low of 1.4% in 1993.

18 INCOME

In 1992, Bangladesh's gross national product (GNP) was $24,672 million at current prices, or $220 per person.

19 INDUSTRY

Total output from major industries for 1991/92 included: jute textiles, 416,400 tons; garments, 17,674 dozen pieces; cotton yarn, 60,516,000 kilograms; cotton cloth, 58,865,000 meters; fertilizer, 1,989,000 tons; cement, 272,500 tons; steel ingots, 36,800 tons; paper and newsprint, 88,300 tons; tea, 45,500 kilograms; and sugar, 195,400 tons.

20 LABOR

The civilian labor force in 1991/92 was estimated at approximately 50 million, of whom slightly over 6% were employed by industry. Average daily wages in 1991/92 averaged less than $2.00 per day, and per person annual income, at about $220, is among the lowest in the world. Unemployment continues to be high, and agricultural workers are not protected by disability compensation. In 1991, 147,131 workers took jobs abroad, mainly in Arab lands. Over 700,000 Bangladeshis work outside the country.

21 AGRICULTURE

Rice production dominates about 80% of all cultivated land in Bangladesh. Total rice production in 1992 was 27,400,000 tons.

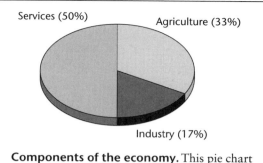

Components of the economy. This pie chart shows how much of the country's economy is devoted to agriculture, industry, or services.

Services (50%)   Agriculture (33%)   Industry (17%)

Jute is the main cash crop of Bangladesh, which produces about one-quarter of the world's total jute supply. Its strong fibers are used to produce carpets, burlap bags, mats, upholstery, and other products. In 1992, 898,000 tons of jute were produced. Tea is the second most important agricultural export, although much of the tea grown is consumed domestically. Total production in 1992 was 45,000 tons.

Crop output in 1992 included sugarcane, 7,446,000 tons; wheat, 1,065,000 tons; potatoes, 1,379,000 tons; bananas, 630,000 tons; sweet potatoes, 470,000 tons; pulses, 506,000 tons; mangoes, 183,000 tons; pineapples, 160,000 tons; coconuts, 82,000 tons; tobacco, 36,000 tons; and barley, 10,000 tons.

22 DOMESTICATED ANIMALS

There were about 23.7 million head of cattle, 820,000 buffaloes, 18,000,000 goats, and 700,000 sheep and poultry in 1992. The shortage of cattle in recent years is the result of lack of vaccines and feed, natural disasters, and an absence of government assistance. In 1992, exports of animal hides totaled $144 million, or 7% of total exports.

23 FISHING

Fish is a staple food of Bangladesh and the main source of protein. There are hundreds of varieties, including carp, salmon, pomfret, shrimp, and catfish. About 892,700 tons of fish (71% from inland waters) were produced in 1991.

24 FORESTRY

Bangladesh has 1,891,000 hectares (4,673,000 acres) of forest, covering some 15% of the land area. About 97% of timber cut is used for firewood. The main forest zone is the Sunderbans area in the southwest, consisting mostly of mangrove forests. Sundari and gewa trees dominate the Sunderban forests. Teak and bamboo are grown in the central forests.

25 MINING

Aside from natural gas, Bangladesh has few mineral resources. Production estimates of mineral commodities in Bangladesh in 1991 included cement, 274,551 tons; marine salt, 300,000 tons; and limestone (mined in the Sylhet and Chittagong regions), 42,484 tons. Reserves of 700 billion cubic meters of natural gas in 13 fields have been found; production totaled 4,893 million cubic meters in 1991.

26 FOREIGN TRADE

Exports of ready-made garments are Bangladesh's leading earner of money from abroad. Leather goods and frozen seafood have also become important

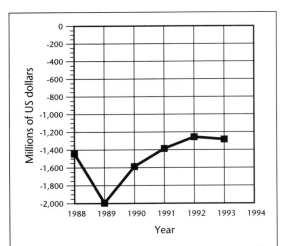

Yearly balance of trade measured in millions of US dollars. The balance of trade is the difference between what a country sells to other countries (its exports) and what it buys (its imports). If a country imports more than it exports, it has a negative balance of trade (a trade deficit). If exports exceed imports, there is a positive balance of trade (a trade surplus).

exports, in addition to tea and more traditional dried fish. Major imports are manufactured goods, food grains, and petroleum. In 1990/91, Bangladesh's main export purchasers were the United States, the Federal Republic of Germany, and the United Kingdom.

27 ENERGY AND POWER

A substantial portion of Bangladesh's electrical supply is met by the country's only hydroelectric plant, at Kaptai, which has a capacity of 130 megawatts. The rest of the country's power is produced by burning coal, gas, and oil. Total power production was 8,930 million kilowatt hours in 1991, of which about 9% was hydroelectric.

Selected Social Indicators

These statistics are estimates for the period 1988 to 1993. For comparison purposes, data for the United States and averages for low-income countries and high-income countries are also given.

Indicator	Bangladesh	Low-income countries	High-income countries	United States
Per capita gross national product†	**$220**	$380	$23,680	$24,740
Population growth rate	**2.0%**	1.9%	0.6%	1.0%
Population growth rate in urban areas	**5.1%**	3.9%	0.8%	1.3%
Population per square kilometer of land	**784**	78	25	26
Life expectancy in years	**56**	62	77	76
Number of people per physician	**5,216**	>3,300	453	419
Number of pupils per teacher (primary school)	**63**	39	<18	20
Illiteracy rate (15 years and older)	**35%**	41%	<5%	<3%
Energy consumed per capita (kg of oil equivalent)	**59**	364	5,203	7,918

† The gross national product (GNP) is the total dollar value of all goods and services produced by a country in a year. The per capita GNP is calculated by dividing a country's GNP by its population. The World Bank defines low-income countries as those with a per capita GNP of $695 or less. High-income countries have a per capita GNP of $8,626 or more. Less than 14% of the world's 5.5 billion people live in high-income countries, while almost 60% live in low-income countries.   > = greater than   < = less than

Sources: World Bank, *Social Indicators of Development 1995,* Baltimore: Johns Hopkins University Press, 1995. Central Intelligence Agency, *World Fact Book,* Washington, D.C.: Government Printing Office, 1994.

28 SOCIAL DEVELOPMENT

The most serious threat to Bangladesh is uncontrolled population growth. In 1976, the National Population Council was formed to develop a population control program, and the Ministry of Health assumed responsibility for family planning. While women have and exercise full voting rights, they receive unequal treatment in many areas, including education, employment, and family matters such as divorce and inheritance.

29 HEALTH

Malaria, tuberculosis, and other serious diseases remain widespread, and public health problems are aggravated by widespread malnutrition and periodic natural disasters. Average life expectancy at birth is about 56 years. In 1993 the government of Bangladesh used a national system to distribute Vitamin A capsules to children. In 1990, there were 8,566 doctors (15 per 1,000 people). In 1992, only 45% of the population had access to health services.

30 HOUSING

The government maintains an urban housing program but does not have any housing development program for villages. As of 1981, 63% of all housing units were straw or bamboo, 20% were mud or unburnt brick, 12% were cement or wood roofed with iron sheets, and 5% were cement or brick.

31 EDUCATION

About 65% of the adult population of Bangladesh can read. Bangladesh has five years of compulsory education. In 1990, the number of primary schools was 45,917, with 189,508 teachers and 11,939,949 students. At the secondary level, there were 130,949 teachers and 3,592,995 students. There are 7 universities, 10 medical colleges, and 10 teacher-training colleges. In 1990, there were 22,447 teachers and 434,309 students in all higher level institutions.

32 MEDIA

There were 241,250 telephones in 1992. The major Bangla daily newspapers (with 1991 circulations), all in Dhaka, are *Ittefaq* (200,000), *Banglar Bani* (125,000), *Sangbad* (75,000), and *Dainik Bangla* (40,000). The largest English dailies, also in Dhaka, are the *Bangladesh Observer* (65,000) and *Bangladesh Times* (35,600). In all, there are 72 dailies, with a total 1991 circulation of 1,016,000.

In 1991, Bangladesh had 26 radio and 11 television stations. Color television was introduced in 1980. As of the same year, there were 4,990,000 radios and 540,000 television sets.

33 TOURISM AND RECREATION

In 1991, 113,242 foreign visitors arrived, 44,890 from South Asia and 18,206 from Eastern Asia. There were 3,063 hotel rooms with a 48.6% occupancy rate. Tourism revenues totaled $9 million. The main tourist attractions include the old Mughal capital at Dhaka, nearby Sonargaon with its ancient architecture, the Buddhist cultural center of Mainamati, and the beach resort of Cox's Bazar.

34 FAMOUS BANGLADESHIS

Sheikh Mujibur Rahman (1920–75) led the successful fight for the independence of East Pakistan and was the first premier of Bangladesh (1972–75). Major General Zia-ur Rahman (1936–81) was military ruler of the country from 1976 until his assassination. As of 1994, the two leading Bangla politicians are women: prime minister Khalida Zia and opposition leader Sheikh Hasina Wajid.

35 BIBLIOGRAPHY

Cobb, Charles E., Jr. "Bangladesh: When the Water Comes." *National Geographic,* June 1993, 118–134.

Heitzman, James and Robert L. Worden, eds. *Bangladesh, a Country Study,* 2d ed. Washington, D.C.: Library of Congress, U.S. Government Printing Office, 1989.

Laurè, J. *Bangladesh.* Chicago: Children's Press, 1992.

Sisson, Richard. *War and Secession: Pakistan, India, and the Creation of Bangladesh.* Berkeley: University of California Press, 1990.

BARBADOS

CAPITAL: Bridgetown.

FLAG: The national flag has three equal vertical bands of ultramarine blue, gold, and ultramarine blue and displays a broken trident in black on the center stripe.

ANTHEM: *National Anthem of Barbados,* beginning "In plenty and in time of need, when this fair land was young. . . ."

MONETARY UNIT: Officially introduced on 3 December 1973, the Barbados dollar (BDS$) of 100 cents is a paper currency officially pegged to the US dollar. There are coins of 1, 5, 10, and 25 cents and 1 dollar, and notes of 1, 2, 5, 10, 20, 50, and 100 dollars. BDS$1 = US$0.4972 (or US$1 = BDS$2.0113)

WEIGHTS AND MEASURES: The metric system is used.

HOLIDAYS: New Year's Day, 1 January; Errol Barrow Day, 23 January; May Day, 1 May; Kadooment Day, 1st Monday in August; CARICOM Day, 1 August; UN Day, 1st Monday in October; Independence Day, 30 November; Christmas Day, 25 December; Boxing Day, 26 December. Movable religious holidays are Good Friday, Easter Monday, and Whitmonday.

TIME: 8 AM = noon GMT.

1 LOCATION AND SIZE

Barbados has an area of 430 square kilometers (166 square miles), slightly less than 2.5 times the area of Washington, D.C., and a total coastline of 101 kilometers (63 miles). The capital city of Barbados, Bridgetown, is located on the country's southwestern coast.

2 TOPOGRAPHY

The coast is almost entirely encircled by coral reefs. The only natural harbor is Carlisle Bay on the southwest coast. The land rises to 340 meters (1,115 feet) at Mt. Hillaby, north of Blackmans.

3 CLIMATE

The tropical climate is tempered by an almost constant sea breeze. Temperatures range from 24° to 29°C (75–84°F). Annual rainfall ranges from about 100 centimeters (40 inches) to 230 centimeters (90 inches).

4 PLANTS AND ANIMALS

Palms, casuarina, mahogany, and almond trees are found on the island. The wide variety of flowers and shrubs includes wild roses, carnations, lilies, and several cacti. Natural wildlife is restricted to a few mammals and birds. Finches, blackbirds, and moustache birds are common.

5 ENVIRONMENT

Soil erosion and coastal pollution from oil slicks are major environmental problems. In 1987, three bird species and the Orinoco crocodile were endangered.

6 POPULATION

The population in 1990 was 257,082. The projected population for the year 2000 was 268,000. In 1990, the population density was 602 persons per square kilometer (1,549 persons per square mile), the highest of all American nations. Bridgetown, the capital, and its suburbs has a population of about 110,000, or over 40% of the island's total.

7 MIGRATION

Most emigrants now resettle in the Caribbean region or along the eastern US coast.

8 ETHNIC GROUPS

About 90% of all Barbadians (called Bajans) are the descendants of former African slaves. Some 5% are mulattos and another 5% are whites.

9 LANGUAGES

English, the official language, is spoken universally, with local pronunciations.

10 RELIGIONS

About 40% of the population is Anglican. Of the remainder, Methodists (7.1%), Pentecostals (8%), and Roman Catholics (4%) predominate.

11 TRANSPORTATION

The highway system had a total length of 1,570 kilometers (976 miles) in 1991. There were 40,951 passenger cars and 6,724 commercial vehicles registered in 1992. Barbados is served through Grantley Adams International Airport by 14 international airlines and one local airline. There is a deepwater harbor at Bridgetown, with docking facilities for cruise ships and freighters.

12 HISTORY

When the British landed on Barbados in 1625, the island was uninhabited. Almost 2,000 English settlers landed in 1627–28. Soon afterward, the island developed a sugar-based economy, supported by a slave population. Slavery was abolished in 1834, and the last slaves were freed in 1838.

During the following 100 years, the economic fortunes of Barbados rose and fell with alternating booms and slumps in the sugar trade. In the 1930s, the dominance of plantation owners and merchants was challenged by a labor movement. The gradual introduction of social and political reforms led to the granting of universal adult suffrage in 1950.

The island was proclaimed an independent republic on 30 November 1966. Political stability has been maintained since that time. In 1973, the nation began issuing its own currency. The country was a staging area in October 1983 for the US-led invasion of Grenada, in which Barbadian troops took part.

13 GOVERNMENT

Barbados has a crown-appointed governor-general (who in turn appoints an advisory Privy Council) and independent executive, legislative, and judicial bodies. The two-chamber legislature consists of a 21-member appointed Senate and a 28-member elected House of Assembly. Voting is universal at age 18. The governor-general appoints as prime minister a member of the House of Assembly.

14 POLITICAL PARTIES

The leading parties are the Barbados Labor Party (BLP), the Democratic Labour Party (DLP), and the National Democratic Party (NDP). The DLP under Prime Minister Erskine Sandiford holds 18 of the 28 seats in the House of Assembly. The BLP retains the remaining 10 seats, leaving the dissident NDP without any representation.

15 JUDICIAL SYSTEM

The Supreme Court of Judicature sits as a high court and court of appeal. Magistrate courts have both civil and criminal jurisdiction. Final appeals are brought to the Committee of Her Majesty's Privy Council in the UK.

16 ARMED FORCES

The Barbados Defense Force and the Royal Barbados Police Force number about 1,000. The defense budget is US$10 million.

17 ECONOMY

The economy has traditionally been dependent on the production of sugar, rum, and molasses. In recent years, however, tourism and manufacturing have surpassed the sugar industry in importance.

As of 1994, Barbados was in the grip of an economic recession that began in mid-1990, spurred by the impact on tourism of the US recession and competition from

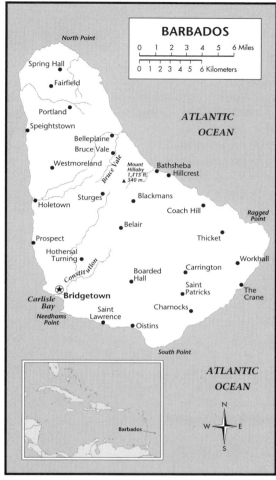

LOCATION: 13°2′ to 13°20′N; 59°25′ to 59°39′W.
TOTAL COASTLINE: 101 kilometers (63 miles).
TERRITORIAL SEA LIMIT: 12 miles.

other Caribbean countries. Unemployment for 1992 was 23%, up from 17.1% in 1991.

18 INCOME

In 1992, Barbados' gross national product (GNP) was US$1,693 million at current prices, or US$6,230 per person. For the period 1985–92 the average inflation rate was 4.3%, resulting in a real growth rate in gross national product (GNP) of 0.6% per person.

19 INDUSTRY

Traditionally, sugar production and related enterprises were Barbados' primary industry, but light industry has also become more important. Items manufactured for export include soap, glycerine, pharmaceuticals, furniture, household appliances, plastic products, fabricated metal products, and cotton garments.

20 LABOR

Total civilian employment as of 1992 was 96,100. In 1992, services accounted for about 39% of the labor force; commerce and tourism, 14.3%; manufacturing, 10%; construction, 7.3%; agriculture, 6%; and other sectors, 23.4%. Unemployment, traditionally high, was reported at 23% in 1992. The legal minimum working age is 16.

21 AGRICULTURE

About 33,000 hectares (81,500 acres), or 76.7% of the total land area, are classified as capable of cultivation. In 1992, 600,000 tons of sugar were produced. In 1990, sugar exports amounted to US$29 million, or 23.7% of total exports. Major food crops are yams, sweet potatoes, corn, eddo, cassava, and several varieties of beans. Some cotton is also grown.

22 DOMESTICATED ANIMALS

Most livestock is owned by individual households. Estimates for 1992 showed 21,000 head of cattle, 56,000 sheep, 45,000 hogs, and 34,000 goats.

23 FISHING

The fishing fleet consists of more than 500 powered boats. The catch in 1991 was 2,697 metric tons. Flying fish, dolphinfish, tuna, turbot, kingfish, and swordfish are among the main species caught.

24 FORESTRY

Fewer than 20 hectares (50 acres) of original forests have survived the 300 years of sugar cultivation. In 1992, imports of forest products totaled US$15.1 million.

25 MINING

Deposits of limestone and coral are quarried to meet local construction needs.

26 FOREIGN TRADE

Main exports include clothing, electronic components, building cement, chemicals, rum, furniture, machinery, transport equipment, and sugar. Barbados' main imports were composed of foodstuffs, other non-durables, fuels and lubricants, building materials, chemicals, textiles, and machinery. Main trade partners were the US, Canada, CARICOM, the UK, and Japan.

27 ENERGY AND POWER

Electricity production in 1991 totaled 527 million kilowatt hours. Oil accounted for more than 70% of energy usage in 1991. Crude oil production in 1991 was 470,000 barrels. Natural gas production was 35 million cubic meters.

28 SOCIAL DEVELOPMENT

A national social security system provides old age and survivors' pensions, sickness, disability, maternity benefits, and employment injury benefits. The Family Planning Association receives government support. The 1992 Domestic Violence law requires a police response to violence against women and children.

29 HEALTH

In 1986, government health facilities included 11 hospitals and 8 public health centers, with a total of more than 2,100 beds. In 1990, there were 294 doctors, and 100% of the population had access to health care services. Life expectancy during 1992 was 75 years.

30 HOUSING

The Barbados Housing Authority constructs housing projects, and redevelops overcrowded areas. In 1980, 90% of all housing consisted of detached homes and 6% of apartments.

31 EDUCATION

Education is compulsory for children between the ages of 5 and 16. In 1991, children in 106 primary schools numbered 26,662. The Barbados branch of the University of the West Indies opened in 1963, and the Barbados Community College was established in 1968. Barbados' adult literacy rate in 1992 was estimated at 99%.

32 MEDIA

There are three AM and two FM radio stations and two television stations (of which one is pay television). An estimated

Photo credit: Barbados Tourism Authority.

Children gather in front of their school.

226,000 radios and 68,000 television sets were in use in 1991, and there were 110,600 telephones. There are two daily newspapers in Bridgetown, the *Advocate-News* (circulation, 32,000 in 1991) and the *Daily Nation* (77,000).

33 TOURISM AND RECREATION

Barbados, with its fine beaches, sea bathing, and pleasant climate, has long been a popular holiday retreat. In 1991, 394,222 tourists visited Barbados, of whom 119,069 were from the US, 46,286 from Canada, and 153,954 from Europe. Tourist spending was an estimated US$453 mil-

Selected Social Indicators

These statistics are estimates for the period 1988 to 1993. For comparison purposes, data for the United States and averages for low-income countries and high-income countries are also given.

Indicator	Barbados	Low-income countries	High-income countries	United States
Per capita gross national product†	$6,230	$380	$23,680	$24,740
Population growth rate	0.4%	1.9%	0.6%	1.0%
Population growth rate in urban areas	1.5%	3.9%	0.8%	1.3%
Population per square kilometer of land	602	78	25	26
Life expectancy in years	75	62	77	76
Number of people per physician	1,121	>3,300	453	419
Number of pupils per teacher (primary school)	17	39	<18	20
Illiteracy rate (15 years and older)	1%	41%	<5%	<3%
Energy consumed per capita (kg of oil equivalent)	1,381	364	5,203	7,918

† The gross national product (GNP) is the total dollar value of all goods and services produced by a country in a year. The per capita GNP is calculated by dividing a country's GNP by its population. The World Bank defines low-income countries as those with a per capita GNP of $695 or less. High-income countries have a per capita GNP of $8,626 or more. Less than 14% of the world's 5.5 billion people live in high-income countries, while almost 60% live in low-income countries.

> = greater than   < = less than

Sources: World Bank, *Social Indicators of Development 1995,* Baltimore: Johns Hopkins University Press, 1995. Central Intelligence Agency, *World Fact Book,* Washington, D.C.: Government Printing Office, 1994.

lion. There were 6,650 hotel rooms with a 50.5% occupancy rate. Cricket is the national sport, followed by surfing, sailing, and other marine pastimes.

34 FAMOUS BARBADIANS

Sir Grantley Adams (1898–1971) was premier of the Federation of the West Indies (1958–62). Erskine Sandiford (b.1938) has been prime minister since 1987. Barbados-born Edwin Barclay (1882–1955) was president of Liberia from 1930 to 1944.

35 BIBLIOGRAPHY

Beckles, Hilary. *A History of Barbados: From Amerindian Settlement to Nation-State.* New York: Cambridge University Press, 1990.

Potter, Robert B. *Barbados.* Oxford, England, and Santa Barbara, Calif.: Clio Press, 1987.

BELARUS

Republic of Belarus
Respublika Belarus

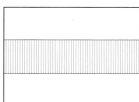

CAPITAL: Minsk.

FLAG: Three horizontal bands of white (top), red, and white.

ANTHEM: *Maladaya Belarus*.

MONETARY UNIT: The Belarus ruble circulates along with the Russian rouble (R). The government has a varying exchange rate for trade between Belarus and Russia.

WEIGHTS AND MEASURES: The metric system is in force.

HOLIDAYS: New Year's Day, 1 January; Orthodox Christmas, 7 January; International Women's Day, 8 March; Labor Day, 1 May; Victory Day, 9 May; Independence Day, 27 July; Day of Commemoration, 2 November; Christmas, 25 December.

TIME: 2 PM = noon GMT.

1 LOCATION AND SIZE

Belarus is a landlocked nation located in eastern Europe, between Poland and Russia. Comparatively, the area occupied by Belarus is slightly smaller than the state of Kansas, with a total area of 207,600 square kilometers (80,154 square miles). The boundary length of Belarus totals 3,098 kilometers (1,925 miles).

The capital city of Belarus, Minsk, is located near the center of the country.

2 TOPOGRAPHY

The topography of Belarus is generally flat and contains much marshland.

3 CLIMATE

The mean temperature is 19.4°C (67°F) in July and −5°C (23°F) in January. Rainfall averages between 57 centimeters (22.5 inches) and 61 centimeters (26.5 inches) annually.

4 PLANTS AND ANIMALS

One-third of the country is forest. Some of the mammals in the forest include deer, brown bears, rabbits, and squirrels. The marshes are home to ducks, frogs, turtles, raccoons, and muskrats.

5 ENVIRONMENT

Belarus was the former Soviet republic most affected by the accident at the Chernobyl nuclear power plant in Ukraine in April 1986. Most experts estimate that 25–30% of Belarus's farmland was affected by radiation and should not be used for agricultural purposes. In addition, Belarus has significant air and water pollution from industrial sources. The soils also contain unsafe levels of lead, zinc, copper, and the agricultural chemical DDT.

6 POPULATION

The population of Belarus was 10,199,709 in 1989. The UN projects a population of 10,811,000 in the year 2000. At the start of 1990, Minsk, the capital, had an estimated population of 1,613,000.

7 MIGRATION

In 1990, emigration to other Soviet republics exceeded immigration by 32,000.

8 ETHNIC GROUPS

In 1989, Belarussians formed 78% of the population. Russians compromised 13%; Poles, 4%; Ukrainians, 3%; and Jews, 1%.

9 LANGUAGES

Belarussian belongs to the eastern group of Slavic languages and is very similar to Russian. The vocabulary has words taken from Polish, Lithuanian, German, Latin, and Turkic.

10 RELIGIONS

The Eastern Orthodox Church is the main church, and there is a Roman Catholic population of 14%. As of 1990, there was a small but significant Jewish population of 75,000.

11 TRANSPORTATION

About 5,570 kilometers (3,460 miles) of railways cross Belarus, connecting it to Russia, Ukraine, Lithuania, Poland, and Latvia. There were 98,200 kilometers (61,000 miles) of highways in 1990.

12 HISTORY

The Belarussians are the descendants of Slavic tribes that migrated into the region in the ninth century AD. They trace their distinct identity from the thirteenth century when the Mongols conquered Russia and parts of Ukraine. During this period, Belarus managed to maintain its identity as part of the Grand Duchy of Lithuania. The combining of the Grand Duchy with Poland in 1569 put the territory of Belarus under Polish rule. After the division of Poland in the late eighteenth century, Belarus fell to the Russian Empire.

The Belarussian National Republic was formed in March 1918 with German military assistance. However, after the German government collapsed in November 1918, Bolshevik troops moved in and set up the Byelorussian Soviet Socialist Republic in January 1919. In 1922, the Belarus SSR became one of the 15 socialist republics to form the Union of Soviet Socialist Republics. Belarus, located between Germany and Russia, was devastated by World War II.

Throughout the early 1990s the Belarussian leadership wanted to keep the Soviet Union intact. However, shortly after the failed August 1991 takeover attempt against Mikhail Gorbachev, the independence of Belarus was declared on 26 August 1991.

Since independence, Belarus has made very little progress toward economic and political reform. The economy is failing and Soviet-era party bosses are struggling to hold power.

13 GOVERNMENT

A new constitution was adopted on 15 March 1994. Until mid-1994, Belarus was the only former Soviet republic not to have a president. In elections held on 19 July 1994, Alyaksandr Lukashenka was elected after promising to clear out the Communist establishment ruling Belarus.

Under the new constitution, Belarus is divided into six regions.

14 POLITICAL PARTIES

The Communist Party was declared illegal after the failed August 1991 takeover attempt, but was re-legalized in February 1993. It and two other pro-Communist parties merged into one political party called the People's Movement of Belarus in May 1993. The primary opposition party, the Belarussian Popular Front, holds only 10% of the seats in parliament.

15 JUDICIAL SYSTEM

The government continues to operate under the judicial system of the former Soviet Union. The courts system consists of district courts, city or province courts, and republic courts.

16 ARMED FORCES

Belarus's armed forces number 125,000 and will be reduced to 90,000, organized as an army, air force, and air defense force.

17 ECONOMY

Belarus's economy is geared toward industrial production, mostly in machinery and metallurgy with a significant weapons industry.

LOCATION: 53°53′N; 28°0′E **BOUNDARY LENGTHS:** Total boundary lengths, 3,098 kilometers (1,925 miles); Latvia 141 kilometers (88 miles); Lithuania 502 kilometers (312 miles); Poland, 605 kilometers (376 miles); Russia 959 kilometers (596 miles); Ukraine, 891 kilometers (554 miles).

Belarus's economy is closely tied in with those of Eastern Europe and the other republics of the former Soviet Union. The break-up of the Soviet Union was highly disruptive to it.

18 INCOME

In 1992, the gross national product was $30,127 million at current prices, or $2,870 per person. For the period 1985–92, the average inflation rate was 41.6%.

A man checks ration coupons he has just bought from a street vendor at the city market in Minsk. A faltering economy after the break-up of the USSR led the government to ration supplies of food and other essential items. Many coupons found their way onto the black market where they were sold for four times the official price.

19 INDUSTRY

Belarus's main industries are engineering, machine tools, agricultural equipment, chemicals, motor vehicles, and some consumer goods, such as watches, televisions, and radios.

20 LABOR

Of the 4,887,400 persons employed in 1992, 21% were engaged in agriculture, 30% in mining, 23% in services, 10% in construction, and 16% in other sectors.

Currently, the minimum age for employment is 16. In certain cases, such as in the death of a family's chief wage earner, people as young as 15 may apply for special permission to take full-time employment.

21 AGRICULTURE

Production levels (in 1,000 tons) for 1992 include: potatoes, 8,000; rye, 2,700; sugar beets, 1,350; oats, 800; wheat, 400; and corn, 25.

22 DOMESTICATED ANIMALS

About 15% of the land area is devoted to pastureland. In 1992, there were approximately 6,600,000 cattle, 4,700,000 pigs, 400,000 sheep, and 50 million chickens.

Belarus produces more dairy products than any other former Soviet republic except Russia. In 1992, 5.8 million tons of milk, 189,800 tons of eggs, and 130,000 tons of butter were produced.

23 FISHING

Fishing is confined to the system of rivers (the Pripyat, the Byarezina, the Nyoman, the Zach Dvina, the Sozh, the Dnieper) that crosses landlocked Belarus.

24 FORESTRY

Radioactive contamination from the 1986 Chernobyl disaster has severely restricted timber output.

Selected Social Indicators

These statistics are estimates for the period 1988 to 1993. For comparison purposes, data for the United States and averages for low-income countries and high-income countries are also given.

Indicator	Belarus	Low-income countries	High-income countries	United States
Per capita gross national product†	**$2,870**	$380	$23,680	$24,740
Population growth rate	**0.0%**	1.9%	0.6%	1.0%
Population growth rate in urban areas	**1.3%**	3.9%	0.8%	1.3%
Population per square kilometers of land	**49**	78	25	26
Life expectancy in years	**71**	62	77	76
Number of people per physician	**246**	>3,300	453	419
Number of pupils per teacher (primary school)	**n.a.**	39	<18	20
Illiteracy rate (15 years and older)	**2%**	41%	<5%	<3%
Energy consumed per capita (kg of oil equivalent)	**3,427**	364	5,203	7,918

† The gross national product (GNP) is the total dollar value of all goods and services produced by a country in a year. The per capita GNP is calculated by dividing a country's GNP by its population. The World Bank defines low-income countries as those with a per capita GNP of $695 or less. High-income countries have a per capita GNP of $8,626 or more. Less than 14% of the world's 5.5 billion people live in high-income countries, while almost 60% live in low-income countries.

n.a. = data not available.   > = greater than   < = less than

Sources: World Bank, *Social Indicators of Development 1995,* Baltimore: Johns Hopkins University Press, 1995. Central Intelligence Agency, *World Fact Book,* Washington, D.C.: Government Printing Office, 1994.

25 MINING

Peat is found throughout the country, and potash is mined in the Salihorsk region.

26 FOREIGN TRADE

In 1988, 91% of Belarus's total exports went to other Soviet republics, and 79% of its total imports came from them.

27 ENERGY AND POWER

Domestic electricity is produced by four thermal plants. Belarus also imports electricity generated by nuclear and hydroelectric plants. In 1991, consumption of electricity totaled 49 billion kilowatt hours. About 40,000 barrels of oil are produced per day.

28 SOCIAL DEVELOPMENT

The government has provided inhabitants with food and other basic goods to preserve social stability. Many factories have given workers mandatory unpaid vacations and four-day work weeks to avoid laying them off or closing down. While there are no legal restrictions on women's participation in public life, social barriers remain substantial.

[29] HEALTH

Between 1988 and 1992, the country had 4.05 doctors per 1,000 people, and between 1985 and 1990, there were 879 hospitals with 13.2 hospitals beds per 1,000 people.

Total health care expenditures in 1990 were $1,613 million. Life expectancy in 1992 was 71 years (76 for females and 66 for males).

The factor most affecting the health of the Belorussian population is the accident at the Chernobyl nuclear power plant in April 1986. An estimated 2.2 million Belorussians were directly affected by radioactive fallout. Continuing radiation weakens the immune systems of individuals in contaminated areas. Many are said to suffer from "Chernobyl AIDS."

[30] HOUSING

In 1990, Belarus had 17.9 square meters of housing space per capita and, as of 1 January 1991, 635,000 households (or 28.8%) were on waiting lists for housing in urban areas.

[31] EDUCATION

In 1990, the literacy rate was 97.9%. Education is compulsory for children between the ages of 7 and 17. Secondary education lasts for five years. In 1991, there were 5,100 primary level schools with 113,100 teachers and 897,000 students. Secondary level schools had 691,300 students.

There are three universities in Belarus. The largest is the Belarussian State University. All higher level institutions combined had 187,400 students and 17,000 teaching staff in 1991.

[32] MEDIA

The government operates one radio station and one television station in Minsk. In 1991, there were 3,170,000 radios and 2,760,000 television sets. There was approximately one telephone for every 17 people as of early 1990.

There are 28 daily newspapers, with a combined 1991 circulation of 2,738,000. The most widely read (with 1991 circulation figures) are *Sovetskaya Belorussiya* (645,500); *Narodnaya Gazeta* (387,000); *Belorusskaya Niva* (130,000); and *Zarya* (107,500).

[33] TOURISM AND RECREATION

The difficult transition to democratic rule and a free market economy has delayed the development of the tourism sector.

[34] FAMOUS BELARUSSIANS

Frantsky Sharyna, who lived in the first quarter of the sixteenth century, translated the Bible into Belarussian. Modern writers include Vladzimir Dubouka and Yazep Pushcha, both poets.

[35] BIBLIOGRAPHY

The Modern Encyclopedia of Russian, Soviet and Eurasian History. Gulf Breeze, Fla.: Academic International Press, 1994.

Zaprudnik, I.A. *Belarus: At a Crossroads in History*. Boulder, Colo.: Westview Press, 1993.

BELGIUM

Kingdom of Belgium

[Dutch:] *Koninkrijk België* [French:] *Royaume de Belgique*

CAPITAL: Brussels (Brussel, Bruxelles).

FLAG: The flag, adopted in 1831, is a tricolor of black, yellow, and red vertical stripes.

ANTHEM: *La Brabançonne (The Song of Brabant),* named after the Duchy of Brabant.

MONETARY UNIT: The Belgian franc (BFr) is a paper currency of 100 centimes. There are coins of 50 centimes and 1, 5, 20, 50, and 500 francs, and notes of 100, 500, 1,000, and 5,000 francs. BFr1 = $0.0291 (or $1 = BFr34.375).

WEIGHTS AND MEASURES: The metric system is the legal standard.

HOLIDAYS: New Year's Day, 1 January; Labor Day, 1 May; Independence Day, 21 July; Assumption Day, 15 August; All Saints' Day, 1 November; Armistice Day, 11 November; Dynasty Day, 15 November; and Christmas, 25 December. Movable holidays are Easter Monday, Ascension, and Whitmonday.

TIME: 1 PM = noon GMT.

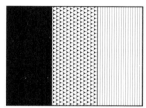

1 LOCATION AND SIZE

Situated in northwestern Europe, Belgium has an area of 30,510 square kilometers (11,780 square miles), slightly larger than the state of Maryland. Belgium has a total boundary length of 1,449 kilometers (900 miles).

Belgium's capital city, Brussels, is located in the north central part of the country.

2 TOPOGRAPHY

The coastal region consists mostly of sand dunes and flat pastureland. Eastward, this region gradually gives way to a gently rolling central plain, whose many fertile valleys are irrigated by an extensive network of canals and waterways. The Ardennes, a heavily wooded plateau, is located in southeast Belgium and continues into France. It reaches an altitude of 694 meters (2,277 feet) at the Signal de Botrange, the country's highest point. Chief rivers are the Schelde and the Meuse.

3 CLIMATE

In the coastal region, the climate is mild and humid. Except in the highlands, rainfall is seldom heavy. The average annual temperature is 8°C (46°F). In Brussels, the mean temperature ranges from 3°C (37°F) in January to 18°C (64°F) in July. Average annual rainfall is 70 centimeters (28 inches).

4 PLANTS AND ANIMALS

The digitalis, wild arum, hyacinth, strawberry, goldenrod, lily of the valley, and other plants common to temperate zones grow in abundance. Beech and oak are the most common trees. Among the mammals found in Belgium are the boar, fox, badger, squirrel, weasel, marten, and hedgehog. The many varieties of aquatic life include pike, carp, trout, eel, barbel, perch, smelt, chub, roach, bream, shad, sole, mussels, crayfish, and shrimp.

5 ENVIRONMENT

Belgium's most significant environmental problems are air, land, and water pollution due to the heavy concentration of industrial facilities in the country. The sources of pollution range from nuclear radiation to mercury from industry and pesticides from agricultural activity.

The country's water supply is threatened by hazardous levels of heavy metals, mercury, and phosphorous. Pollution of rivers and canals was considered the worst in Europe as of 1970, when strict water-protection laws were enacted. Air pollution reaches dangerous levels due to high concentrations of lead and hydrocarbons.

By 1994, two species of mammals and 13 species of birds were endangered. Nine plant species were also threatened.

6 POPULATION

One of the most densely populated countries in the world, Belgium had a population of 9,978,681 in 1991, with a density of 327 persons per square kilometer (847 persons per square mile). The UN population projection for the year 2000 was 10,084,000. In 1989, the population of Brussels (including suburbs) was 964,385, while Antwerp's was 470,349.

7 MIGRATION

At the end of 1991, 922,502 persons of foreign nationality were living in Belgium. The major nationalities, in order of ranking, were Italian, French, Moroccan, Dutch, and Spanish. In 1989 there were 59,169 immigrants and 33,458 emigrants. Migration within Belgium came to 386,359.

8 ETHNIC GROUPS

The Salian Franks, who settled there during the fourth century AD, are considered the ancestors of Belgium's present population. Among the native population, the ratio of Flemings (of Dutch descent) to Walloons (of French descent) is about 5 to 3.

9 LANGUAGES

According to a 1970 constitutional revision, there are three official languages in Belgium—French, Dutch (also called Flemish), and German. Dutch is the language of the four northern provinces, while French is the language of the four southern Walloon provinces. The majority of people in the Brussels metropolitan area are French-speaking.

The relationship between the two major language groups has been tense at times. This is especially true for Brussels, a mostly French-speaking territory surrounded by a Dutch-speaking region.

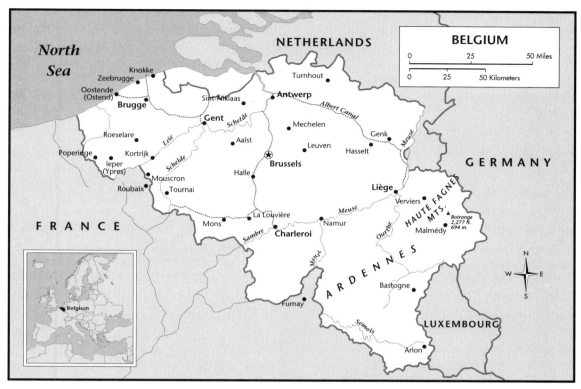

LOCATION: 49°29′52″ to 51°30′21″N; 2°32′48″ to 6°25′38″E. **BOUNDARY LENGTHS:** Netherlands, 450 kilometers (280 miles); Germany, 162 kilometers (101 miles); Luxembourg, 148 kilometers (92 miles); France, 620 kilometers (385 miles); North Sea, 66 kilometers (41 miles). **TERRITORIAL SEA LIMIT:** 12 miles.

10 RELIGIONS

According to 1993 estimates, 86% of the population is Roman Catholic and less than 1% is Protestant. Most of the remainder is nonreligious. In 1993, there were also 250,000 Muslims living in Belgium, and more than 32,000 Jews.

11 TRANSPORTATION

The railway network comprises 3,667 kilometers (2,279 miles) of track operated by the government-controlled Belgian National Railway Co. The road network comprises 103,396 kilometers (64,250 miles), of which 11,717 kilometers (7,281 miles) are national highways. Motor vehicles in 1991 included 3,928,906 passenger cars and 363,850 trucks.

Inland waterways comprise 2,043 kilometers (1,270 miles) of rivers and canals, and are linked with those of France, Germany, and the Netherlands. The chief port, Antwerp, handles three-fourths of the country's foreign cargo.

In 1992, the Belgian national airline, Sabena, flew 6,207 million passenger-kilometers and 386 million ton-kilometers of

Photo credit: Susan D. Rock

People promenade along the Schelde River in Antwerp.

freight. Brussels' National Airport is served by more than 30 major airlines.

12 HISTORY

Belgium is named after the Belgae, a Celtic people whose territory Julius Caesar conquered in 57 BC and ruled as Gallia Belgica. In the fifth century AD, it was overrun by the Franks, and in the eighth century, it became part of Charlemagne's empire. By the tenth century this empire had declined, and feudal powers ruled the land. During the next three centuries, trade flourished. Antwerp, Bruges, Ypres, and Ghent became especially prosperous.

The territories that currently form Belgium, the Netherlands, and Luxembourg—now called the Benelux countries—have been called the Low Countries. Beginning in the fifteenth century, these territory, or parts of them, were ruled at various times by France, Austria, and Spain for some 400 years.

On 4 October 1830, Belgium was declared independent. The following year its parliament chose Prince Leopold of Saxe-Coburg-Gotha as ruler of the new kingdom. In 1865, Leopold I was followed by Leopold II (r.1865–1909), who financed exploration and settlement in the Congo River Basin of Africa, laying the foundations of Belgium's colonial empire.

At the outbreak of World War I, German troops invaded Belgium (4 August 1914). The Belgian army offered fierce resistance, but by the end of November 1914, most of the country was occupied by the Germans. Belgium, on the side of the Allies, continued to struggle against the occupation. Ypres (Ieper), in particular, was the scene of fierce fighting. Nearly 100,000 men lost their lives at a battle near there in April and May 1915.

The Allies won the war and under the Treaty of Versailles (1919), Belgium acquired the German-speaking districts of Eupen, Malmédy, St. Vith, and Moresnet. The country made a remarkable recovery from the war, and by 1923, manufacturing industries were nearly back to normal.

Belgium was again attacked early in World War II. On 10 May 1940, without warning, the Germans invaded the country and bombed Belgian airports, railroad stations, and communications centers. King Leopold III surrendered unconditionally on 28 May and was taken prisoner of war. The country was liberated from the Germans in 1944, and the Belgian government returned to Brussels in September of that year.

The country was economically better off after World War II than after World War I. However, a split had developed during the war years between Leopold III, who had surrendered to the Germans, and the Belgian government-in-exile, operating from London. The government-in-exile had rejected the king's surrender to Germany. On 22 July 1950, Leopold came back from exile, but much of the country opposed his return. On 1 August 1950, he agreed to give up the throne in favor of his son, Baudouin I.

In 1960, the Belgian Congo (now Zaire), a major portion of Belgium's colonial empire, became independent. The event was followed by two years of brutal civil war, involving mercenaries from Belgium and other countries. Another Belgian territory in Africa, Ruanda-Urundi, became independent as the two states of Rwanda and Burundi in 1962.

Belgium shared fully in the European prosperity of the first three postwar decades. However, domestic political conflict during this period centered on the unequal distribution of wealth and power between Flemings (Dutch speakers) and Walloons (French speakers). Today, the country is divided into three regions (Flanders, Wallonia, and Brussels) and three linguistic communities (Flemish, French, and German).

Labor unrest and political violence have erupted in recent years. Vigorous trade-union protests have taken place to protest the freezing of wages and cuts in social security payments. Belgium has one of the largest national debts in Western Europe. In 1994, the government began an environment tax on a range of goods based on the amount of pollution caused in their production.

King Baudouin died suddenly on 31 July 1993, while vacationing in Spain. He was 62 years old. Since he had no children, he was succeeded by his brother, Prince Albert of Liège. King Baudouin had abdicated for a day in April 1990 to avoid having to sign legislation legalizing abortion.

13 GOVERNMENT

Belgium is a hereditary monarchy governed under the constitution of 1831. This document has been frequently amended in recent years to grant recognition and autonomy to the Dutch- and French-speaking communities. Executive power is held by the king, who also holds legislative power jointly with the two-chamber Parliament. The Chamber of Representatives has 212 members, and the Senate, 185 members.

In accordance with the constitutional reform of 1980, there are three communities: the Dutch-, the French-, and the German-speaking communities. They each have independent responsibility for cultural affairs and for matters concerning the individual. There are also three regions in the northwest that have partial responsibility for economic, energy, housing, environmental and other matters.

Belgium is divided into nine provinces. Each has a council of 50 to 90 members and a governor appointed by the king.

14 POLITICAL PARTIES

The Belgian political system operates through "twin" sets of French- and Dutch-speaking parties. Each French-speaking group has a Dutch-speaking counterpart. The three major political alliances are the Christian Social parties, consisting of the Parti Social Chrétien (PSC) and the Christelijke Volkspartij (CVP); the Socialist parties, the Parti Socialiste (PS) and Socialistische Partij (SP); and the Liberal parties, Parti Réformateur et Liberal (PRL) and Partij voor Vrijheid en Vooruitgang (PVV).

The People's Union (Volksunie, or VU) is the Flemish nationalistic party, while the French-speaking Democratic Front (Front Démocratique des Francophones—FDF) affirms the rights of the French-speaking population of Brussels. Ecology parties (ECOCO/AGALEV) have become important political actors by gaining seats in the Chamber and Senate. The environment tax passed in 1993 was a key demand in return for their support of constitutional reforms.

15 JUDICIAL SYSTEM

Belgian law is modeled on the French legal system. The judiciary is an independent branch of government on an equal footing with the legislative and the executive branches.

Minor offenses are dealt with by justices of the peace and police tribunals. More serious offenses and civil lawsuits are brought before district courts of first instance. Other district courts are commerce and labor tribunals. Verdicts given by these courts may be appealed before 5 regional courts of appeal or the 5 regional labor courts in Antwerp, Brussels, Gent, Mons, and Liège.

The highest courts are 5 civil and criminal courts of appeal and the supreme Court of Cassation, which must verify that the law has been properly applied and interpreted. A system of military tribunals, including appellate courts, handle both military and common law offenses involving military personnel.

16 ARMED FORCES

Belgium's active armed forces in 1993 numbered 80,700, including 32,300 draftees and 2,950 women. Combat forces include one armored brigade, two mechanized infantry brigades, and a parachute–commando regiment, which together form an important part of NATO forces in Western Europe.

In 1993, the army had 54,000 personnel, the air force 17,300, and the navy 4,400. In 1991, Belgium spent $4.7 billion on defense, but almost half of the budget comes from NATO allies.

17 ECONOMY

In relation to its size and population, Belgium is among the most highly industrial-

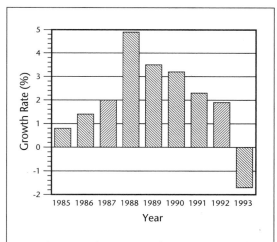

Yearly growth rate of the economy. This economic indicator tells by what percent the economy has increased or decreased when compared with the previous year.

ized countries in Europe. Poor in natural resources, it imports raw materials in great quantity and processes them largely for export. Belgium's highly developed transportation systems are closely linked with those of its neighbors. Its chief port, Antwerp, is one of the world's busiest.

Real growth averaged 2.6% during 1984–91 and was 0.9% in 1992. It fell by about 1.3% in 1993. Public debt in 1993 was the highest in the European Community. However, Belgium has had the highest rate of private savings in the European Community. Consumer prices rose only 15.8% between 1988 and 1993. The unemployment rate was 9.4% in 1993.

18 INCOME

In 1992, Belgium's gross national product (GNP) was $209,594 million at current prices, or $21,650 per person. For the period 1985–92 the average inflation rate was 3.0%, resulting in a real growth rate in gross national product (GNP) of 2.4% per person.

19 INDUSTRY

Steel production is the single most important type of industry, with Belgium ranking high among world producers of iron and steel. Production of crude steel was 11.3 million tons in 1991, while the output of finished steel was 8.98 million tons. In 1991, Belgium produced 477,972 tons of crude copper, 383,053 tons of crude zinc, and 110,684 tons of crude lead.

The textile industry, dating from the Middle Ages, produces cottons, woolens, linens, and synthetic fibers. In 1991, spinning industry production (including cotton, wool, linen, and jute) totaled 172,329 tons of yarn, and the weaving industry produced 520,616 tons of fabric. Brussels and Bruges are noted for fine linen and lace.

The chemical industry manufactures a wide range of products, from heavy chemicals and explosives to pharmaceuticals and photographic supplies. Production in 1991 included sulfuric acid, 1,935,921 tons; nitric acid, 1,439,533 tons; synthetic ammonia, 505,380 tons; and crude tar, 177,230 tons.

The diamond-cutting industry in Antwerp supplies most of the US industrial diamond requirements. Belgium has one of the largest glass industries in the world, and is especially known for its fine crystal glassware.

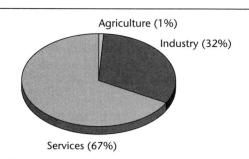

Agriculture (1%)

Industry (32%)

Services (67%)

Components of the economy. This pie chart shows how much of the country's economy is devoted to agriculture (includes forestry, hunting, and fishing), industry, or services.

20 LABOR

As of 1991, the Belgian work force totaled 4,100,000. Of the 1991 total, about 3,700,000 persons were employed, of whom 1,000,000 were in industry and 2,600,000 in services. The number of people receiving unemployment compensation was 472,900 as of January 1992. Unemployment is expected to increase to 9.3% by 1996.

Workers enjoy unemployment insurance, medical insurance, paid holidays, four weeks' annual vacation (for which a bonus is paid from the social security fund), family benefits, severance pay, and workers' compensation.

21 AGRICULTURE

Agriculture's role in the economy is decreasing. In 1990, 2.4% of the employed population worked on farms. Belgium supplies about 80% of its own food needs. As of 1990, about 1,290,000 hectares (3,187,600 acres), or 45.5% of Belgium's total area, were under cultiva-tion. Over half the land cultivated was used for pasture land or green fodder. One quarter was used for the production of food grains.

Government price policy encourages increased production of wheat and barley with decreasing production of rye and oats. Increased emphasis is being placed on the growing of fruits and vegetables. Nearly all fruits found in temperate climates are grown in Belgium. Chief among these are apples, pears, and cherries.

22 DOMESTICATED ANIMALS

Livestock raising is the most important single area of Belgian agriculture. In 1992 there were about 3.1 million head of cattle, 6.5 million hogs, 133,000 sheep, and 18,000 horses. The country supplies its own butter, milk, meat, and eggs. Some cheese is imported, mainly from the Netherlands. Milk production amounted to 3.5 million tons in 1992.

23 FISHING

The chief fishing ports are Zeebrugge and Ostend. The total catch in 1991 was 40,226 tons. Principal species caught are herring, sole, cod, haddock, shrimp, sprat, plaice, and ray.

24 FORESTRY

Forests cover 21% of the area of Belgium. Commercial production of timber is limited. The combined output for Belgium and Luxembourg was 5 million cubic meters in 1991. Belgium serves as a large shipping center for temperate hardwood logs, softwood lumber, and softwood plywood.

25 MINING

Coal, the only mineral resource of major importance, is now mined in the Sambre–Meuse Valley. The shift to alternate sources of energy, as well as foreign competition in coal, has led to a steady decline in output. Production fell from 8.8 million tons during 1973 to 634,000 tons in 1991.

The refining of copper, zinc, and minor metals and the production of steel are the most developed mineral industries in Belgium. Belgium is also an important producer of several industrial minerals, including limestone, dolomite, whiting, soda ash, sodium sulfate, silica sand, and marble.

26 FOREIGN TRADE

Foreign trade plays a greater role in the Belgian economy than in any other EU (European Union) country except Luxembourg. Belgium's chief exports are iron and steel (semifinished and manufactured), foodstuffs, textiles, machinery, road vehicles and parts, nonferrous metals, diamonds, and chemicals. Its imports are general manufactures, foodstuffs, diamonds, metals and metal ores, petroleum and petroleum products, chemicals, clothing, machinery, electrical equipment, and motor vehicles.

Partnered with Luxembourg in the BLEU (Belgium Luxembourg Economic Union), Belgium does not issue separate statistics on foreign trade. In 1992, more than 87% of Belgium-Luxembourg's foreign trade was carried on with the OECD (Organization for Economic Cooperation and Development) countries, chiefly mem-

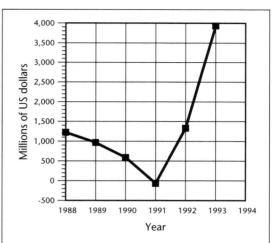

Yearly balance of trade measured in millions of US dollars. The balance of trade is the difference between what a country sells to other countries (its exports) and what it buys (its imports). If a country imports more than it exports, it has a negative balance of trade (a trade deficit). If exports exceed imports, there is a positive balance of trade (a trade surplus).

bers of the European Community. Germany was the leading customer in 1992, followed by France and the Netherlands. Germany is the chief supplier of imports.

27 ENERGY AND POWER

In 1991, there were 118 power stations operating in Belgium. Of a total power output of 71,945 million kilowatt hours that year, 39% was conventional thermal, 60% was nuclear (25% in 1981), and 1% was hydroelectric. The principal sources of primary energy for conventional power production are low-grade coal and by-products of the oil industry. Belgium is heavily dependent on imports of crude oil.

Selected Social Indicators

These statistics are estimates for the period 1988 to 1993. For comparison purposes, data for the United States and averages for low-income countries and high-income countries are also given.

Indicator	Belgium	Low-income countries	High-income countries	United States
Per capita gross national product†	$21,650	$380	$23,680	$24,740
Population growth rate	0.3%	1.9%	0.6%	1.0%
Population growth rate in urban areas	0.4%	3.9%	0.8%	1.3%
Population per square kilometer of land	327	78	25	26
Life expectancy in years	76	62	77	76
Number of people per physician	311	>3,300	453	419
Number of pupils per teacher (primary school)	10	39	<18	20
Illiteracy rate (15 years and older)	<1%	41%	<5%	<3%
Energy consumed per capita (kg of oil equivalent)	4,989	364	5,203	7,918

† The gross national product (GNP) is the total dollar value of all goods and services produced by a country in a year. The per capita GNP is calculated by dividing a country's GNP by its population. The World Bank defines low-income countries as those with a per capita GNP of $695 or less. High-income countries have a per capita GNP of $8,626 or more. Less than 14% of the world's 5.5 billion people live in high-income countries, while almost 60% live in low-income countries.

> = greater than   < = less than

Sources: World Bank, *Social Indicators of Development 1995,* Baltimore: Johns Hopkins University Press, 1995. Central Intelligence Agency, *World Fact Book,* Washington, D.C.: Government Printing Office, 1994.

28 SOCIAL DEVELOPMENT

Belgium has a highly developed social security system dating back to mutual benefit societies begun in 1894. The central coordinating organ for welfare is the National Social Security Office. It collects all workers' and employers' contributions for old age pensions and life insurance. It also collects management's payments for family allowances, paid vacations, and other benefits.

The government, which actively promotes women's rights, provided for a National Women's Center in its 1994 budget. In 1992, a royal decree was issued barring sexual harassment in both the public and private sectors.

29 HEALTH

Every city or town in Belgium has a committee in charge of health and hospital services. These committees organize clinics and visiting nurse services, run public hospitals, and pay for relief patients in private hospitals. There is a national health insurance plan, membership in which includes practically the whole population. Average life expectancy in 1992 was 76 years (80 years for females and 73 years for males).

From 1988 to 1992, Belgium had 3.21 doctors per 1,000 people (in 1990, 34,300 physicians). From 1985 to 1990, there were approximately 9 hospital beds per 1,000 people. In 1988, there were nearly 400 hospitals, with a total bed capacity of nearly 10,000. Belgium's total health care expenditures for 1990 were about $14,500 million.

30 HOUSING

Public funds have been made available in increasing amounts to support the construction of low-cost housing, with low-interest mortgages. Housing starts totaled 46,645 in 1992, up from 44,484 in 1991. The total number of dwellings in 1991 was 4,198,000.

31 EDUCATION

Adult illiteracy is practically nonexistent. Education is free and compulsory for children between the ages of 6 and 16. The teaching language is that of the region, for example, French, Dutch, or German.

More than half the school population is in private schools, largely Roman Catholic. Both public and private systems are presently financed with government funds. In 1991, Belgium had 4,158 primary schools with 72,589 teachers and 711,521 students. Secondary level schools had 765,672 students and 110,599 teachers.

Higher education centers on the eight main universities: the state universities of Gent, Liège, Antwerp, and Mons; the two branches of the Free University of Brussels; the Catholic University of Brussels; and the Catholic University of Louvain.

Photo credit: Susan D. Rock

A view of the Old City of Antwerp.

The higher level institutions had 271,007 students in 1989.

32 MEDIA

There are two national radio stations—one broadcasting in French, the other in Dutch. In addition, there are five Dutch-language and three French-language regional stations. Belgium has four national television stations, two in each language. In 1991, there were 4,500,000 television sets and 7,675,000 radio sets in use. In the same year, there were 5,138,282 telephones.

Newspapers are published in French and Dutch, and generally reflect the views of one of the major parties. In 1991, there were 23 daily newspapers with a total circulation estimated at 2.2 million copies. *De Standaard* is Belgium's largest daily newspaper with a circulation of 377,900.

33 TOURISM AND RECREATION

Belgium has three major tourist regions: the seacoast, the old Flemish cities, and the Ardennes Forest in the southeast.

Ostend is the largest North Sea resort. Among Flemish cities, Brugge, Gent, and Ypres stand out, while Antwerp also has many sightseeing attractions.

Brussels, home of the European Community headquarters, is a modern city with historic and cultural landmarks including the Grand'Place, the Palais des Beaux-Arts, the Théâtre Royal de la Monnaie, St. Michael's Cathedral, and Notre Dame du Sablon.

34 FAMOUS BELGIANS

Belgium has produced many famous artists, including Jan van Eyck (1390?–1441), Hans Memling (1430?–94), and Pieter Brueghel the Elder (1525?–69), the ancestor of a long line of painters. Generally considered the greatest of Flemish painters are Peter Paul Rubens (1577–1640) and Anthony van Dyck (1599–

1641). René Magritte (1898–1967) was a famous 20th-century artist.

Belgium made contributions to the development of music through the works of such outstanding 15th- and 16th-century composers as Johannes Ockeghem (1430?–95), Josquin des Prés (1450?–1521), and Orlando di Lasso, (1532–94). César Franck (1822–90) was a well-known 19th-century composer.

Eight Belgians have won the Nobel Prize in various fields. The poet and playwright Maurice Maeterlinck (1862–1949), whose symbolist dramas have been performed in many countries, received the prize for literature in 1911. Jules Bordet (1870–1961) received the physiology or medicine award in 1919 for his contributions to immunology. The same award went to Corneille J. F. Heymans (1892–1968) in 1938, and was shared by Albert Claude (1898–1983) and Christian de Duve (b.1917) in 1974.

Three Belgians have won the Nobel Peace Prize: Auguste Beernaert (1829–1912) in 1909, Henri Lafontaine (1854–1943) in 1913, and Father Dominique Pire (1910–69) in 1958.

35 BIBLIOGRAPHY

Hargrove, J. *Belgium.*, Chicago: Children's Press, 1988.

Wee, Herman van der. *The Low Countries in Early Modern Times*. Brookfield, Vt.: Variorum, 1993.

BELIZE

CAPITAL: Belmopan.

FLAG: The national flag consists of the Belize coat of arms on a white disk centered in a blue rectangular field with a narrow red stripe at the top and the bottom.

ANTHEM: *Land of the Free.*

MONETARY UNIT: The Belize dollar (B$), formerly tied to the UK pound sterling and now pegged to the US dollar, is a paper currency of 100 cents. There are coins of 1, 5, 10, 25, 50 cents and 1 dollar, and notes of 1, 5, 10, 20, 50, and 100 dollars. B$1=US$0.50 (or US$1=B$2.00).

WEIGHTS AND MEASURES: Imperial weights and measures are used. The exception is the measuring of petroleum products, for which the US gallon is standard.

HOLIDAYS: New Year's Day, 1 January; Baron Bliss Day, 9 March; Labor Day, 1 May; Commonwealth Day, 24 May; National Day, 10 September; Independence Day, 21 September; Columbus Day, 12 October; Garifuna Day, 19 November; Christmas, 25 December; Boxing Day, 26 December. Movable holidays are Good Friday and Easter Monday.

TIME: 6 AM = noon GMT.

1 LOCATION AND SIZE

Belize (formerly British Honduras), on the Caribbean coast of Central America, has an area of 22,960 square kilometers (8,865 square miles), slightly larger than the state of Massachusetts. Belize has a total boundary length of 902 kilometers (560 miles). The capital city of Belize, Belmopan, is located in the center of the country.

2 TOPOGRAPHY

The Maya Mountains (which reach a high point of 1,122 meters/3,681 feet at Victoria Peak) form the backbone of the country, which is drained by 17 rivers. The coastal waters are sheltered by a line of reefs.

3 CLIMATE

The climate is tempered by northeast trade winds that keep temperatures between 16° and 32°C (61–90°F) in the coastal region. Annual rainfall averages vary from 127 centimeters (50 inches) to more than 380 centimeters (150 inches).

4 PLANTS AND ANIMALS

Most trees are mixed hardwoods—mainly mahogany, cedar, and sapodilla (the source of chicle). There are pines in the flat regions and mangroves on the coastal lands. Native animals include armadillo, opossum, deer, and monkeys.

5 ENVIRONMENT

Forest lands have been destroyed, and water quality remains a problem. It is esti-

Photo credit: Mary A. Dempsey

A Belizean girl stands in the doorway of her home.

mated that 47% of the country's rural population does not have access to pure water. Pollutants also threaten Belize's coral reefs. Of 504 bird species, four are endangered, as are 36 plant species.

6 POPULATION

As of 1991, the total population was 189,392, with 59,220 living in Belize City. The population density was 9 persons per square kilometer (21.4 persons per square mile), the lowest in Central America.

7 MIGRATION

By the end of 1992, Belize had some 20,000 refugees and perhaps as many non-refugee illegal aliens from Central America. As many as 65,000 Belizeans were living in the US by mid-1988.

8 ETHNIC GROUPS

Some 29.8% of the population was Creole (of African descent) in 1991, while 43.6% was Mestizo (mixed White and Maya). Another 14.6% was Maya and 6.6% Garifuna (Carib). There were also people of European, Chinese, Asian Indian, and Syrian-Lebanese ancestry.

9 LANGUAGES

The official language is English. At least 80% of the people can speak standard English and/or a Creole patois (dialect). Spanish is spoken by approximately 60% of the population. Other languages spoken include Garifuna, Mayan and other Amerindian languages.

10 RELIGIONS

In 1993, 62% of the inhabitants were Roman Catholic and 4% were Maronite Catholic. Thirty percent were members of various Protestant denominations, including Anglicans (12%) and Methodists (6%). Afro-American spiritists, Hindus, Baha'is, Muslims, and Jews are also represented.

11 TRANSPORTATION

In 1991, Belize had 2,575 kilometers (1,600 miles) of roads and about 4,800 motor vehicles. Belize City is the main port. International airports at Belize City and Punta Gorda handle service to the US and Central America. The P.S.W. Goldson Airport handled 272,000 passengers in 1991.

[12] HISTORY

The area now called Belize was once heavily populated by Maya Indians, whose civilization collapsed around AD 900. The first permanent European settlement was established in 1638 by shipwrecked English seamen. Later immigrants included African slaves and British sailors.

England struggled with Spain over possession of the area, with the British winning by the 19th century. In 1862, they created the colony of British Honduras. For the next century, forestry was the main enterprise until eventually replaced by the sugar industry.

After attaining self-government on 1 January 1964, the country adopted Belize as its official name in 1973, although not fully independent yet. The UK granted Belize independence as of 21 September 1981. Guatemala, which claimed the southern quarter of the area, refused to recognize the new nation and severed diplomatic relations with the UK. In December 1986, the UK and Guatemala resumed full diplomatic ties, but an 1,800-member British garrison remained in Belize.

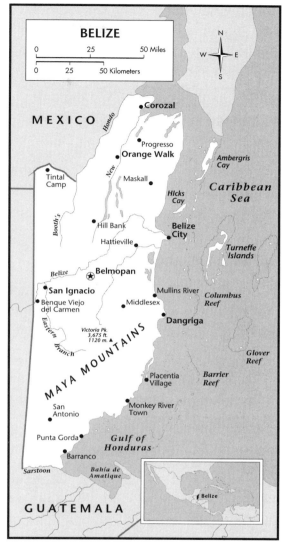

LOCATION: 15°53′ to 18°31′N; 87°16′ to 89°8′W.
BOUNDARY LENGTHS: Mexico, 251 kilometers (156 miles); Caribbean coastline, 475 kilometers (295 miles); Guatemala, 269 kilometers (167 miles). **TERRITORIAL SEA LIMIT:** 3 miles.

[13] GOVERNMENT

Governmental authority is vested in a governor-general appointed by the UK monarch, a cabinet headed by a prime minister, and a two-chamber National Assembly. The National Assembly consists of a 28-member House of Representatives elected by universal adult voting, and a Senate of eight members appointed by the governor-general. The voting age is 18. Belize is divided into six administrative districts.

14 POLITICAL PARTIES

The two major parties in Belize are the current majority People's United Party (PUP) and the United Democratic Party (UDP).

15 JUDICIAL SYSTEM

There is a Supreme Court and a court of appeals. Final appeal is to the UK Privy Council. Six summary jurisdiction courts (criminal) and six district courts (civil) are presided over by magistrates.

16 ARMED FORCES

The Belize Defense Force consists of 1,160 men in five regular and three reserve companies and a training organization. The defense budget is around US$9 million.

17 ECONOMY

The economy is dependent on agriculture and fishing. The country continues to import most of its consumer goods, including much of its food and all of its petroleum requirements. Belize recorded healthy economic growth during 1992 due to good agricultural production.

18 INCOME

In 1992, Belize's gross national product (GNP) was US$442 million at current prices, or US$2,450 per person. For the period 1985–92, the average inflation rate was 3.2%, resulting in a real growth rate in gross national product (GNP) of 6.3% per person.

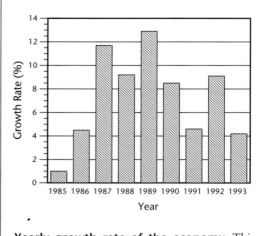

Yearly growth rate of the economy. This economic indicator tells by what percent the economy has increased or decreased when compared with the previous year.

19 INDUSTRY

The industrial sector is small but has been expanding. Industrial products in 1985 included 3,670 tons of fertilizer, 2,734,000 garments, 2,528,000 pounds of wheat flour, 102,000 tons of sugar, 28,100 tons of molasses, and 600,000 gallons of beer.

20 LABOR

The labor force in 1992 was estimated at 60,000. About 30% of the labor force is employed in agriculture, forestry, and fishing. Labor legislation covers minimum wages, work hours, employment of young persons, and workers' safety and compensation.

The minimum age for employment is 14, except in jobs involving dangerous machinery, where the minimum age is 17. Children between the ages of 5 and 14 are required to attend school, although in reality there are many dropouts.

21 AGRICULTURE

Because agriculture is not diversified enough, the country relies heavily on food imports. Sugar and citrus are the leading agricultural exports. Sugarcane production totaled 984,000 tons in 1992. The 1992 citrus output included 70 million pounds of oranges and 40 million pounds of grapefruit. Belize hopes eventually to supply its own rice, beans, and corn.

22 DOMESTICATED ANIMALS

Mennonite farms account for much of Belize's dairy and poultry output. In 1992, the nation had an estimated 26,000 hogs, 4,000 sheep, and 1,000,000 chickens. Some 4,000 tons of poultry meat and 7,000 tons of milk were produced in 1992.

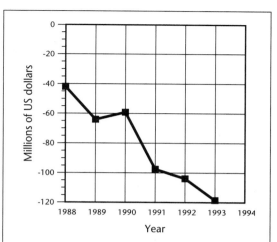

Yearly balance of trade measured in millions of US dollars. The balance of trade is the difference between what a country sells to other countries (its exports) and what it buys (its imports). If a country imports more than it exports, it has a negative balance of trade (a trade deficit). If exports exceed imports, there is a positive balance of trade (a trade surplus).

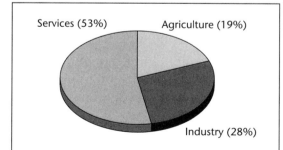

Components of the economy. This pie chart shows how much of the country's economy is devoted to agriculture (includes forestry, hunting, and fishing), industry, or services.

23 FISHING

In 1991, the total catch was 1,639 tons. Lobster is the leading product. Marine exports (including shrimp, lobster, fish, and conch) totaled 998,000 tons in 1992.

24 FORESTRY

The principal varieties of trees cut are mahogany, pine, cedar, and rosewood. In 1991 exports of forest produce (including chicle) comprised about 3% of total export earnings.

25 MINING

In 1991, clay production amounted to 2 million tons; dolomite, 100,000 tons;

Photo credit: Mary A. Dempsey

A view of the Mayan site of Xunantunich.

limestone, 300,000 tons; sand and gravel, 200,000 tons; and gold, 5 kilograms.

26 FOREIGN TRADE

In 1992, Belize's merchandise imports reached $243 million, while exports totaled $141 million. Belize's most important imports were machinery, food, fuels, chemicals, and other manufactured goods. The country's major exports included sugar, garments, citrus concentrate, seafood, vegetables, lumber, and bananas. Belize's major trade partners were the US, the UK, Mexico, CARICOM, the European Community (EC), Japan, and the Netherlands.

27 ENERGY AND POWER

Electric power is supplied by ten diesel-powered generators and is inadequate. In 1991, total capacity of the government-operated generators was 25,000 kilowatts.

28 SOCIAL DEVELOPMENT

Workers' compensation covers agricultural workers. A social security system is in effect. Employed persons aged 14–64 are eligible to make contributions for old age, disability, survivor, and health benefits. Women are active in all areas of national life, but they face domestic violence and discrimination in the business sector.

Selected Social Indicators

These statistics are estimates for the period 1988 to 1993. For comparison purposes, data for the United States and averages for low-income countries and high-income countries are also given.

Indicator	Belize	Low-income countries	High-income countries	United States
Per capita gross national product†	$2,450	$380	$23,680	$24,740
Population growth rate	2.5%	1.9%	0.6%	1.0%
Population growth rate in urban areas	2.1%	3.9%	0.8%	1.3%
Population per square kilometer of land	9	78	25	26
Life expectancy in years	74	62	77	76
Number of people per physician	1,562	>3,300	453	419
Number of pupils per teacher (primary school)	26	39	<18	20
Illiteracy rate (15 years and older)	9%	41%	<5%	<3%
Energy consumed per capita (kg of oil equivalent)	426	364	5,203	7,918

† The gross national product (GNP) is the total dollar value of all goods and services produced by a country in a year. The per capita GNP is calculated by dividing a country's GNP by its population. The World Bank defines low-income countries as those with a per capita GNP of $695 or less. High-income countries have a per capita GNP of $8,626 or more. Less than 14% of the world's 5.5 billion people live in high-income countries, while almost 60% live in low-income countries.

> = greater than   < = less than

Sources: World Bank, *Social Indicators of Development 1995,* Baltimore: Johns Hopkins University Press, 1995. Central Intelligence Agency, *World Fact Book,* Washington, D.C.: Government Printing Office, 1994.

29 HEALTH

Belize is relatively free of widespread diseases. Since 1976, however, there has been an increase in reported malaria cases. The government maintains a hospital in Belize City and rural health centers throughout the country. As of 1988, there were 85 physicians, and 10 hospitals. Life expectancy was 74 years in 1992.

30 HOUSING

Housing is inadequate, and the situation has been aggravated by hurricane devastation. The government has put aside small sums for low-cost housing programs.

31 EDUCATION

The adult literacy rate presently exceeds 91%. Primary education is free and compulsory for children between the ages of 6 and 14. In 1991, there were 46,023 pupils in 236 primary schools, and 8,557 in 32 secondary schools. The University College of Belize was opened in 1986. There are also several colleges providing specialized training.

32 MEDIA

The Belize National Radio Network transmits in English and Spanish. Altogether, there are 6 AM and 5 FM radio stations and

1 television station. In 1991, there were 112,000 radios and 32,000 television sets. In 1993, Belize had 21,000 telephones. There is no daily newspaper. There were five weeklies in 1991.

33 TOURISM AND RECREATION

Belize is attracting growing numbers of tourists to its Mayan ruins, its barrier reef (the longest in the Western Hemisphere), and its beaches, forests, and wildlife. Tourist arrivals totaled 222,779 in 1991, 26,016 from Europe and 84,033 from the Americas. In 1991, tourist expenditures totaled US$95 million. There were 2,922 hotel rooms and 4,990 beds. In May, 1992, Belize was the site of the First World Congress on Tourism and the Environment.

34 FAMOUS BELIZEANS

George C. Price (b.1919), leader of the PUP, became the country's first premier in 1964. Manuel Esquivel (b.1940), leader of the UDP, became prime minister in December 1984.

35 BIBLIOGRAPHY

Merrill, Tim, ed. *Guyana and Belize: Country Studies*. 2nd ed. Washington, D.C.: Government Printing Office, 1993.

O'Neill, Thomas. "New Sensors Eye the Rain Forest." *National Geographic*, September 1993, 118–130.

Wright, Ronald. *Time among the Maya: Travels in Belize, Guatemala, and Mexico*. New York: Weidenfeld & Nicolson, 1989.

BENIN

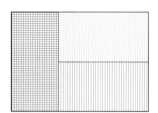

Republic of Benin
République du Bénin

CAPITAL: Porto-Novo.

FLAG: Two equal horizontal bands of yellow (top) and red with a vertical green band on the hoist side.

ANTHEM: *L'Aube Nouvelle (The New Dawn).*

MONETARY UNIT: The Communauté Financière Africaine franc (CFA Fr) is a paper currency. There are coins of 1, 2, 5, 10, 25, 50, 100, and 500 CFA francs, and notes of 50, 100, 500, 1,000, 5,000, and 10,000 CFA francs. CFA Fr1 = $0.0017 (or $1 = CFA Fr586.20).

WEIGHTS AND MEASURES: The metric system is the legal standard.

HOLIDAYS: New Year's Day, 1 January; Anniversary of Mercenary Attack on Cotonou, 16 January; Labor Day, 1 May; Independence Day, 1 August; Armed Forces Day, 26 October; National Day, 30 November; Harvest Day, 31 December. Most religious holidays have been abolished, but Good Friday, Easter Monday, Christmas, 'Id al-Fitr, and Id al-'Adha' remain public holidays.

TIME: 1 PM = noon GMT.

1 LOCATION AND SIZE

The People's Republic of Benin (formerly Dahomey) is situated in West Africa on the northern coast of the Gulf of Guinea. It has an area of 112,620 square kilometers (43,483 square miles), extending 665 kilometers (413 miles) north to south and 333 kilometers (207 miles) east to west. Comparatively, Benin is slightly smaller than the state of Pennsylvania. The capital city of Benin, Porto-Novo, is located in the southeastern corner of the country.

2 TOPOGRAPHY

The coast of Benin is difficult to reach because of sandbanks. It has no natural harbors, river mouths, or islands. Behind the coastline is a network of lagoons. The Ouémé is Benin's longest river. Benin's northern rivers, the Mékrou, Alibori, Sota, and Pendjari, are torrential and broken by rocks.

3 CLIMATE

Southern Benin's climate is typically equatorial—hot and humid, with a long dry season from December to March, in which a dry desert wind, the *harmattan*, blows in a northeasterly to southwesterly direction. Temperatures range between 22°C (72°F) and 35°C (95°F), averaging 27°C (81°F). The great rains fall from March to July.

Northern Benin has only one wet season (May to September, with most rain in August) and a hot dry season in which the harmattan blows for three or four months. Temperatures range from a maximum of 40°C (104°F) in January to a minimum of 13°C (56°F) in July.

4 PLANTS AND ANIMALS

Apart from small isolated patches, little true forest remains. Trees include coconut, oil palm, ronier palm, ebony, shea nut, kapok, fromager, and Senegal mahogany. Among the mammals in Benin are the elephant, lion, panther, monkey, and wild pig, as well as many kinds of antelope. Crocodiles and many species of snakes (including python, puff adder, and mamba) are widely distributed. Partridge, guinea fowl, and wild duck, as well as many kinds of tropical birds, are common. Insects include varieties of tsetse fly and other carriers of epidemic disease.

5 ENVIRONMENT

Benin has two national parks and several game reserves. In addition, the government has set aside 5,900 hectares (14,580 acres) for tree nurseries to help with reforestation. In 1994, the main environmental issues facing the people of Benin were desertification (land turning to desert), deforestation (loss of trees), wildlife endangerment, and water pollution. Regular droughts speed up the spread of the desert into agricultural lands in the north. By 1994, of the 187 species of mammals, 11 were threatened with extinction. Of 630 bird species, one was endangered. Three plant species out of a total of 2,000 were also threatened.

6 POPULATION

Total population in mid-1994 was estimated at 5,338,095. A population of 6,269,000 is projected for the year 2000. Almost three-fourths of the population are clustered in the southern half of the country. An estimated 42% of the population lived in cities in 1995. Porto-Novo, the capital, had a population of about 213,000 in 1990.

7 MIGRATION

Many people move with the seasons to both Nigeria and Ghana for work. Thousands of Beninese were expelled from Nigeria in early 1983, and thousands were expelled from Gabon in 1977–78. It was estimated in 1984 that over 100,000 Beninese people living abroad could be regarded as political refugees.

8 ETHNIC GROUPS

Although several of the larger groups in southern Benin are culturally and socially related, there is a marked division between the peoples of the south and those of the north. The largest ethnic group is that of the Fon or Dahomeyans.

9 LANGUAGES

The official language is French. Many African languages are spoken. Fon and Yoruba are the most important in southern Benin. Bariba and Fulani are most common in the north.

10 RELIGIONS

In 1992, it was estimated that 70% of the people of Benin follow traditional African religions, particularly those that give an object (a fetish) magic power. Fetishes may take the form of images, trees, or animals (the python is considered sacred in southern Benin). In 1992, about 20% of the population was Roman Catholic; some

13% of the people, mainly those in the north, are Muslims.

11 TRANSPORTATION

In 1991, Benin had 578 kilometers (359 miles) of meter-gauge railroad. Of Benin's 5,050 kilometers (3,138 miles) of roads, only about 920 kilometers (572 miles) are tarred. In 1992, Benin had about 25,000 passenger cars and 13,000 commercial vehicles.

Cotonou is Benin's one deepwater port, capable of handling three million tons of cargo annually. There is an international airport at Cotonou and another major airport at Parakou.

12 HISTORY

Benin's (formerly Dahomey) borders were determined by Anglo-French rivalry in the late-nineteenth-century partition of Africa. The Portuguese—the first Europeans to establish trading posts on the West African coast—founded the trading post of Porto-Novo on what is now the Benin coast. They were followed by English, Dutch, Spanish, and French traders as the slave trade developed. In the mid-nineteenth century, the slave trade was gradually replaced by trade in palm oil. Anglo-French rivalry in Porto-Novo, in which successive local kings took different sides, eventually ended with a French protectorate there (1882).

From 1892 to 1898, the territory took its modern shape with the exploration and extension of French control in the north. The construction of the railroad to the north was begun in 1900. Dahomey

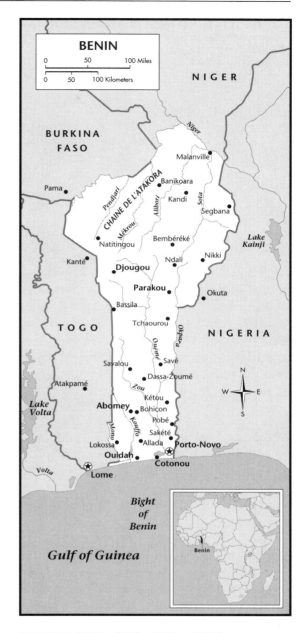

LOCATION: 0°47′ to 3°47′E; 6°15′ to 12°25′N. **BOUNDARY LENGTHS:** Niger, 190 kilometers (118 miles); Nigeria, 750 kilometers (466 miles); Atlantic coastline, 125 kilometers (78 miles); Togo, 620 kilometers (385 miles); Burkina Faso, 270 kilometers (168 miles). **TERRITORIAL SEA LIMIT:** 200 miles.

became a colony of the federation of French West Africa in 1904. The French ruled the country until 1 August 1960, when Dahomey proclaimed its independence.

After independence, the country suffered from extreme political instability, with military coups in 1963, 1965 (twice), 1967, 1969, and 1972. The coup on 26 October 1972 established Major Mathieu Kérékou as the leader of a military regime. It represented a clear break with all earlier Dahomeyan governments, introducing revolutionary changes in the political and economic life of the country. In late 1974, President Kérékou said that the national revolution would follow a Marxist-Leninist course, and the state took over many industries. On 1 December 1975, the country's name was changed to the People's Republic of Benin.

In 1980, Kérékou made an official visit to Libya. During the visit, he converted to the Islamic faith in the presence of the Libyan leader, Colonel Mu'ammar al-Qadhafi, and accordingly took the first name Ahmed. The two countries then signed a major bilateral cooperation agreement.

Through the years, hundreds of government opponents have been imprisoned, often without trial. Opposition came mostly from the banned Communist Party (Parti Communiste du Dahomey—PCT) and student protesters. However, in 1989 Kérékou announced that the country would no longer follow a Marxist-Leninist philosophy. Democratic reforms were instituted and on 2 December 1990, a new constitution was adopted by popular referendum. Presidential and parliamentary elections were held on 10 March 1991. This was Benin's first free election in 30 years. Kérékou lost the presidential election to his opponent Nicephore Soglo. However no one party was able to gain control of the National Assembly. A working coalition was formed to run the government, but in 1993 it fell apart. Since then, there have been tensions between the president and the legislature.

13 GOVERNMENT

The 1990 Constitution led to multiparty elections. The president is elected by popular vote for a five-year term. A directly elected National Assembly has a maximum life of four years.

14 POLITICAL PARTIES

Partisan politics are characterized by frequent splits and mergers. Party allegiances in the National Assembly are fluid. The 1990 multiparty general elections produced a National Assembly in which the largest bloc of votes (12 of 64) were held by a Coalition of Democratic Forces (RFD). It was replaced on 30 October 1993 by the African Assembly for Progress (RAP), which is composed of eleven parties and associations. The second largest bloc, with nine seats, is the Alliance of the National Party for Democracy and Development (PNDD) and the Democratic Renewal Party (PRD).

The National Convention for the Forces of Change, formed in February 1993, is an alliance of opposition groups.

The Communist Party of Benin was registered in October 1993.

15 JUDICIAL SYSTEM

Each district has a court with the power to try cases, and each province has a court to handle appeals. At the lowest level, each commune, village, and city ward has its own court. The highest court is the Supreme Court. Under the new constitution, people who are arrested must be brought before a magistrate (judge) within 48 hours.

16 ARMED FORCES

In 1993, the armed forces had some 4,350 personnel. The army of 3,800 included three infantry battalions, a parachute/commando battalion, a service battalion, an engineering battalion, an artillery battery, and an armored squadron. There were 350 personnel in the air force, which had one attack helicopter and fourteen support helos and aircraft. There was a navy of 150 personnel and one patrol boat. A paramilitary police force totaled 2,000.

17 ECONOMY

Benin's economy is recovering from the economic problems that led to the collapse of the socialist government in power between 1974 and 1989. Companies that were state-owned are being returned to private ownership. However, recovery efforts are complicated by the fact that Benin's economy is strongly influenced by economic trends in Nigeria.

Agriculture is the most important sector in the Benin economy, accounting for

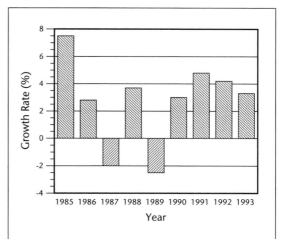

Yearly growth rate of the economy. This economic indicator tells by what percent the economy has increased or decreased when compared with the previous year.

some 35.4% of gross domestic product (1990). About 90% of this output is produced on family farms using little technology. They mainly produce domestically consumed crops such as maize, sorghum, millet, paddy rice, cassava, yams, and beans. Typically, Benin is self-sufficient in food. Cotton, palm oil, and groundnuts are grown and exchanged for cash.

Livestock, forestry, and fishing make up another 10% of gross domestic product. Not enough wood is produced to meet the national demand for fuel. The fishing sector has overissued the stock and is in decline.

Benin's mineral resources are limited. Limestone, marble, and petroleum reserves are exploited commercially. Gold is produced for local crafts only. Phosphates, chromium, rutile, and iron ore

Photo credit: AP/Wide World Photos

A rural youth club leader encourages the children to salvage even the smallest amount of cotton clinging to the stalks. Frugality is important in a country where the population must depend on the land for its living.

have been located in the north but remain undeveloped resources.

18 INCOME

In 1992 Benin's gross national product (GNP) was $2,058 million at current prices, or $430 per person.

19 INDUSTRY

Benin's industrial sector accounts for 9% of gross domestic product and centers primarily on construction materials and the processing of agricultural products. In 1986, Benin produced only 12,096 tons of oil, 704 tons of palm-kernel oil, and 896 tons of palm cake, out of a total palm oil production capacity of 215,000 metric tons per year. Benin's electricity needs are met by hydroelectric power from Akosombo dam in Ghana and the Nangbeto dam on the Mono River.

20 LABOR

The Labor Code of Benin prohibits child labor (under the age of 18) in any form, but the code is not well enforced. Many children work on family farms, and even in cities underage children often work as street vendors.

21 AGRICULTURE

Benin is predominantly an agricultural country with about 75% of the population engaged in the agricultural sector.

The main food crops are manioc, yams, corn, sorghum, beans, rice, sweet potatoes, pawpaws, guavas, bananas, and coconuts. Production estimates for the main food crops for 1992 were yams, 1,177,000 tons; manioc, 932,000 tons; corn, 399,000 tons; millet and sorghum, 129,000 tons; beans, 50,000 tons; sweet potatoes, 28,000 tons; and rice, 9,000 tons.

Palm products have long been Benin's principal export crop, but in recent years cotton has increased in importance, with production increasing tenfold since 1981. Despite improved production, however, cotton storage and ginning capacity are still insufficient. In 1992, cotton production was 65,000 tons. Peanut production has also become important recently; in 1992, 70,000 tons of shelled groundnuts were produced. Other crops with their 1992 production figures were cashews, 1,200 tons; bananas, 13,000 tons; mangoes, 12,000 tons; and coconuts, 20,000 tons.

22 DOMESTICATED ANIMALS

In 1992 there were an estimated 1 million head of cattle, 920,000 sheep, 1,120,000 goats, 750,000 hogs, and 25 million chickens. Estimated output of livestock products in 1992 included 14,000 tons of beef and veal, 6,000 tons of sheep and goat meat, and 8,000 tons of pork. Although the livestock population has increased by 40% over the last decade, Benin still imports substantial amounts of meat and poultry to meet local demand.

23 FISHING

Ocean fishing, which had been carried on largely by Ghanaian fishers, is gaining importance at Cotonou and other coastal centers. Lagoon and river fishing remain

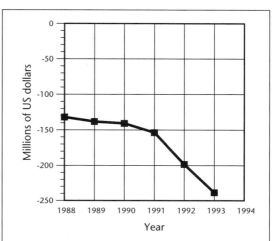

Yearly balance of trade measured in millions of US dollars. The balance of trade is the difference between what a country sells to other countries (its exports) and what it buys (its imports). If a country imports more than it exports, it has a negative balance of trade (a trade deficit). If exports exceed imports, there is a positive balance of trade (a trade surplus).

of primary importance. Of an estimated catch of 41,000 tons in 1991, 32,000 tons were from inland waters. The production of fish has steadily declined since the 1980s due to overfishing and ecological abuses.

24 FORESTRY

There are about 3.4 million hectares (nearly 8.4 million acres) classified as forest and woodland, about 31% of the total land area. Most forests are in northern Benin, and use of them is subject to public control. Timber production is small. Firewood, charcoal, and building wood for local use are the most important forest products.

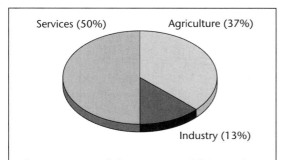

Components of the economy. This pie chart shows how much of the country's economy is devoted to agriculture (includes forestry, hunting, and fishing), industry, or services.

Selected Social Indicators

These statistics are estimates for the period 1988 to 1993. For comparison purposes, data for the United States and averages for low-income countries and high-income countries are also given.

Indicator	Benin	Low-income countries	High-income countries	United States
Per capita gross national product†	$430	$380	$23,680	$24,740
Population growth rate	3.1%	1.9%	0.6%	1.0%
Population growth rate in urban areas	4.7%	3.9%	0.8%	1.3%
Population per square kilometer of land	43	78	25	26
Life expectancy in years	48	62	77	76
Number of people per physician	13,312	>3,300	453	419
Number of pupils per teacher (primary school)	35	39	<18	20
Illiteracy rate (15 years and older)	77%	41%	<5%	<3%
Energy consumed per capita (kg of oil equivalent)	20	364	5,203	7,918

† The gross national product (GNP) is the total dollar value of all goods and services produced by a country in a year. The per capita GNP is calculated by dividing a country's GNP by its population. The World Bank defines low-income countries as those with a per capita GNP of $695 or less. High-income countries have a per capita GNP of $8,626 or more. Less than 14% of the world's 5.5 billion people live in high-income countries, while almost 60% live in low-income countries.

> = greater than   < = less than

Sources: World Bank, *Social Indicators of Development 1995,* Baltimore: Johns Hopkins University Press, 1995. Central Intelligence Agency, *World Fact Book,* Washington, D.C.: Government Printing Office, 1994.

25 MINING

With the exception of oil, Benin is relatively poor in mineral resources. Exports of mineral goods accounted for 9.5% of total estimated 1991 exports of $291.4 million. There is iron ore in the north, but of low-grade quality; limestone is quarried for use in cement plants.

26 FOREIGN TRADE

Benin consistently runs a trade deficit; this pattern continued in 1991 when the deficit reached $191.1 million on $291.4 million worth of exports. Exports declined by 50% in the 1985 to 1987 period and declined another 28% between 1987 and 1990.

27 ENERGY AND POWER

Production from the Sémé offshore oil field began in October 1982 by Saga Petroleum, a Norwegian firm working under a service contract. The field yielded 1,353,000 barrels of oil in 1991. In 1990, Benin exported an estimated 1,270,000 barrels of crude oil.

Electrical power generated in Benin is entirely thermal. Installed capacity in 1991 was an estimated 15,000 kilowatts;

total domestic power output in 1991 was 5 million kilowatt hours.

28 SOCIAL DEVELOPMENT

All public employees receive family allowances for up to six children. There is also a system of old-age benefits, and medical care is free.

29 HEALTH

Most serious epidemic diseases have been brought under control by mobile health units and other facilities. In 1990, 35% of children under 5 years old suffered from malnutrition, and by 1991 only 51% of the population had access to safe water. Estimated average life expectancy in 1992 was only 48 years.

In 1992, only 18% of the population had access to health services. Total health care expenditures for Benin were $79 million in 1990.

30 HOUSING

In rural areas, the typical dwelling of northern Benin is a round hut of beaten mud with a cone-shaped thatch roof. In southern Benin, rectangular huts with sloping roofs of palm or straw thatch are more usual. Along the coastal lagoons, houses are often built on stilts.

As of 1979, 24% of housing units were modern houses, 74% were traditional dwellings, and less than 1% were categorized as flats or villas.

31 EDUCATION

Since 1975, all education has been free, public, secular, and compulsory from ages

Photo credit: AP/Wide World Photos

This mother and her sons have access to safe clean water from a well. Families like hers in Benin's arid north know frequent shortages of water in the best of times. During the Sahelian droughts, the situation became critical. Children, as always, suffered the most.

6 to 12. In 1988–89, enrollment of children at the primary level was 52%, and 13% at the secondary level. In 1991, there were 2,952 primary schools with 505,970 pupils enrolled. In the general secondary schools, there were 76,672 pupils and 2,178 teachers.

The National University of Benin at Cotonou, founded in 1970, offers courses in agriculture, medicine, liberal arts, science, law, economics, and politics.

[32] MEDIA

Virtually all media in Benin are controlled by the government. The state provides telegraph and telephone service, and a government-owned radio and television service broadcasts in French, English, and eighteen native languages. In 1991, there were about 428,000 radios and 24,000 television sets in use and 16,918 telephones.

In 1991, the only daily newspaper was *La Nation* (formerly *Ehuzu),* the government publication, with a daily circulation of about 12,000.

[33] TOURISM AND RECREATION

Tourist attractions include the lake village of Ganvie, two game parks in the north, the ancient royal city of Abomey, several museums, and beaches. Hunting lodges have been built to promote safaris in the two national parks, where strong efforts have also been made to preserve wild game. In the south are picturesque villages built on stilts over the waters of the coastal lagoons.

[34] FAMOUS BENINESE

Perhaps the most famous historical ruler in the area now known as Benin was Béhanzin (d.1906), who was king of Abomey from 1889 until he was defeated by the French in 1894.

[35] BIBLIOGRAPHY

Decalo, Samuel. *Historical Dictionary of Benin,* 2nd ed. Metuchen, N.J.: Scarecrow Press, 1987.

Ronen, Dov. *Dahomey: Between Tradition and Modernity.* Ithaca, N.Y.: Cornell University Press, 1975.

BHUTAN

Kingdom of Bhutan

Druk-Yul

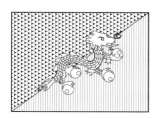

CAPITAL: Thimphu (Tashi Chho Dzong).

FLAG: The flag is divided diagonally into an orange-yellow field above and a crimson field below. In the center is a wingless white Chinese dragon.

ANTHEM: *Gyelpo Tenjur,* beginning "In the Thunder Dragon Kingdom, adorned with sandalwood."

MONETARY UNIT: The ngultrum (N) is a paper currency of 100 chetrum. There are coins of 5, 10, 25, and 50 chetrum and 1 ngultrum, and notes of 1, 5, 10, and 100 ngultrum. The ngultrum is at par with the Indian rupee (R), which also circulates freely. N1 = $0.0319 (or $1 = N31.370).

WEIGHTS AND MEASURES: The metric system is the legal standard, but some traditional units are still in common use.

HOLIDAYS: King's Birthday, 11–13 November; National Day, 17 December. Movable Buddhist holidays and festivals are observed.

TIME: 5:30 PM = noon GMT.

1 LOCATION AND SIZE

Bhutan, a landlocked country in the Himalaya mountain range, has an area of 47,000 square kilometers (18,147 square miles), slightly more than half the size of the state of Indiana, with a total boundary length of 1,075 kilometers (668 miles). The capital city, Thimphu, is located in the west central part of the country.

2 TOPOGRAPHY

Bhutan is a mountainous country of extremely high altitudes and uneven terrain. The highest peaks include Kula Kangri (7,554 meters/24,783 feet) and Chomo Lhari (7,314 meters/23,997 feet). Bhutan has many rivers, including the Amo, the Wong, and the Mo.

3 CLIMATE

Rainfall is moderate in the central valleys, while the higher elevations are relatively dry. In general, the mountainous areas are cold most of the year. Temperatures in the mountains average 4°C (39°F) in January and 17°C (63°F) in July.

4 PLANTS AND ANIMALS

Plants include dense jungle growth; forests of beech, ash, birch, maple, yew, oak, and rhododendron; and firs and pines at the timber line. Primulas, poppies (including the rare blue variety), magnolias, and orchids abound. The abundance of wild animals has been linked to the Buddhist reluctance to take life. Mammals include the cheetah, bear, rhinoceros, and several kinds of deer.

5 ENVIRONMENT

In 1994, the main environmental problems in Bhutan were soil erosion and water pollution. The Manas Game Sanctuary is located along the banks of the Manas River. By 1994, fifteen species of mammals were endangered; ten bird species, as well as fifteen species of plants, were threatened with extinction.

6 POPULATION

The population of Bhutan was estimated by the United Nations at 1,612,000 in 1992. The projected population for the year 2000 was 1,942,000. The capital, Thimphu, had an estimated population of 27,000 in 1990.

7 MIGRATION

Bhutan forbids the entry of new settlers from Nepal. Since 1959, the border with Tibet has been closed to immigration. The border between Bhutan and India is open, and citizens of Bhutan are free to live and work in India.

8 ETHNIC GROUPS

Bhutanese are mainly of Tibetan stock, and are also known as Buotias. Other groups include the Ngalop (also called Bhobe) and the Sharchop. Aboriginal or native tribal peoples live in villages scattered throughout Bhutan. The remaining peoples are Nepalese settlers.

9 LANGUAGES

Four main languages are spoken in Bhutan. The official language is Dzongkha, a Tibetan dialect. Bumthangkha, an aboriginal language, is spoken in central Bhutan, while Sharchopkha is spoken in eastern Bhutan. The Nepalese mostly keep their own language, Nepali.

10 RELIGIONS

About 70% of the Bhutanese are Buddhists. They mainly belong to the Drukpa (people of the dragon) subsect of the Kagyupa Buddhist sect, introduced from Tibet in the twelfth century. About 25% of the population are Hindus, and Muslims make up most of the remaining 5%.

11 TRANSPORTATION

Before the 1961–66 development plan, there were no surfaced roads in Bhutan. In 1991, there were about 1,304 kilometers (810 miles) of roads. The national air carrier, Druk Airlines, began operations in 1983 with regular flights between Calcutta and Bhutan's main airfield at Paro.

12 HISTORY

The ancestors of the Bhotes (or Bhotias) came from Tibet, probably in the ninth century. In the fifteenth century, Shabdung Ngawang Nangyal, a Tibetan lama, united the country and built most of the fortified villages (dzongs). During the eighteenth and nineteenth centuries, British efforts to trade with Bhutan proved unsuccessful. In 1910, British India agreed explicitly not to interfere in Bhutanese internal affairs, while Bhutan accepted British "guidance" in handling foreign matters. After 1947, India took over this role.

In the 1960s, India helped Bhutan prepare economic plans to modernize the country and end its isolation. Relations with Nepal have grown difficult in recent years because of tensions surrounding ethnic Nepalese living in Bhutan. Cross-border attacks between Bhutan and Nepal through a narrow corridor of India have forced thousands of ethnic Nepalese—both illegal immigrants and Bhutanese citizens—to migrate in recent years.

13 GOVERNMENT

Bhutan has functioned as a limited monarchy since 1969. The king, who is chief of state and head of government, may be removed at any time by a two-thirds vote of the National Assembly. The Royal Advisory Council is the country's chief administrative body. There is also a 7-member Council of Ministers. The National Assembly, known as the Tsongdu, consists of 151 members. It meets twice a year at Thimphu, the capital. The country is divided into 4 regions, 18 districts (*dzongkhas*), and 192 blocks, or *gewog*.

14 POLITICAL PARTIES

Political parties are illegal in Bhutan. Opposition groups, composed mainly of ethnic Nepalese, include the Bhutan State Congress (BSC), the People's Forum for Democratic Rights, and the Bhutan People's Party (BPP), a militant group.

15 JUDICIAL SYSTEM

Local headmen and magistrates (*thrimpon*) hear original cases. Appeals may be made to an eight-member High Court. From here, a final appeal may be made to the king.

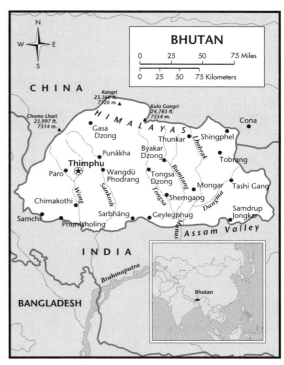

LOCATION: 26°42′ to 28°21′N; 88°45′ to 92°8′E.
BOUNDARY LENGTHS: India, 607 kilometers (377 miles); China, 412 kilometers (256 miles).

16 ARMED FORCES

India is responsible for Bhutan's defense. The army consists of about 4,000 lightly armed soldiers in the army and palace guard.

17 ECONOMY

Isolated Bhutan has one of the smallest economies in the world. Farming or herding supports 91% of the labor force. The country supplies most of its food needs through the production of grains, fruits, some meat, and yak butter.

Photo credit: AP/Wide World Photos

Two young girls swing together at a playground.

[20] LABOR

About 95% of all workers are farmers and herders. There is a severe shortage of skilled labor, no legislated minimum wage, no standard workweek, and no health and safety standards. Most salaried workers are employed by the government.

There are no child labor laws in Bhutan. Road crew workers, for example, are accepted on the basis of height, not age. So sometimes children as young as eleven, who are tall, may be put to work at heavy labor.

[21] AGRICULTURE

Since there is little level space available for cultivation, fields are generally terraced. Stone aqueducts carry irrigation water. In 1992, output of paddy rice was estimated at 43,000 tons. Other crops include wheat, maize, millet, buckwheat, barley, potatoes, sugarcane, cardamom, walnuts, and oranges.

[18] INCOME

Bhutan's gross domestic product was estimated to be about $250 million in 1991, or about $180 per person. The inflation rate of consumer prices was estimated at 10% in 1991.

[19] INDUSTRY

Crafts are the principal industrial occupation. Homespun textiles—woven and embroidered cottons, wools, and silks—are the most important products. Also produced in Bhutan are cement, carbide, and particle board. A large number of sawmills operate throughout the country.

[22] DOMESTICATED ANIMALS

In 1992, there were an estimated 422,000 head of cattle, 74,000 hogs, 52,000 sheep, and 40,000 goats. Also, 49 tons of greasy wool and 25 tons of scoured wool were produced.

[23] FISHING

Freshwater fish are found in most waterways. The total catch averages 1,000 tons annually.

[24] FORESTRY

About 54% of Bhutan is covered with forests. Roundwood production in 1991 totaled 1,560,000 cubic meters, about 82% of which was used for fuel.

25 MINING

For centuries, silver and iron have been mined in Bhutan for handicrafts. In 1991, dolomite production amounted to 50,000 tons. Slate is also quarried for use as a stone that can be cut to a specific size.

26 FOREIGN TRADE

After the 1960 government ban on trade with Tibet, Bhutan came to trade almost exclusively with India. Recently, however, exports to other countries have grown rapidly. Trade with countries other than India now accounts for about 20% of Bhutan's total.

Bhutan's principal exports to India include vegetables, dolomite, timber, coal, oranges, cardamom, some preserved food, handicraft items, yak tails for fly whisks, and yak hair. The main imports from India are petroleum products (mainly kerosene), motor vehicles, cereals, and cotton textiles. In 1989/90, total exports were estimated at $44 million and imports at $40 million.

27 ENERGY AND POWER

About 85% of Bhutan's energy requirement is derived from firewood. Of commercial energy sources, petroleum accounts for 60%, coal 30%, and electricity only 10%.

28 SOCIAL DEVELOPMENT

There is no national social welfare system, except for a modest maternal and child welfare program begun in the early 1980s, which includes family planning. Bhutan's culture does not isolate or disenfranchise (deprive of voting and other rights) women.

29 HEALTH

Bhutan suffers from a shortage of medical personnel. Only 65% of the population has access to any form of medical care. In 1990, there were 141 doctors. The average life expectancy in 1993 was only 48 years. Malaria, tuberculosis, and venereal disease remain widespread.

30 HOUSING

Traditional houses are built of blocks or layers of stone set in clay mortar, with roofs formed of pine shingles kept in place by heavy stones. As of 1990, 60% of urban and 30% of rural dwellers had access to a public water supply.

31 EDUCATION

Bhutan's estimated rate of adult literacy in 1990 was 38.4%. In 1988, primary schools numbered 150 with 1,513 teachers and 55,340 pupils. General secondary schools had 695 teachers and 3,456 students. There was one junior college, two teacher training colleges, and one college affiliated with the university at Delhi in India.

32 MEDIA

In 1988, Bhutan had only 1,990 telephones. Bhutan did not have its own television station as of 1992 but received broadcasts from India and Bangladesh. In 1991, the country had an estimated 25,000 radios. A weekly government newspaper, *Kuensel*, is published in

Selected Social Indicators

These statistics are estimates for the period 1988 to 1993. For comparison purposes, data for the United States and averages for low-income countries and high-income countries are also given.

Indicator	Bhutan	Low-income countries	High-income countries	United States
Per capita gross national product†	$180	$380	$23,680	$24,740
Population growth rate	2.4%	1.9%	0.6%	1.0%
Population growth rate in urban areas	5.4%	3.9%	0.8%	1.3%
Population per square kilometer of land	15	78	25	26
Life expectancy in years	48	62	77	76
Number of people per physician	13,110	>3,300	453	419
Number of pupils per teacher (primary school)	31	39	<18	20
Illiteracy rate (15 years and older)	62%	41%	<5%	<3%
Energy consumed per capita (kg of oil equivalent)	33	364	5,203	7,918

† The gross national product (GNP) is the total dollar value of all goods and services produced by a country in a year. The per capita GNP is calculated by dividing a country's GNP by its population. The World Bank defines low-income countries as those with a per capita GNP of $695 or less. High-income countries have a per capita GNP of $8,626 or more. Less than 14% of the world's 5.5 billion people live in high-income countries, while almost 60% live in low-income countries.

> = greater than   < = less than

Sources: World Bank, *Social Indicators of Development 1995*, Baltimore: Johns Hopkins University Press, 1995. Central Intelligence Agency, *World Fact Book*, Washington, D.C.: Government Printing Office, 1994.

Dzongkha, English, and Nepali, with a circulation of about 12,500 as of 1991.

33 TOURISM AND RECREATION

In 1974, Bhutan opened its door to tourists, but strict entry regulations and the country's remoteness have restricted the number of visitors. Income from tourism totaled approximately $2 million in 1990. In 1991, there were 2,106 foreign visitors. The beautiful Thimphu, Paro, and Punākha valleys, with their many monasteries, are accessible to tourists. Archery is the national sport.

34 FAMOUS BHUTANESE

Jigme Dorji Wangchuk (1928–72) instituted numerous social reforms during his reign as king of Bhutan.

35 BIBLIOGRAPHY

Bunting, Bruce W. "Bhutan, Kingdom in the Clouds." *National Geographic,* May 1991, 79–101.

Dogra, R. C. *Bhutan.* Oxford, England; Santa Barbara, Calif.: Clio Press, 1990.

Foster, L. *Bhutan.* Chicago: Children's Press, 1989.

Pommaret-Imaeda, Françoise, and Yoshiro Imaeda. *Bhutan: A Kingdom in the Eastern Himalayas.* Translated by Ian Nobel. Boston: Shambhala, 1985.

BOLIVIA

Republic of Bolivia

República de Bolivia

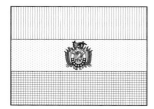

CAPITALS: La Paz (administrative capital); Sucre (legal and judicial capital).

FLAG: The flag is a horizontal tricolor of red, yellow, and green stripes, representing the animal, mineral, and vegetable kingdoms, with the coat of arms centered on the yellow band.

ANTHEM: *Himno Nacional,* beginning "Bolivianos, el hado propicio coronó nuestros volos anhelos" ("Bolivians, propitious fate crowned our outcries of yearning").

MONETARY UNIT: The boliviano (B) was introduced on 1 January 1987, replacing the peso at a rate of P1,000,000 = B1. There are coins of 2, 5, 10, 20, and 50 cents and 1 boliviano and notes of 2, 5, 10, 20, 50, 100, and 200 bolivianos. B1 = $0.2186 (or $1 = B4.5750).

WEIGHTS AND MEASURES: The metric system is the legal standard, but some Spanish weights are still used in retail trade.

HOLIDAYS: New Year's Day, 1 January; Labor Day, 1 May; National Festival, 5–7 August; Columbus Day, 12 October; All Saints' Day, 1 November; Christmas, 25 December. Movable holidays include Carnival, Ash Wednesday, Holy Thursday, Good Friday, Holy Saturday, and Corpus Christi.

TIME: 8 AM = noon GMT.

1 LOCATION AND SIZE

Situated in South America just north of the Tropic of Capricorn, Bolivia has a total area of 1,098,580 square kilometers (424,164 square miles), slightly less than three times the size of the state of Montana. Completely landlocked, Bolivia has a total boundary length of 6,743 kilometers (4,190 miles).

The capital city of Bolivia, La Paz, is located in the west-central part of the country.

2 TOPOGRAPHY

Bolivia has three geographic zones: the Andean highlands in the west, running north to south; the moist slopes and valleys on the eastern side of the Andes, called the Yungas and Valles; and the eastern tropical lowland plains, or Oriente. In Bolivia, the Andes divide into two chains—the Cordillera Occidental and the Cordillera Oriental—that make up about one-third of the country.

Between the two chains lies a broad sedimentary plateau about 4,000 meters (13,000 feet) above sea level, called the Altiplano, which contains about 28% of Bolivia's land area and more than half of its population. In the north of this plateau, astride the border with Peru, lies Lago Titicaca, the highest navigable lake in the world at an altitude of more than 3,660 meters (12,000 feet).

3 CLIMATE

Although Bolivia lies entirely in the tropics, extreme differences in altitude and rainfall give it a great variety of climates. The mean annual temperature of La Paz, at 3,697 meters (12,130 feet), is about 8°C (46°F). That of Trinidad, in the eastern lowlands, is 26°C (79°F). Around Lake Titicaca, rainfall is adequate, but there is less than 5 centimeters (2 inches) a year in the extreme southwest. The fertile valleys in the Cordillera Oriental have a warmer, drier Mediterranean climate.

The Yungas and Valles have a semi-tropical, moist climate. Rainfall is heavy in the northeast. The lowland plain becomes drier to the south, until it reaches drought conditions near the Argentine border.

4 PLANTS AND ANIMALS

Because of the wide range in altitude, Bolivia has plants of every climatic zone, from arctic growth high in the mountains to tropical forests in the Amazon basin. On the high plateau above 3,050 meters (10,000 feet) grows a coarse bunch grass called ichu, used for pasture, thatching, and weaving mats. The Lake Titicaca region is believed to be the original home of the potato.

In the tropical forest, the quinine-producing quina tree grows, as does the Pará rubber tree. There are more than 2,000 species of hardwoods. Aromatic shrubs are common, as are vanilla, sarsaparilla, and saffron plants. Useful native plants include palms, sweet potatoes, manioc, peanuts, and an astonishing variety of fruits.

On the Altiplano, the most important animal is the llama, one of the most efficient carrier animals known. Alpaca are found there, too. In the tropical Amazon region are the puma, tapir, armadillo, sloth, peccary, capiguara (river hog), and ant bear, as well as several kinds of monkeys. Bird life is rich and varied.

5 ENVIRONMENT

As of 1994, the chief environmental problem in the densely populated Altiplano was soil erosion, resulting from poor cultivation methods and overgrazing. Almost 24% of the city dwellers and 70% of rural people do not have pure water. The main sources of water pollution are fertilizers, pesticides, and mining.

As of 1994, 21 mammals, 34 species of birds, 4 species of reptiles, and 1 species of fish were considered endangered.

6 POPULATION

The total population as of the last national census in 1992 was 6,420,792. The projected population for the year 2000 was 9,038,000. The population density in 1992 was 6 persons per square kilometer (15.1 per square mile). Three-fourths of the total population lives on the Altiplano or in the western mountain valleys. The southeastern lowlands are sparsely populated. In 1988, La Paz, the administrative capital, had an estimated population of 1,049,800. Sucre, the legal and judicial capital, had 95,635.

BOLIVIA

0	50	100	150	200 Miles	
0	50	100	150	200 Kilometers	

LOCATION: 9°40′ to 22°53′s; 57°29′ to 69°35′w. **BOUNDARY LENGTHS:** Brazil, 3,125 kilometers (1,942 miles); Paraguay, 756 kilometers (470 miles); Argentina, 742 kilometers (461 miles); Chile, 861 kilometers (535 miles); Peru, 1,048 kilometers (651 miles).

7 MIGRATION

Aside from Spaniards during the colonial period, European immigration has been insignificant. Since the 1950s, migration to neighboring countries has increased. About 675,000 Bolivians were estimated to reside outside the country in the late 1980s, in search of employment and better

Photo credit: Anne Kalosh

A frontal view of the ornate San Francisco Church in La Paz.

economic opportunities. A number of Bolivian braceros (contract agricultural laborers) go to northwestern Argentina to work in rice and sugar harvests.

Within the country, migration is swelling the sparsely populated lowlands. High unemployment among agricultural laborers and miners has caused significant migration to the cities.

8 ETHNIC GROUPS

Estimates of the make-up of the Amerindian population are Quechua, about 30% and Aymará, 25%. Cholos (Bolivians of mixed white and Amerindian lineage) make up another 25 to 30%, and those of wholly European background account for nearly all the rest. The distinction between Amerindian, cholo, and white has gradually become blurred, making these estimates at least somewhat subjective.

Other Amerindians include the Chiriguanos, Mojenos, Chiquitanos, and Sirionós. In all, Amerindians number about 100,000.

9 LANGUAGES

Spanish, Quechua, and Aymará are all official languages. About 40% of Bolivians speak Spanish as a mother tongue. Approximately 37% of the people still speak Quechua, and 24% speak Aymará, although an increasing number of Amerindians also speak Spanish.

10 RELIGIONS

The 1961 constitution abolished state support of the Roman Catholic Church, thus formally separating church and state. In 1993, an estimated 92.1% of the population was Roman Catholic. Most Amerindians combine their own religious symbols with Christian observance. An active Protestant minority totaled 335,000 when last counted in 1985. There were also about 65,900 tribal religionists, 2,800 Buddhists, and 600 Jews.

11 TRANSPORTATION

The shortage of transportation facilities is one of the most serious barriers to economic development. Railroads are single-track meter gauge, totaling 3,675 kilometers (2,284 miles) in 1991. Of a total of 38,836 kilometers (24,133 miles) of roads, less than 4% were paved. In 1992, there were 335,000 motor vehicles, of which 270,000 were passenger cars, and 65,000 were commercial vehicles.

The hub of air traffic is El Alto airport near La Paz, the world's highest commercial airport. The other international airport is at Santa Cruz. Little use has been made of Bolivia's 14,000 kilometers (8,700 miles) of navigable waterways. Because Bolivia does not have access to the ocean, it has been granted port privileges at Antofagasta and Arica in Chile, at Mollendo in Peru, and at Santos in Brazil.

12 HISTORY

Following the decline of the highly developed Tiahuanaco civilization, Quechua-speaking Incas conquered the region surrounding Lake Titicaca and colonized villages in most of what is now Bolivia by 1300 AD. The Spaniard Francisco Pizarro led the Western conquest of the Inca Empire in 1532–33.

In 1545, silver was discovered in the Andean region of Bolivia, then called Alto Peru, or Upper Peru, at a mine named the Cerro Rico (Rich Hill) de Potosí. The mines continued to produce vast amounts of wealth for the Spanish Empire, and for years Potosí was the largest city in the Western Hemisphere. In 1776, the region was added to the Viceroyalty of La Plata, a group of Spanish possessions with its center at Buenos Aires.

Upper Peru gained its freedom after Simón Bolívar's 1924 liberation of Peru. Bolívar sent his young general, Antonio José de Sucre, to free Upper Peru. Upper Peru was formally proclaimed the Republic of Bolívar on 6 August 1825 (the name was soon changed to Bolivia).

Sucre was chosen as the first president in 1826, and the capital city, Chuquisaca, was renamed Sucre in his honor. He was succeeded by General Andrés de Santa Cruz, who conquered Peru in 1836 and formed the Peruvian-Bolivian Confederation. In 1839, Chilean forces defeated and dissolved the confederation and ended the presidency of Santa Cruz.

A period of instability followed. The almost constant civil war slowed Bolivia's economic progress and resulted in the loss of much of its land. At the close of the War of the Pacific (1879–84), which pitted Chile against Bolivia and Peru, Chile seized what was then the Bolivian port of Antofagasta. Deprived of its only coastal territory, Bolivia was forever after a land-locked country.

After a silver boom in the late 19th century, silver production gave way to tin mining. The nation was controlled by a few wealthy mine and plantation owners, allied with various foreign interests, while the Amerindians, excluded from the system, found their lot unchanged after almost 400 years.

World War II brought further strains to Bolivia. As world demand skyrocketed, the tin market boomed, but working conditions in Bolivia's mines remained miserable and wages remained low. In December of 1943, a coalition of the army and the Nationalist Revolutionary Movement (Movimiento Nacionalista Revolucionario—MNR) engineered a successful takeover of the government. However, the tin market collapsed at the war's end, weakening the new government's power base. The new government, in turn, was overthrown and a conservative government favoring the wealthy mine and land owners was installed.

The MNR returned to power in the early 1950s, dominating Bolivian politics from 1952 to 1964. Its first government, led by Víctor Paz Estenssoro, made dramatic moves to transform Bolivian society. The tin holdings of the three dominant families were taken over by the government, and a comprehensive land reform program was begun, along with large-scale welfare and literacy programs. Industry was encouraged, and the search for oil deposits was hastened.

In addition, a new policy gave Amerindians the right to vote and tried to integrate the Amerindian community more fully into the national economy. The right to vote, previously restricted to literate Bolivian males (who constituted less than ten per cent of the population), was made universal for all Bolivians over 21.

After his initial term in office, Paz became more and more dictatorial, and divisions within the MNR worsened. After Paz tried to rig the presidential elections in June 1964, he was removed from office by a military takeover. For the next 20 years, a series of military and civilian governments ruled Bolivia.

In 1985, former prime minister Paz, now 77, was returned to office. Faced with runaway inflation, which reached an annual rate of 14,000% in August 1985, the two leading parties agreed to cooperate, allowing a comprehensive economic reform package to pass through the legislature. Inflation and interest rates fell and the economy stabilized.

More importantly, Paz got competing political parties to cooperate in support of a continuing democracy. Paz's successor, Jaime Paz Zamora, who took office in 1989, was able to hold together a coalition and serve a full four-year presidential term.

Following the 1993 elections, Gonzalo Sánchez de Lozada assumed the presidency. His vice president, Victor Hugo Cárdenas, is the first Amerindian in Bolivian history to hold that office.

13 GOVERNMENT

The constitution of 3 February 1967 provides for a representative democracy, with its government divided into an executive branch, a two-chamber legislature (consisting of a Chamber of Deputies and a Senate), and the judiciary.

In practice, the constitution has not been consistently observed. Military takeovers and states of siege have been frequent. Congress was dissolved by the armed forces from 1969–79 and again between 1980 and 1982. Between 1966 and 1978, no presidential elections were held.

14 POLITICAL PARTIES

Numerous parties and coalitions have formed and dissolved over the years, usually tied to the personalities of the various leaders.

The leading party is the Nationalist Revolutionary Movement (Movimiento Nacionalista Revolucionario—MNR). It was originally a militant organization, but the years have moderated the party's stance. The other leading party is the Movement of the Revolutionary Left (Movimiento de la Izquierda Revolucionaria—MIR), which won the presidency in 1989 under leader Jaime Paz Zamora.

The right-wing Democratic Nationalist Alliance (Alianza Democrática Nacionalista—ADN) is closely tied to former President Hugo Banzer Suarez. The United Left (Izquierda Unida—IU) is a coalition of leftist parties. The center-right Christian Democratic Party (PDC) and far-right "Conscience of the Fatherland" party (CONDEPA) complete the list of parties with significant electoral support.

15 JUDICIAL SYSTEM

Judicial power is exercised by the Supreme Court, the superior district courts in each department, and the local courts. The Supreme Court, which sits at Sucre, is divided into four chambers: two deal with civil cases, one with criminal cases, and one with administrative, mining, and social cases.

The district courts usually hear appeals from the local courts. There is also a separate national labor court.

16 ARMED FORCES

As of 1993, armed strength totaled 31,500 men (army, 23,000; a navy for lake and river patrol, 4,500; air force, 4,000), and

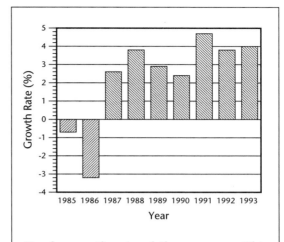

Yearly growth rate of the economy. This economic indicator tells by what percent the economy has increased or decreased when compared with the previous year.

paramilitary police of 16,200. Defense expenditures in 1993 were $80 million.

17 ECONOMY

As of 1994, Bolivia was in its second decade of democratic rule and its tenth consecutive year of economic expansion. Market reforms are firmly in place, investment is growing steadily, and inflation is under control. Growth was led by construction, manufacturing, and services. Inflation was reduced from the amazing 14,000% in 1985 to only 10.7% in 1992.

18 INCOME

In 1992, Bolivia's gross national product (GNP) was $5,084 million at current prices, or $760 per person.

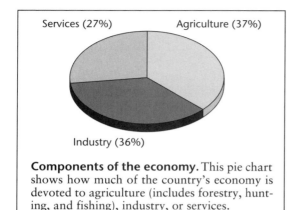

Services (27%)   Agriculture (37%)

Industry (36%)

Components of the economy. This pie chart shows how much of the country's economy is devoted to agriculture (includes forestry, hunting, and fishing), industry, or services.

19 INDUSTRY

Industrial development has been severely restricted by political instability, the small domestic market, the uncertain supply of raw materials, and the lack of technically trained labor. Over one-half of output is in nondurable consumer goods—food, beverages, tobacco, and coffee. Handicrafts and hydrocarbons account for much of the remainder.

20 LABOR

The economically active population was 2.4 million in 1991. Of that total, 27.2% worked in industry, 36.4% in agriculture, and 36.4% in services.

Practically the entire nonagricultural labor force, as well as part of the peasantry, is unionized. The Central Bolivian Workers' Organization (Central Obrera Boliviana—COB) is the central labor federation, to which nearly all unions belong.

21 AGRICULTURE

An estimated 2.1% of Bolivia's land area was under cultivation in 1991. Another 24% was permanent pasture. Agricultural development has been handicapped by extremely low productivity, poor distribution of the population in relation to productive land, and a lack of transportation facilities.

The most important crops are potatoes, corn, barley, quinoa (a milletlike grain), habas (broad beans), wheat, alfalfa, and oca (a tuber). The potato is the main staple; dehydrated and frozen to form chuño or tunta, it keeps indefinitely. The most profitable crop in the Yungas is coca, which is chewed by the local population and from which cocaine is extracted. It has been estimated that from 1982 through 1986, about 71,000 hectares (175,000 acres), twice as much land as in 1980, were planted with coca and that some 100,000 people were engaged in its cultivation.

Coffee, cacao, bananas, yucca, and aji (a widely used chili pepper) are also important. In the fertile irrigated valleys, the important crops are corn, wheat, barley, vegetables, alfalfa, and oats. The Tarija area is famous for grapes, olives, and fruit.

22 DOMESTICATED ANIMALS

In 1992 there were an estimated 5.7 million head of cattle, 7.3 million sheep, 1.4 million goats, 2.2 million hogs, 6,340,000 donkeys, and 323,000 horses. Poultry numbered 28 million in 1992.

The Amerindians of the high plateau depend on the llama because it can carry loads at any altitude and provides leather, meat, and dung fuel. Leading animal product exports are hides, alpaca and vicuña wool, and chinchilla fur.

23 FISHING

Fishing is a minor activity in Bolivia. A few varieties of fish are caught in Lake Titicaca by centuries-old methods and sent to La Paz. The catch was estimated at 5,637 tons in 1991.

24 FORESTRY

Bolivia is potentially one of the world's most important forestry nations. Trees are mostly evergreens and deciduous hardwoods. There are more than 2,000 species of tropical hardwoods of excellent quality, such as mahogany, jacaranda, rosewood, palo de balsa, quina, ironwood, colo, and cedar. Sawmills are few, however, and the almost total lack of transportation facilities has made harvesting expensive. Roundwood production in 1991 was only 1,632,000 cubic meters, up from 1,412,000 cubic meters in 1986 and 1,369,000 cubic meters in 1981. Exports of wood and wood products accounted for only $29.8 million in 1992. Bolivia is one of South America's leading rubber exporting countries.

25 MINING

Bolivia is the fourth largest tin-producing nation, after Brazil, Malaysia, and Indonesia. Mineral exports usually make up about 70% of the nation's exports, when natural gas is included. Total mine pro-

Photo credit: Anne Kalosh

A young woman poses with her llama near Lake Titicaca on Bolivia's border with Peru.

duction in Bolivia was 16,830 tons in 1991. Smelter production was 14,663 tons.

Silver, zinc, tungsten, bismuth, lead, copper, gold, asbestos, and other metals are also exported. Bolivia was the world's second largest producer of antimony in 1991, with 7,287 tons mined.

26 FOREIGN TRADE

Bolivia depends primarily on its mineral exports, especially tin and natural gas. Tin exports, however, have been gradually decreasing since 1946. In 1993, export earnings increased to $630 million while imports reached $1,131 million. Bolivia's

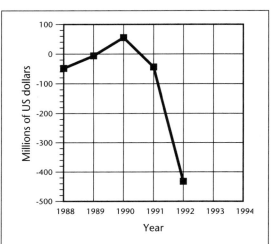

Yearly balance of trade measured in millions of US dollars. The balance of trade is the difference between what a country sells to other countries (its exports) and what it buys (its imports). If a country imports more than it exports, it has a negative balance of trade (a trade deficit). If exports exceed imports, there is a positive balance of trade (a trade surplus).

major trading partners include the US, Brazil, and Japan.

27 ENERGY AND POWER

Total electric power output in 1991 was 2,150 million kilowatt hours, of which 59% was hydroelectric. Electricity consumption grew by 7% in 1992, more than triple the population growth. In 1991, the total average daily production of crude oil was 22,174 barrels, while production of natural gas was estimated at 5,432,000 cubic meters.

28 SOCIAL DEVELOPMENT

Social security coverage is compulsory for both salaried employees and rural work-

ers. Those covered by the program receive medical, hospital, dental, and pharmaceutical care for themselves and their families. The government also provides old age pensions, survivors' benefits, maternity benefits, and family allowances.

Although women are guaranteed equal protection under the Constitution, in most cases, they earn less than men for doing similar work.

29 HEALTH

Health conditions have been notably poor, owing to poor hygiene and an insufficient number of doctors and hospitals, especially in rural areas. The most common disorders are acute respiratory diseases, tuberculosis, malaria, hepatitis, and Chagas' disease. Malnutrition is a serious and growing problem, with 18% of children under age five considered malnourished in 1990. Life expectancy in 1992 was estimated at 60 years.

In 1992, 63% of the population had access to health care. The country's total health care expenditures for 1990 were $181 million.

30 HOUSING

As of 1988, 67% of all housing units were detached private dwellings, 25% were detached rooms for rent with common facilities, 5% were huts, and 2% were apartments. Only about 50% of the population had access to piped indoor water, and about 26% lived in dwellings with adequate sanitary facilities.

Selected Social Indicators

These statistics are estimates for the period 1988 to 1993. For comparison purposes, data for the United States and averages for low-income countries and high-income countries are also given.

Indicator	Bolivia	Low-income countries	High-income countries	United States
Per capita gross national product†	$760	$380	$23,680	$24,740
Population growth rate	2.1%	1.9%	0.6%	1.0%
Population growth rate in urban areas	3.9%	3.9%	0.8%	1.3%
Population per square kilometer of land	6	78	25	26
Life expectancy in years	60	62	77	76
Number of people per physician	1,446	>3,300	453	419
Number of pupils per teacher (primary school)	25	39	<18	20
Illiteracy rate (15 years and older)	23%	41%	<5%	<3%
Energy consumed per capita (kg of oil equivalent)	310	364	5,203	7,918

† The gross national product (GNP) is the total dollar value of all goods and services produced by a country in a year. The per capita GNP is calculated by dividing a country's GNP by its population. The World Bank defines low-income countries as those with a per capita GNP of $695 or less. High-income countries have a per capita GNP of $8,626 or more. Less than 14% of the world's 5.5 billion people live in high-income countries, while almost 60% live in low-income countries.

> = greater than   < = less than

Sources: World Bank, Social Indicators of Development 1995, Baltimore: Johns Hopkins University Press, 1995. Central Intelligence Agency, World Fact Book, Washington, D.C.: Government Printing Office, 1994.

31 EDUCATION

In 1990, Bolivia's estimated adult literacy rate was 77% (males, 84.7%; and females, 70.7%). Primary education, which lasts for eight years, is compulsory and free of charge. Secondary education lasts for another four years. In 1990, there were 1,278,775 students enrolled at the primary level with 51,763 teachers. There were also 219,232 secondary students with 12,434 teachers.

Bolivia has eight state universities, one in each departmental capital except Cobija. There are also two private universities. The University of San Francisco Xavier in Sucre, dating from 1624, is one of the oldest universities in Latin America.

32 MEDIA

There were 129 AM radio stations in 1992 and 43 television stations. A government-owned television station broadcasts from La Paz. In 1991, Bolivia had an estimated 4,590,000 radio receivers and 755,000 television sets. Bolivia had about 194,180 telephones in 1991.

In 1991 there were 14 daily newspapers. The most important La Paz daily newspapers, with their estimated circulations in 1991, are *El Diario,* 45,000; *Hoy,*

Photo credit: Mary A. Dempsey

Fraile (friar) monolith at Tiahuanaco ruins.

20,000; and *Última Hora,* 20,000. Important provincial dailies are *Los Tiempos* (Cochabamba), with 15,000 circulation; and *El Mundo* (Santa Cruz), with 18,000.

33 TOURISM AND RECREATION

In 1991 there were 220,902 tourist arrivals in hotels and other establishments, of which 16% came from Peru, 12% from the United States, and 11% from Argentina. There were 11,013 rooms in hotels and other facilities. Tourism receipts totaled $90 million.

La Paz and Sucre have many colonial churches and buildings, and there are Inca ruins on the islands of Lake Titicaca, which also offers opportunities for fishing and sailing. The world's highest ski run is located at Chacaltaya, and mountain climbing and hiking are available on the country's Andean peaks.

34 FAMOUS BOLIVIANS

Andrés de Santa Cruz (1792–1865), who considered himself the "Napoleon of the Andes," dominated the early years of the independent nation. Simón Patiño (1861–1947), the richest of the "big three" tin barons, began his career as a loan collector and acquired his first mine by chance. He later became one of the world's wealthiest men.

Bolivia's outstanding literary figure is Gabriel René-Moreno (1836–1909), a historian, sociologist, and literary critic. The highly original poet and philosopher Franz Tamayo (1879–1956), although belonging to the landed aristocracy, was a champion of the downtrodden Amerindian. Tamayo was elected president in 1935, but an army revolt prevented him from taking power.

35 BIBLIOGRAPHY

Blair, David Nelson. *The Land and People of Bolivia.* New York: J.B. Lippincott, 1990.
Hudson, Rex A., and Dennis M. Hanratty, *Bolivia, a Country Study.* 3rd ed. Washington, D.C.: Government Printing Office, 1991.
Morrison, M. *Bolivia.* Chicago: Children's Press, 1988.
Yeager, Gertrude Matyoka. *Bolivia.* Oxford, England; Santa Barbara, Calif.: Clio Press, 1988.

BOSNIA AND HERZEGOVINA

Republic of Bosnia and Herzegovina
Republika Bosnia i Herzegovina

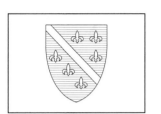

CAPITAL: Sarajevo.

FLAG: White with a large blue shield; the shield contains white Roman crosses with a white diagonal band.

ANTHEM: A new national anthem was being prepared in late fall 1994.

MONETARY UNIT: The dinar was introduced October 1994. No exchange rate was available at the time of publication.

WEIGHTS AND MEASURES: The metric system is the legal standard.

HOLIDAYS: New Year's Day, 1–2 January; Labor Days, 1–2 May; 27 July; 25 November.

TIME: 1 PM = noon GMT.

1 LOCATION AND SIZE

Bosnia and Herzegovina is located in southeastern Europe on the Balkan Peninsula, between Croatia and Serbia and Montenegro. Bosnia and Herzegovina is slightly larger than the state of Tennessee, with a total area of 51,233 square kilometers (19,781 square miles). It has a total boundary length of 1,389 kilometers (863 miles).

Bosnia and Herzegovina's capital city, Sarajevo, is located near the center of the country.

2 TOPOGRAPHY

The topography of Bosnia and Herzegovina features hills, mountains, and valleys. Approximately 50% of the land is forested; about 20% can be cultivated. Bosnia and Herzegovina is subject to frequent and destructive earthquakes.

3 CLIMATE

The climate features hot summers and cold winters. In July, the mean temperature is 22.5°C (72.5°F). January's mean temperature is 0°C (32°F). Annual rainfall averages 62.5 centimeters (24.6 inches).

4 PLANTS AND ANIMALS

Ferns, flowers, mosses, and common trees populate the landscape. Wild animals include deer, brown bears, rabbits, fox, and wild boars.

5 ENVIRONMENT

Metallurgical factories contribute to air pollution. Water is scarce, as are landfill sites.

6 POPULATION

The population of Bosnia and Herzegovina was 4,365,639 in 1991 and was estimated at 4,618,804 in July 1993 by the United States government. The population density in 1991 was 85 per square kilometer (221 per square mile). Sarajevo, the capital, had a population of 415,631.

7 MIGRATION

Many people living in Bosnia and Herzegovina fled the war that followed independence from the Yugoslav federation in 1990. In 1994, there were over 800,000 refugees outside of Bosnia and Herzegovina. In addition, the US government estimates that as many as 1.2 million persons have been displaced within the country due to the ongoing conflict.

8 ETHNIC GROUPS

In 1991, 43.7% of the people were South Slavs of the Islamic faith. Serbs comprised 31.4%, and Croats, 17.3%. Some 239,845 (5.5%) declared themselves as Yugoslavs.

9 LANGUAGES

The native language of all the major ethnic groups is Serbo–Croatian, which belongs to the southern Slavic group.

10 RELIGIONS

Sunni Muslims comprise over 40% of the population, Serbian Orthodox 31%, and Roman Catholics some 19%. A small Baha'i community is present as well.

11 TRANSPORTATION

The main railway is a one meter gauge track which connects the Croatian port at Dubrovnik to Sarajevo and crosses the Sava River before returning into Croatia at the northern border. In 1991, there were 21,168 kilometers (13,154 miles) of highways, 54% of which were paved.

12 HISTORY

Origins

Bosnia was populated in ancient times by Thracians, Illyrians, and Celts, with Greek colonies since 400 BC. It was taken over by the Romans around 168 BC. Slavic tribes began raiding and settling in the Balkan area in large numbers in the fifth century AD. They were joined in the seventh century by Croatian and Serbian tribes. By the ninth century, most of the Bosnian area came under the influence of Rome. The Croats became Catholic, while most Serbs fell under the influence of the Byzantine Empire and became Eastern Orthodox Christians.

Between the ninth and eleventh centuries, Croatians competed with Bulgarians, Serbs, and the Byzantine empire for control of Bosnia. Hungary took over in 1136 and ruled for much of the next 100 years.

Beginning in the late thirteenth century, a series of Bosnian princes gained control, beginning with Stjepan Kotroman around 1288. The greatest was Tvrtko, who was crowned King of Bosnia and Serbia in 1377.

The Ottoman Turks conquered Bosnia in 1443. The Turks gradually occupied Herzegovina, taking full control by 1482. The two regions were subject to the Ottoman Empire for the next 400 years.

LOCATION: 44°17′N; 17°30′E. **BOUNDARY LENGTHS:** Total boundary lengths, 1,389 kilometers (863 miles); Croatia (northern), 751 kilometers (467 miles); Croatia (south), 91 kilometers (57 miles); Serbia, 312 kilometers (194 miles); Montenegro, 215 kilometers (134 miles).

Under Ottoman Rule

The Ottomans introduced their administration, property concepts, and customs into Bosnia and Herzegovina. Most Bosnian Christians converted to Islam because it gave them privileged status under the

Ottomans. Followers of Islam were the ruling class, regardless of their national or ethnic backgrounds. Christian peasants practically became serfs to Muslim landlords. In spite of this, communities of followers of the Orthodox (Serbian) Church and Catholic (Croatian) Church survived into the late nineteenth century. In 1878, Austria occupied Bosnia and Herzegovina, putting an end to four centuries of Ottoman rule.

Under Austro-Hungarian Rule

The Austrian approach to the administration of Bosnia and Herzegovina was to keep things mostly as they were while gradually introducing Western administrative and education models. Bosnia and Herzegovina was annexed by Austria in 1908, leading to the adoption of a constitution, legal recognition of political parties, and a Bosnian Parliament in 1910. However ethnic minorities never accepted Austrian rule and on 28 June 1914, Austrian Archduke Ferdinand was assassinated by a Serbian radical. This act led to the beginning of World War I. Austria immediately attacked Serbia, and the Serbian community of Bosnia and Herzegovina was subjected to a regime of terror that included indiscriminate executions by the Austrian authorities.

First (Royal) Yugoslavia

After World War I, the Bosnian National Council decided to unite with the Kingdom of Serbia in 1918. Bosnia and Herzegovina ceased to exist as a distinct political unit. After ten stormy years of parliamentary government, King Alexander established a royal dictatorship in 1929 called "Yugoslavia." What once was Bosnia and Herzegovina was split among four of the new units (Vrbaska, Drinska, Primorska, and Zetska). Serb and Croat peasants were finally freed from their feudal obligations to Muslim landlords through the agrarian reforms decreed in 1919 and slowly implemented over the next twenty years.

World War II

Germany, Italy, and their allies Hungary, Romania, and Bulgaria, attacked Yugoslavia on 6 April 1941 and divided the country among themselves. The Croatian terrorist Ustaša organization collaborated with the aggressors and was allowed to proclaim an Independent State of Croatia on 10 April 1941. This new state incorporated all of Bosnia and Herzegovina. Of its total population of 6.3 million, one-third were Serbian and one-twelfth were Muslim. Once in power, the Ustaša troops began to "cleanse" Greater Croatia of the Serbian population. Their tactics included the use of terror, mass deportations, and genocidal massacres.

The Serbian population responded by joining the Partisan resistance movement led by Josip Broz-Tito, head of the Yugoslav Communist Party. Bosnia and Herzegovina suffered terrible losses in attacks by the Germans, as well as through internal civil war among Communist-dominated Partisans, nationalist Serbs (Cetniks), and Croatian terrorists (Ustaše), with the Muslim population caught in the middle.

Soviet armies entered Yugoslavia from Romania and Bulgaria in the fall of 1944, and Communist-led forces took control of all of Yugoslavia.

Second (Communist) Yugoslavia

The World War II Partisan resistance movement, controlled by the Communist Party of Yugoslavia and led by Marshal Tito, won control of the country. Under Tito, Yugoslavia developed its own brand of Marxist economy based on workers' councils and self-management of enterprises and institutions. Tito ruled Yugoslavia until his death in 1980. During that time, Tito managed to maintain peace among the Croats, Serbs, and Muslims. After his death there was an economic crisis which led to tensions between the different groups. They demanded a reorganization of the Yugoslav federation into a confederation of sovereign states and a shift to a market economy.

On 1 August 1990, Bosnia and Herzegovina declared itself a "sovereign and democratic state." However, by 1991 Yugoslavia was dissolved, as Slovenia, Croatia, Bosnia and Herzegovina, and Macedonia declared independence individually, leaving only Serbia and Montenegro together in a new Federal Republic of Yugoslavia.

Independence and War

The coalition government of Bosnia and Herzegovina had a very difficult time maintaining the spirit of ethnic cooperation. The Serbian and Croatian parties each wanted a temporary confederation as a transition to unification with their "mother state" of Serbia or Croatia. The Muslim party favored a united Bosnia and Herzegovina. Ultimately war broke out among the parties.

War spread in Bosnia in mid-1992. While Serbs took over control of some 70% of the country, Croats kept control of western Herzegovina. Their Muslim allies tried to resist Serbian attacks on mostly Muslim cities and towns full of refugees. Despite peacekeeping efforts by the European Community, the United States, the United Nations, and the North Atlantic Treaty Organization (NATO), Bosnia and Herzegovina was engaged in a civil war that has continued into 1995.

13 GOVERNMENT

The war being waged in Bosnia and Herzegovina since April 1992 has prevented the working out of a constitution agreeable to the three main groups. So far none of the constitutional plans submitted for terminating the hostilities has been accepted by all three parties to the ongoing conflict.

14 POLITICAL PARTIES

The elections of November–December 1990 for the parliament of Bosnia and Herzegovina gave 87 seats in the parliament to the Muslim Party of Democratic Action (SDA); 71 to the Serbian Democratic Party (SDS); 44 to the Croatian Democratic Union (HDZ); 18 to the Communist Party; and 13 to the Alliance of Reform Forces.

Photo credit: AP/Wide World Photos

Two young Muslim refugees work their way through barbed wire which surrounds a UN supply depot in Zenica. The boys were forced from their home by fighting between Muslims and Serbs.

15 JUDICIAL SYSTEM

The Bosnian conflict has disrupted the ordinary functioning of courts in most areas.

16 ARMED FORCES

There is no national force, although the official Muslim government controls 30,000–50,000 militia men, who face 50,000 Croats and 67,000 Serbs. The Serbs control most of the Russian weapons abandoned by the former Yugoslavian army. A major portion of the United Nations Protection Force (about 10,000 personnel from 29 nations) has been sent to Bosnia and Herzegovina.

17 ECONOMY

Bosnia and Herzegovina ranked next to Macedonia as the poorest republic of the former Yugoslav federation. Although industry accounts for over 50% of its income, Bosnia and Herzegovina is primarily agricultural. Farms have been small and inefficient, making it necessary to import food. Metallic ore and coal production, timber production, and textiles are also important.

18 INCOME

In 1991, Bosnia and Herzegovina's gross domestic product (GDP) was an estimated $1,400 millions, or $3,200 per person. In

1991, the average inflation rate was 80% per month, resulting in a real growth rate in GDP of –37%.

19 INDUSTRY

Mining and mining-related activities make up the bulk of Bosnia and Herzegovina's industry. Steel production, vehicle assembly, textiles, tobacco products, wooden furniture, and domestic appliances are also important industries. Industrial production has plunged since 1990 because of the civil war.

20 LABOR

Before the civil war, the labor force in 1991 amounted to 1,026,254, with 2% engaged in agriculture, 45% in industry and mining, and the remainder in other sectors. In February 1992, unemployment was estimated at 28%.

21 AGRICULTURE

About 19.8% (1,015,000 hectares/ 2,508,000 acres) of the total area was considered as possible farm land in 1991; another 27.6% (1,400,000 hectares/ 3,459,000 acres) was estimated to be used as permanent pasture land. Since the disintegration of the Yugoslav SFR, civil fighting in the major agricultural areas has often interrupted harvests and caused major crop losses.

22 DOMESTICATED ANIMALS

As of 1991, there were some 1.4 million hectares (3.5 million acres) of permanent pasture land, representing about 27% of the country's total area. Because of the breakup of the Yugoslav SFR and civil war that followed, the livestock population has fallen considerably since 1990.

23 FISHING

With no ports on its twenty kilometers (12 miles) of Adriatic coastline, marine fishing is not commercially important. Inland fishing occurs on the Sava, Una, and Drina Rivers.

24 FORESTRY

In 1991, about 2.3 million hectares (5.7 million acres) were forested, accounting for nearly 46% of the total area. Much of the timber output has been used for fuel since the civil war began.

25 MINING

Nonfuel mineral resources include copper, lead, zinc, gold, and iron ore. Iron ore is mined at Vareš, Ljubija, and Radovan. Bauxite is also mined at Vlasenica, Jajce, Bosanska Krupa, Posusje, Lištica, and Citluk. There was a lead-zinc mine at Srebrenica and a manganese mine at Buzim in 1991. Salt is produced from brine at Tuzla, and mined at Tušanj.

26 FOREIGN TRADE

International trade with Bosnia and Herzegovina has been limited since the beginning of the civil war.

27 ENERGY AND POWER

As of 1991, total installed electrical capacity was 14,400 million kilowatts. Electrical generation has been irregular since the beginning of the civil war. Brown coal and lignite mines are located around Tuzla. In 1991, the annual capacity for the brown coal mines totaled 12 million tons; lignite mine capacity was 7 million tons.

28 SOCIAL DEVELOPMENT

Bosnia's economy and social fabric have been devastated by the war. In spite of minimum wage guarantees, delays and partial payments are widespread. Serbia has imposed an embargo on food deliveries. Enforcement of sick leave and other benefit programs, as well as occupational health and safety measures, has been inadequate.

By October 1993, over 800,000 Bosnian refugees had fled the country, while another 1.2 million were displaced within its borders. In 1993, rape and other forms of physical abuse were inflicted on women, including the strip-searching of Muslim women in the town of Mostar.

29 HEALTH

There have been over 200,000 war-related deaths. In 1992 alone, Bosnia suffered 120,000 war-related deaths. Figures for war-related deaths after 1993 were not available at the time of publishing.

30 HOUSING

No recent information is available.

31 EDUCATION

Education at the elementary level is free and compulsory for eight years. At the secondary level, children have the option to take up general, vocational, or technical education. General secondary education lasts for four years and qualifies the students for university education.

32 MEDIA

Communications facilities in Sarajevo and other Bosnian cities have been almost destroyed by the ongoing civil war. Radio-Television Sarajevo administers radio and television broadcasts. In 1991, Sarajevo had four radio and two television stations, all broadcasting in Serbo-Croatian. In Sarajevo, the daily newspaper *Oslobodjenje* has managed to publish continuously throughout the siege of that city despite poweroutages, newsprint shortages, and direct attacks on its offices.

33 TOURISM AND RECREATION

The civil war has disrupted the development of a tourist industry in Bosnia and Herzegovina. Sarajevo, the capital city, was the site of the 1984 Winter Olympics.

34 FAMOUS PERSONS

Dr. Alija Izetbegović has been the president of Bosnia and Herzegovina since December 1991. Haris Silajdžić was the prime minister in 1994. Dzemd Bijedic (1917–1977) was a leader of Yugoslavia from 1971 until 1977, when he was killed in a plane crash.

35 BIBLIOGRAPHY

Cataldi, Anna. *Letters from Sarajevo: Voices of a Besieged City.* Shaftesbury, Eng.: Element, 1994.

Filipović, Zlata. *Zlata's Diary: A Child's Life in Sarajevo.* New York: Viking, 1994.

Glenny, Michael. *The Fall of Yugoslavia: The Third Balkan War.* New York: Penguin, 1992.

Gutman, Roy. *A Witness to Genocide: The 1993 Pulitzer Prize-winning Dispatches on the "Ethnic Cleansing" of Bosnia.* New York: Macmillan, 1993.

BOTSWANA

Republic of Botswana

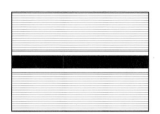

CAPITAL: Gaborone.

FLAG: The flag of Botswana consists of five horizontal stripes. The top and bottom stripes are light blue and wider than the middle stripe, which is black. The blue stripes are separated from the black by thin white stripes.

ANTHEM: *Fatshe La Rona (Blessed Country).*

MONETARY UNIT: On 23 August 1976, the pula (P) of 100 thebe replaced the South African rand (R) as Botswana's legal currency. There are coins of 1, 2, 5, 10, 25, 50 thebe and 1 pula, and notes of 2, 5, 10, 20, 50 and 100 pula. P1 = $0.3899 (or $1 = P1.5878).

WEIGHTS AND MEASURES: The metric system is the legal standard.

HOLIDAYS: New Year's Day, 1 January; Good Friday; Easter Monday; Ascension; President's Day, 15 July; Botswana Days, 30 September–1 October; Christmas, 25 December; Boxing Day, 26 December.

TIME: 2 PM = noon GMT.

1 LOCATION AND SIZE

Botswana is a landlocked country in southern Africa. It covers an area of 600,370 square kilometers (231,804 square miles). Comparatively, Botswana is slightly smaller than the state of Texas. It meets Zambia at a point in the north and is bordered on the northeast by Zimbabwe, on the southeast and south by South Africa, and on the west and north by Namibia (South West Africa). Its total boundary length is 4,013 kilometers (2,494 miles).

2 TOPOGRAPHY

Botswana is a broad tableland with a mean altitude of 1,000 meters (3,300 feet). A vast plateau about 1,200 meters (4,000 feet) in height, extending north from Kanye to the Zimbabwean border, divides the country into two distinct regions. The eastern region is hilly bush country and grassland (veld). To the west lies the swampy Okavango Delta and the Kalahari Desert. The only sources of year-round surface water are the Chobe River in the north, the Limpopo in the east, and the Okavango in the northwest. In seasons of heavy rainfall, floodwaters flow into the Makgadikgadi Salt Pans, Lake Ngami, and Lake Xau.

3 CLIMATE

Most of the country has a subtropical climate, with cooler temperatures at higher altitudes. Winter days are warm and nights are cool, with heavy frost common in the desert. Temperatures range from average maximums of 33°C (91°F) in January and 22°C (72°F) in July to average minimums of 18°C (64°F) in January and

Photo credit: Cynthia Bassett

Botswana's elephant population is second only to Zaire. This elephant is harking the tree so he can feast on the pods. Although elephants damage trees through this action, they also help the ecosystem by shaking the pods from the trees.

5°C (41°F) in July. Beginning in August, seasonal winds blow from the west and carry sand and dust across the country. Rainfall normally averages 45 centimeters (18 inches), ranging from 69 centimeters (27 inches) in the north to less than 25 centimeters (10 inches) in the Kalahari. Drought conditions existed in the early and mid-1980s.

4 PLANTS AND ANIMALS

About 90% of Botswana is covered by savanna (grassland). Even the Kalahari

Desert contains enough vegetation to support tens of thousands of wild animals. Common trees are the mopane, camelthorn, motopi (shepherd's tree), and baobab. Botswana is a natural game reserve for most animals found in southern Africa, including lions, leopards, cheetahs, elephants, giraffes, zebras, hippopotamuses, rhinoceroses, African buffalo, hyenas, and 22 species of antelope. The duiker (a small, horned antelope), wildebeest (gnu), and springbok (gazelle) are familiar. Some 549 bird species are also native to Botswana.

5 ENVIRONMENT

Because of the rapid increase in the cattle population, overgrazing is a serious threat to the vegetation and wildlife of Botswana. Other environmental concerns include the preservation of wildlife and water shortages. There are 5 game reserves, 3 game sanctuaries, and 40 controlled hunting areas. Almost 20% of the land has been set aside for national parks and game reserves. A major factor in Botswana's water supply problem is that 66% of the country falls within the Kalahari desert. As of 1994, nine mammal species (including the African elephant and the black rhinoceros), six bird species, one reptile species, and four plant species were threatened with extinction.

6 POPULATION

According to the official 1991 census, the population was 1,326,796, with the 1994 population estimated at 1,359,413. The average population density in 1991 was two persons per square kilometer (six per

BOTSWANA

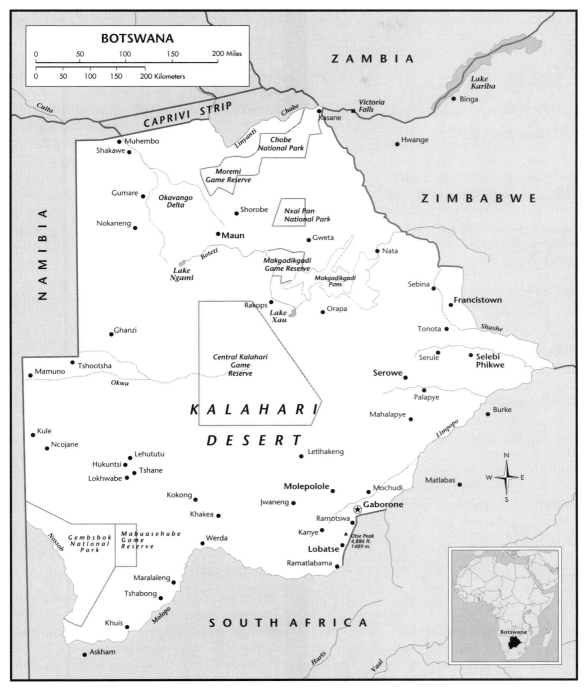

BOTSWANA

| 0 | 50 | 100 | 150 | 200 Miles |
| 0 | 50 | 100 | 150 | 200 Kilometers |

ZAMBIA

Cuito

CAPRIVI STRIP

Chobe

Victoria
Falls

*Lake
Kariba*

● Binga

● Muhembo

● Shakawe

Linyanti

Kasane

**Chobe
National Park**

● Hwange

**Moremi
Game Reserve**

ZIMBABWE

● Gumare

*Okavango
Delta*

● Shorobe

**Nxai Pan
National Park**

● Nokaneng

● **Maun**

Boteti

● Gweta

● Nata

● Sebina

Francistown

*Lake
Ngami*

**Makgadikgadi
Game Reserve**

*Makgadikgadi
Pans*

● Ghanzi

Rakops ●

*Lake
Xau*

● Orapa

● Tonota

Shashe

● Serule

● **Selebi
Phikwe**

● Mamuno

● Tshootsha

Okwa

**Central Kalahari
Game
Reserve**

Serowe ●

● Palapye

● Mahalapye

● Burke

K A L A H A R I

D E S E R T

● Letlhakeng

● Kule

● Ncojane

● Lehututu

● Hukuntsi

● Tshane

● Lokhwabe

● Kokong

● Khakea

Molepolole ●

Jwaneng ●

● Mochudi

● Matlabas

★ **Gaborone**

Ramotswa ●

● Werda

Nossob

*Mabuasehube
Game
Reserve*

Kanye ●

▲ Otse Peak
4,886 ft.
1489 m.

*Gembsbok
National
Park*

Lobatse ●

● Maralaleng

● Ramatlabama

● Tshabong

● Khuis

Molopo

S O U T H   A F R I C A

● Askham

Harts

Vaal

Limpopo

NAMIBIA

N
W E
S

Botswana

LOCATION: 17°47′ to 26°54′s; 20° to 29°21′e. **BOUNDARY LENGTHS:** Zimbabwe, 813 kilometers (505 miles); South Africa (including Bophuthatswana), 1,778 kilometers (1,105 miles); Namibia (South West Africa), 1,461 kilometers (908 miles).

square mile), but nearly 80% of the population lives on the better soils of the eastern strip of the country. One-third of the population lives in urban areas. Gaborone, the capital, had an estimated population of 138,471 in 1991.

7 MIGRATION

At least 50,000 Botswanans are working in South Africa at any particular time. In 1991, the number of South African residents listed as born in Botswana was 21,468. Botswana had some 500 refugees at the end of 1992, about 40% from South Africa.

8 ETHNIC GROUPS

The population of Botswana is distributed among eight tribes: the Bamangwato, Batswana, Bakwena, Bangwaketsi, Bakgatla, Barolong, Bamalete, and Batlokwa. Each tribe has its own territory. Tribal land comprises about 71% of the country. Other native peoples include the Kalanga, Yei, Mbukushu, Subiya, Herero, Kgalagadi, Basarwa (Bushmen), and Hottentots. In the mid-1980s, the non-African population included small numbers of Asians, Europeans, and people of mixed race.

9 LANGUAGES

English is the official language. Setswana, however, is spoken by most Botswanans.

10 RELIGIONS

About half the population practices traditional African religions, and the rest are Christian. Nearly 12% of the Christians belong to African churches, and 3.6% are Roman Catholics. The largest church is the United Congregational Church of Southern Africa. Freedom of religion is constitutionally guaranteed.

11 TRANSPORTATION

In 1991, Botswana had 11,514 kilometers (7,154 miles) of roads: 1,700 kilometers (1,056 miles) were gravel, 1,600 kilometers (994 miles) asphalt, and 8,214 kilometers (5,104 miles) earth or sand. Paved roads have been extended to the Zambian and Zimbabwean borders. There were some 60,000 registered road motor vehicles in 1991, of which 42% were passenger cars and the rest commercial vehicles. The main railroad from Cape Town in South Africa to Bulawayo in Zimbabwe runs through Botswana for a distance of 641 kilometers (398 miles). Two branch lines totaling 71 kilometers (44 miles) connect with the main line, and in 1991, a new 165 kilometer (103 mile) spur was completed.

The government-owned Air Botswana operates internal flights and international service to Johannesburg, South Africa; Mbabane, Swaziland; and Harare, Zimbabwe. A total of 111,200 passengers arrived and departed via Air Botswana in 1992.

12 HISTORY

Early History

According to tradition, the founder of the Batswana tribe was a fourteenth-century chief named Mogale. His great-great-grandson Malope had three sons: Kwena, Ngwaketse, and Ngwato. They became the chiefs of the major tribes that now inhabit Botswana.

The foundation of the modern state began in the late 1800s. Up to that time, the Batswana had had no permanent contact with Europeans, except for the missionaries Robert and Mary Moffat and David Livingstone, who had established missions in the first half of the nineteenth century. When the European powers began to invade southern Africa in the latter half of the nineteenth century, hostility developed between the Batswana and the European settlers. Khama III, who in 1872 became chief of the Bamangwato people, appealed to the United Kingdom for assistance. In response, the whole of what was then known as Bechuanaland was placed under the protection of England's Queen Victoria in 1885.

The territory south of the Molopo River was established as the crown colony of British Bechuanaland. In 1895, it was incorporated into South Africa. The northern part of the territory, the Bechuanaland Protectorate, which stayed British, was governed by the high commissioner in South Africa beginning in 1891. The South African Act of Union of 1909, which created the Union (now Republic) of South Africa, provided for the eventual transfer to South Africa of Bechuanaland along with Basutoland and Swaziland.

Modern History

The first significant political progress was made in 1921–22 with the creation of European and African advisory councils, together with a joint advisory council. In 1961, executive and legislative councils were created. Seretse Khama was elected prime minister in Bechuanaland's first general elections. Then in 1965 a constitution was written. Final constitutional talks were held in London in February 1966. On 30 September 1966, under the leadership of President Khama, the newly named Republic of Botswana came into being.

During this first decade of independence, Botswana refused to support United Nations, sanctions against South Africa. Although officially opposed to apartheid (a policy of political and economic discrimination based on race), Botswana was economically dependent on South Africa. After the 1969 elections, President Khama banned imports from white-minority-ruled Rhodesia (now Zimbabwe). Tensions were high in the 1970s as Botswana sheltered 20,000 refugees from Rhodesia, and Rhodesian armed forces crossed into Botswana on raids against guerrillas.

South Africa accused Botswana of allowing rebels to terrorize South Africa. In 1985, South African commandos killed several South African refugees in Gaborone. Further South African border violations and attacks in Botswana continued, but by 1992 the two countries established formal diplomatic relations.

13 GOVERNMENT

Botswana is a republic. Under its constitution, the president is elected by the National Assembly and is chief of state, chief executive, and commander-in-chief of the armed forces. The president appoints a cabinet from among the National Assembly members. The president can veto any bill, but if it is passed again within six months, the president must either sign it or dissolve the Assembly. All citizens over the age of 21 can vote. Both the president and the Assembly are elected for five-year terms.

The House of Chiefs consists of the chiefs of the eight principal tribes, and four chiefs elected from minority districts. Botswana has both a High Court and traditional village councils, called *kgotla*, where villagers can express opinions. Botswana is one of Africa's few stable multiparty democracies and has a commendable human rights record.

14 POLITICAL PARTIES

Botswana's leading party, the Botswana Democratic Party (BDP), was founded in late 1961, pledging itself to democracy, nonracialism, and a multiparty state. Other parties include the Botswana People's Party (BPP), the Botswana Independence Party (BIP), and the Botswana National Front (BNF). Botswana is an active member of the Southern Africa Development Community (SADC).

15 JUDICIAL SYSTEM

The constitution provides for a high court, a court of appeal, and lower courts. The African Courts Proclamation of 1961 provides for courts knowledgeable in tribal law and custom, presided over by chiefs. The judiciary is independent of the executive and the legislative branches.

16 ARMED FORCES

The Botswana Defense Force (ground and air units) is estimated at over 6,000 members, armed with North Atlantic Treaty

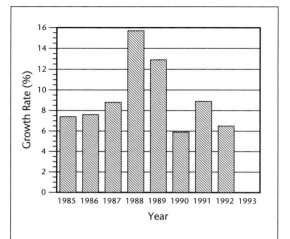

Yearly growth rate of the economy. This economic indicator tells by what percent the economy has increased or decreased when compared with the previous year.

Organization (NATO) weapons in 1993. There are about 1,000 paramilitary police.

17 ECONOMY

Botswana's economy was dependent almost entirely on livestock production until the 1970s, when the country became an important exporter of diamonds and other minerals. Foreign investment in agriculture, tourism, and industry, together with the rapid growth in diamond production, helped Botswana achieve average annual economic growth of 8.4% from independence through 1984. Real growth of 10% was recorded between 1985 and 1987. However, it slowed to 8.7% in the following two years (1987–89). Agriculture employs an estimated 62.1% of the labor force (1991). Intense competition

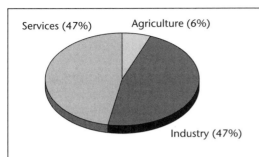

Components of the economy. This pie chart shows how much of the country's economy is devoted to agriculture (includes forestry, hunting, and fishing), industry, or services.

for water resources has affected industrial development plans.

18 INCOME

In 1992, Botswana's gross national product (GNP) was $3,797 million at current prices, or $2,790 per person.

19 INDUSTRY

Botswana has a small manufacturing sector, which produces textiles, beverages, chemicals, metals, plastics, and electrical products.

20 LABOR

The vast majority of the estimated labor force of 443,455 in 1991 worked with livestock and agriculture. In 1992, there were 227,500 paid employees. In addition, about 16,000 citizens of Botswana were working in South African mines.

The employment of children under age thirteen by anyone except members of the child's immediate family is prohibited. No young person under the age of fifteen may be employed in any industry, and no one under the age of sixteen may be employed in night work. No person age sixteen or younger may be employed in hazardous jobs like mining. The hours and working conditions of children in rural areas are difficult to monitor. Such employment is almost always in family businesses or on family farms, where child labor laws do not apply.

21 AGRICULTURE

Only about 2.4% of the total land area is used for agriculture, mostly in the eastern region. Crop production is limited by traditional farming methods, frequent drought, erosion, and disease. Principal crops for domestic use are sorghum, corn, and millet. Grain is usually imported from Zimbabwe and South Africa. Smaller quantities of cowpeas, beans, and other seed crops are also grown. The 1985–86 crop output totaled 25,000 tons. Botswana imported 70% more (by value) than it exported in agricultural products in 1992.

22 DOMESTICATED ANIMALS

In 1991, the cattle population was about 2,500,000. Other livestock included 2,090,000 goats, 2,000,000 poultry, 325,000 sheep, 153,000 donkeys, and 34,000 horses.

23 FISHING

Inhabitants of the Limpopo River Valley and the Okavango region caught about 1,900 tons of fish for local consumption in 1991.

24 FORESTRY

The forests of the north include the valuable mukwa, mukusi, and mopane woods. Roundwood production was an estimated 1,440,000 cubic meters in 1991.

25 MINING

Botswana is the world's third-largest diamond producer, mining a total of 16.5 million carats in 1991. Botswana also contains base and precious metals including silver, copper, and nickel. Smelted nickel-copper-cobalt matte is another valuable mineral commodity. Diamond reserves were reported to be 300 million carats, or 20 years' worth at current production. Nickel-copper ore reserves were reported as 95 million tons at the end of 1991. Soda ash production amounted to 62,000 tons in 1991.

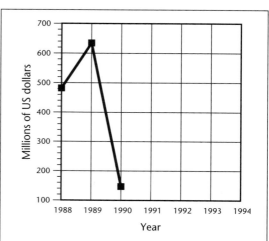

Yearly balance of trade measured in millions of US dollars. The balance of trade is the difference between what a country sells to other countries (its exports) and what it buys (its imports). If a country imports more than it exports, it has a negative balance of trade (a trade deficit). If exports exceed imports, there is a positive balance of trade (a trade surplus).

26 FOREIGN TRADE

Botswana's primary exports, most of which went to Europe (85.9%) and African countries (13.5%) in 1988, include diamonds, beef, copper-nickel matte and textiles. Primary imports include machinery and electrical goods, vehicles, transport equipment, food, beverages, and tobacco products. Botswana imports much of its food and other basic needs, primarily through the South African Customs Union countries (77%) and the United Kingdom (6.1%).

27 ENERGY AND POWER

Most electric power is generated thermally, totalling 630 million kilowatt hours in 1991. Coal production was 783,873 tons in 1991, mostly for the production of electricity. The government is considering constructing a plant with which to export power to South Africa beginning in the next century. Several companies are prospecting for oil, but none was discovered as of 1993.

28 SOCIAL DEVELOPMENT

Many social welfare needs are provided by tribal custom. Social security on a national scale has not yet been introduced. Women made up about 28% of the wage labor force in 1983. Drinking water supplies, public schools, and health clinics have been established in almost every village.

Selected Social Indicators

These statistics are estimates for the period 1988 to 1993. For comparison purposes, data for the United States and averages for low-income countries and high-income countries are also given.

Indicator	Botswana	Low-income countries	High-income countries	United States
Per capita gross national product†	$2,790	$380	$23,680	$24,740
Population growth rate	3.2%	1.9%	0.6%	1.0%
Population growth rate in urban areas	7.1%	3.9%	0.8%	1.3%
Population per square kilometer of land	2	78	25	26
Life expectancy in years	65	62	77	76
Number of people per physician	5,139	>3,300	453	419
Number of pupils per teacher (primary school)	29	39	<18	20
Illiteracy rate (15 years and older)	26%	41%	<5%	<3%
Energy consumed per capita (kg of oil equivalent)	388	364	5,203	7,918

† The gross national product (GNP) is the total dollar value of all goods and services produced by a country in a year. The per capita GNP is calculated by dividing a country's GNP by its population. The World Bank defines low-income countries as those with a per capita GNP of $695 or less. High-income countries have a per capita GNP of $8,626 or more. Less than 14% of the world's 5.5 billion people live in high-income countries, while almost 60% live in low-income countries.

> = greater than   < = less than

Sources: World Bank, *Social Indicators of Development 1995,* Baltimore: Johns Hopkins University Press, 1995. Central Intelligence Agency, *World Fact Book,* Washington, D.C.: Government Printing Office, 1994.

29 HEALTH

In 1992, fifteen general hospitals provided comprehensive health services for about 90% of the population, with one doctor for every 5,139 people. Tuberculosis is a major health problem, as is malnutrition, which in 1990 affected 15% of children under 5 years of age. The average life expectancy in 1992 was 65 years, with a death rate of 9.3 per 1,000 people in 1993. The infant mortality rate in 1992 was 45 per 1,000 live births.

30 HOUSING

There is no overcrowding in tribal villages, but slums have developed in the larger towns. The Botswana Housing Corp., a public enterprise, concentrates its efforts on major urban areas.

31 EDUCATION

Education, not compulsory, lasts for seven years at the primary level, followed by five years of secondary school. In 1992, Botswana had 654 primary schools, with 308,840 students and 9,708 teachers. Secondary schools had 78,804 students and 4,437 teachers in 1991. There were 3,567 pupils and 376 teachers at the university level in 1991. The University of Botswana offers studies in social sciences, education, sciences, agriculture, and humanities.

Photo credit: Cynthia Bassett

A group of college educated Botswanas who travel around the country teaching English in the villages.

32 MEDIA

The government publishes the *Daily News* (circulation 32,000 in 1991) in both English and Setswana, and the bilingual monthly magazine *Kutlwaro* (circulation 24,000). There were 5 independent newspapers in 1991.

That year Botswana's fifteen radio transmitters broadcast to 155,000 radios, with Radio Botswana providing a variety of programs. There was no television service as of 1991, but the 21,000 owners of television sets could receive South African programming. There were 34,318 telephones in use in 1991.

33 TOURISM & RECREATION

In 1991, 899,000 tourists visited Botswana, 46% from South Africa and 37% from Zimbabwe. Botswana's beautiful and well-stocked game reserves are its principal tourist attraction, with both hunting and photographic safaris available. The Okavango Delta region is a maze of waterways, islands, and lakes during the rainy season. It includes the Moremi Game Reserve. Nearby is Chobe National Park.

The Kalahari Desert is another attraction, as are the country's tapestry weavers, potters, and rugmakers. The Tsodilo Hills have cave paintings by the ancestors of the Basarwa (Bushmen), the earliest known inhabitants of Botswana. The government's "National Conservation Strategy and Tourism Policy" is intended to promote tourism while protecting wildlife areas.

34 FAMOUS BOTSWANANS

Khama III (1837–1923), chief of the Bamangwato and a Christian convert, reigned for 48 years. His grandson, Sir Seretse Khama (1921–80), was Botswana's first president. Quett Ketumile Joni Masire (b.1925) succeeded him in 1980.

35 BIBLIOGRAPHY

Lanting, Frans. "A Gathering of Waters and Wildlife." *National Geographic,* December 1990, 5–37.
Lauré. J. *Botswana.* Chicago: Children's Press, 1993.
Morton, Fred. *Historical Dictionary of Botswana.* Metuchen, N.J.: Scarecrow Press, 1989.
Stedman, Stephen John (ed). *Botswana: the Political Economy of Democratic Development.* Boulder, Colo.: L. Rienner Publishers, 1993.
Wiseman, John A. *Botswana.* Oxford, Eng.; Santa Barbara, Calif.: Clio Press, 1992.

BRAZIL

Federative Republic of Brazil
República Federativa do Brasil

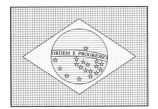

CAPITAL: Brasília.

FLAG: The national flag consists of a green field upon which is a large yellow diamond twice as wide as it is high. Centered within the diamond is a blue globe showing constellations of the southern skies dominated by the Southern Cross. Encircling the globe is a white banner bearing the words *Ordem e Progresso*.

ANTHEM: *Hino Nacional Brasileiro,* beginning "Ouviram do Ipiranga" ("Listen to the cry of Ipiranga").

MONETARY UNIT: On 3 March 1990, the cruzeiro (CR$), a paper currency of 100 centavos, replaced the cruzado (CZ$) at the rate of CR$1:CZ$1,000 (the cruzado had replaced an older cruzeiro at the same rate in 1986). There are currently no coins in circulation, with notes of 50, 100, 200, 500, 1,000, 5,000, 10,000, 50,000, 100,000, and 500,000 cruzeiros. CR$1 = US$0.0011 (or US$1 = CR$913.345).

WEIGHTS AND MEASURES: The metric system is the legal standard, but some local units are also used.

HOLIDAYS: New Year's Day, 1 January; Tiradentes, 21 April; Labor Day, 1 May; Independence Day, 7 September; Our Lady of Aparecida (Patroness of Brazil), 12 October; All Souls' Day, 2 November; Proclamation of the Republic, 15 November; Christmas, 25 December. Movable holidays include the pre-Lenten carnival, usually in February, Good Friday, and Corpus Christi.

TIME: At noon GMT, the time in Fernando de Noronha is 10 AM; Rio de Janeiro, 9 AM; Manaus, 8 AM; Rio Branco, 7 AM.

1 LOCATION AND SIZE

Situated in east-central South America, Brazil is the largest country in Latin America and the fourth-largest in the world in continuous area, ranking after Russia, Canada, and China (the US is larger with Alaska, Hawaii, and the dependencies included). Occupying nearly half of the South American continent, it covers an area of 8,511,965 square kilometers (3,286,488 square miles). Sharing borders with all continental South American countries except Ecuador and Chile, Brazil has a total boundary length of 22,182 kilometers (13,783 miles).

Brazil's capital city, Brasília, is located in the southeastern part of the country.

2 TOPOGRAPHY

The northern part of Brazil is dominated by the basin of the Amazon River and its many tributaries, which occupies two-fifths of the country. The Amazon River is, at 6,280 kilometers (3,900 miles), the world's second-longest river after the Nile, although the Amazon ranks first in the volume of water carried. The Amazon lowlands east of the Andes mountains make up the world's largest tropical rainforest.

In the northernmost part of the Amazon Basin lie a series of mountain ranges, known as the Guiana Highlands, where Brazil's highest mountain, Pico da Neblina (3,014 meters/9,888 feet), is located. South of the Amazon Basin is a large plateau called the Brazilian Highlands. The highlands meet the Atlantic Ocean in a steep, wall-like slope, the Great Escarpment.

3 CLIMATE

Brazil is a tropical country but extends well into the temperate zone. The Amazon Basin has a typically hot, tropical climate, with annual rainfall exceeding 250 centimeters (100 inches) in some areas. The Brazilian Highlands, which include roughly half of the total area, are subtropical. The narrow coastal lowland area ranges from tropical in the north to temperate in the south. The cool upland plains of the south have a temperate climate and an occasional snowfall.

Rainfall is heavy in the lowlands and in the upper Amazon Basin, along the northern coast, at certain points on the east coast, and in the southern interior, while there are periodic droughts in the northeast. The average high temperature in Rio de Janeiro in February is 29°C (84°F). The average low in July is 17°C (63°F).

4 PLANTS AND ANIMALS

About one-fourth of the world's known plant species are found in Brazil. The Amazon Basin, the world's largest tropical rainforest, includes tall Brazil nut trees, brazilwood, myriad palms, kapok-bearing ceiba trees enlaced with vines and creepers, rosewood, orchids, and water lilies, and is the home of the wild rubber tree.

The characteristic flora of the northeast interior is the carnauba wax-yielding palm and the thorn scrub. Along the humid coast are many mango, cajú, guava, coconut, and jack-fruit trees, as well as large sugar and cotton plantations. In the southern states are exotic flowers, such as papagaias; flowering trees, such as the quaresma, which blossoms during Lent; and the popular ipê tree with its yellow petals. The pampas of Rio Grande do Sul are extensive grasslands.

The Amazon rainforest is host to a great variety of tropical animals, including hundreds of types of macaws, toucans, parrots, and other brightly colored birds; brilliant butterflies; many species of small monkeys; anacondas, boas, and other large tropical snakes; crocodiles and alligators; and such distinctive animals as the Brazilian "tiger" (onca), armadillo, sloth, and tapir. The rivers in that region abound with turtles and exotic tropical fish, and the infamous "cannibal fish" (piranha) is common. In all, more than 2,000 fish species have been identified.

5 ENVIRONMENT

As of 1986, it was estimated that the forests of the Amazon were being cleared for grazing, timber, human habitation, and other commercial purposes at a rate of up to 20 million hectares (50 million acres) a

BRAZIL

BRAZIL

| 0 | 200 | 400 | 600 Miles |
| 0 | 200 | 400 | 600 Kilometers |

VENEZUELA

COLOMBIA

GUYANA

GUIANA HIGHLANDS

SURINAME FRENCH GUIANA

Negro

Japurá

A M A Z O N

Branco

Jari

Macapá

Ilha Caviana
Ilha Mexiana

Ilha Marajó

Belém

São Luís

ATLANTIC
OCEAN

Javari

Juruá

S E L V A S

Manaus

Santarém

Amazon

Represa de Tucuruí

Fortaleza

B A S I N

Tapajós

Imperatriz

Teresina

Natal

Purus

Madeira

Jacare-Acanga

Parnaíba

João Pessoa

Recife

Rio Branco

Pôrto Velho

Vila Murtinho

Cachimbo

Xingu

Araguaia

Represa de Sobradinho

Juàzeiro

Maceió

Iberia

Santa Rosa

Guaporé

Tocantins

Aracaju

PERU

Juruena

B R A Z I L I A N

Ibotirama

São Francisco

Salvador

Ilhéus

Mato Grosso

Cuiabá

Pôrto Seguro

Ponta de Corumbau
Ponta de Baleia

BOLIVIA

Plateau

Anápolis

⍟ **Brasília**

Goiânia

HIGHLANDS

Taquari

Purto Suárez

Corumbá

Paranaíba

Uberlândia

Grande

Represa de Furnas

Vitória

Belo Horizonte

Campo Grande

Paraná

Tietê

Ribeirão Prêto

▲ *Pico da Bandeira 9,482 ft./2890 m.*

Campos

Campinas

Volta Redonda

Londrina

Bauru

São Paulo

Rio de Janeiro

Sorocaba

Santos

CHILE

PARAGUAY

Itaipú Resevoir

IGUAZÚ FALLS

Barracão

Curitiba

Florianópolis

PACIFIC OCEAN

Uruguay

Erexim

Tubarão

ARGENTINA

Santana do Livramento

Porto Alegre

Pelotas

ATLANTIC
OCEAN

URUGUAY

N
W   E
S

Brazil

LOCATION: 5°16′19″N to 33°45′9″S; 34°45′54″ to 73°59′32″W. **BOUNDARY LENGTHS:** Venezuela, 1,495 kilometers (929 miles); Guyana, 1,606 kilometers (998 miles); Suriname, 593 kilometers (368 miles); French Guiana, 655 kilometers (407 miles); Atlantic coastline, 7,408 kilometers (4,603 miles); Uruguay, 1,003 kilometers (623 miles); Argentina, 1,263 kilometers (785 miles); Paraguay, 1,339 kilometers (832 miles); Bolivia, 3,126 kilometers (1,942 miles); Peru, 2,995 kilometers (1,861 miles); Colombia, 1,644 kilometers (1,022 miles). **TERRITORIAL SEA LIMIT:** 12 miles.

year. In 1994, this figure had decreased, although no exact figures were available.

Other environmental problems in Brazil include water pollution from mercury, toxic industrial wastes, untreated waste, and the threat to agricultural soil by erosion from the clearing of the forests.

The damage to the rainforest environment is reflected in the number of extinct and endangered species. Between 1900 and 1950, 60 species of birds and mammals became extinct. Currently, 40 species of birds and 318 plant species are endangered.

Among endangered amphibians and reptiles were the Anegada ground iguana, the American crocodile, and three species of turtle. Endangered bird species included the tundra peregrine falcon, red-tailed parrot, Lear's macaw, and cherry-throated tanager.

6 POPULATION

Brazil is the most populous country in Latin America and the fifth most populous in the world. According to the 1991 census, the total population was 146,917,459. A population of 172,777,000 was projected by the UN for the year 2000. Population density in 1991 was 18 per square kilometer (45 per square mile). Major cities and their 1991 populations are as follows: São Paulo, 9,626,894; Rio de Janeiro, 5,473,909; and the capital, Brasília, 1,598,415.

7 MIGRATION

Between 1821 and 1945, approximately 5.2 million European immigrants entered Brazil, most of them settling in the south. Brazil has the largest Japanese colony in the world, numbering more than one million. In recent years, because of the increasing prosperity of Europe and Japan, there has been less desire to migrate to underdeveloped rural Brazil or its inflation-plagued industrial cities. Also, immigration is controlled by laws limiting the annual entry of persons of any national group to 2% of the total number of that nationality that had entered in the preceding 50 years.

8 ETHNIC GROUPS

The original inhabitants were Indians, chiefly of Tupi-Guaraní stock. The Portuguese settlers had few taboos against race mixture, and centuries of large-scale intermarriage have produced a tolerant and distinctly Brazilian culture.

Within the Brazilian nationality are blended the various aboriginal Indian cultures; the Portuguese heritage, with its diverse strains; the traditions of millions of persons of African descent; and European elements resulting from sizable immigration since 1888 from Italy, Spain, Germany, and Poland. The arrival of Japanese and some Arabs during the 20th century has contributed to the complex Brazilian melting pot.

According to the 1991 census, 55% of Brazil's population was white, 39% mixed, and 5% black. The remaining 1% consisted of Japanese, Indians, and other groups. The Indian population was estimated at 250,000 in 1993.

9 LANGUAGES

The language of Brazil is Portuguese, which is spoken by practically all inhabitants except some isolated Indian groups. Substantial variations in pronunciation and word meaning, however, distinguish it from the language as it is spoken in Portugal. German, Italian, and Japanese are also spoken in immigrant communities.

10 RELIGIONS

Brazil is the largest Catholic nation in the world, with an estimated 88% of the population professing the Roman Catholic faith. Protestants constituted upwards of 6% of the population. Two other large religious groups are the Spiritists (about 2%), followers of the writings of Allan Kardec; and the Afro-American Spiritists (about 2%), whose rites evolved from the spirit worship of black Africans.

Brazil's Japanese and Okinawan population includes some 395,000 Buddhists, but the younger generation has tended to embrace Christianity. There are approximately 194,000 Orthodox Christians and, in 1990, some 100,000 Jews.

11 TRANSPORTATION

Roads are the primary carriers of freight and passenger traffic. Brazil's road system totaled 1,448,000 kilometers (899,787 miles) in 1991. Motor vehicles registered as of 1992 included 12,974,991 passenger cars, and 1,371,127 commercial vehicles. Brazil's railway system has been declining since 1945, when emphasis shifted to highway construction. The total extension of railway track was 28,828 kilometers (17,914 miles) in 1991.

Photo credit: Susan D. Rock.

These boats are docked at an Amazon River town.

Coastal shipping links widely separated parts of the country. Of the 36 deep-water ports, Santos and Rio de Janeiro are the most important, followed by Paranaguá, Recife, Vitória, Tubarão, Maceió, and Ilhéus. There are 50,000 kilometers (31,070 miles) of navigable inland waterways.

Air transportation is highly developed. In 1992, Brazilian airlines performed more than 28,000 million passenger-kilometers (17,600 million passenger-miles) of service. Of the 48 principal airports, 21 are international. Of these, Rio de Janeiro's Galeão international airport and Guarulhos International Airport at São Paulo are by far the most active.

[12] HISTORY

The original inhabitants of Brazil were hunter-gatherers, except in the lower Amazon, where agriculture developed. After the European discovery of the New World, Spain and Portugal became immediate rivals for the vast new lands. On Easter Sunday in 1500, the Portuguese admiral Pedro Álvares Cabral landed in the present-day state of Bahia in Brazil and formally claimed the land for the Portuguese crown.

Cabral's ship returned to Portugal with a cargo of red dyewood, and from the name of the wood, pau-brasil, the new land acquired the name Brazil. In 1532, the first Portuguese colonists arrived.

Other Europeans began to move in on the Portuguese colony. In 1555, the French established a settlement in the Bay of Rio de Janeiro. In 1624, the Dutch attacked Bahia and began to extend their territory throughout northeastern Brazil. Under the Dutch, who remained until being driven out in 1654, the area thrived economically. The sugar plantations of northeastern Brazil became the world's major source of sugar.

The discovery of gold in 1693 and diamonds in about 1720 opened up new lands for colonization in the colony's interior. From their coastal base in São Paulo, Brazilian pioneers pushed inland in search of mineral riches and Indian slaves.

By the early 18th century, Portugal's oppressive policies toward the colonists brought about a strong movement for independence, which Pedro, the Portuguese prince regent, supported. He proclaimed Brazil's independence on 7 September 1822, and later that year was crowned Emperor Pedro I. In 1831, a military revolt forced him to abdicate, and the throne passed to his five year-old son, Pedro.

In 1840, the new Emperor was crowned. Under Pedro II, Brazil enjoyed half a century of peaceful progress. New frontiers were opened, many immigrants arrived from Europe, railroads were built, and the gathering of rubber in the Amazon Basin led to the growth of cities. The abolition of slavery in 1888 brought about an economic crisis that disrupted the Brazilian Empire.

In 1889, a bloodless revolution deposed Pedro II and established the Republic of the United States of Brazil. At first, the republic was ruled by military regimes, but by 1894 a constitutional civilian government was in place. By the end of the 19th century, coffee had become the nation's principal source of wealth.

Brazil soon entered a period of economic and political turmoil, aggravated by regional and military rivalries. By 1930, a military takeover with widespread civilian support placed into power Getúlio Vargas. Vargas' government sought reforms for Brazil's middle and lower classes, but discouraged dissent.

Vargas was ousted by the military in 1946 but returned to the presidency in 1950. He was succeeded from 1955 to 1961 by Juscelino Kubitschek de Oliveira, whose most ambitious project was building a new federal capital, Brasília, in the highlands of central Brazil.

Ten years of military government, starting in 1964, brought Brazil rapid economic expansion, but there was a dramatic reversal during the oil crisis of 1973–74. During the late 1970s, continuing economic difficulties led to labor unrest and numerous strikes. In November 1982, Brazil had its first democratic elections since 1964. Opposition parties won the governorships of 10 heavily populated states and a majority in the lower house of Congress.

In January 1985, the electoral college chose Tancredo Neves as Brazil's first civilian president in a generation. When Neves fell gravely ill and died just before his inauguration, Vice-President José Sarney was allowed to take office as president. A new constitution, passed in 1988, was followed by elections a year later. Brazil's first direct presidential elections in 29 years resulted in the victory of Fernando Collor de Mello.

Collor took office in March 1990, and launched a major economic reform program. However, Collor was forced to resign in December 1992 after massive corruption was revealed inside his administration. Itamar Franco took over, promising to continue Collor's programs.

13 GOVERNMENT

The Federative Republic of Brazil is a constitutional republic composed of 26 states and a Federal District, which surrounds the federal capital, Brasília. The constitu-

tion of October 1988 establishes a strong presidential system.

The president is the head of the armed forces and is in charge of the executive branch, assisted in that task by a cabinet of ministers. He also appoints justices to the Supreme Federal Tribunal, the highest court in Brazil. The Congress consists of the 81-member Senate and the 503-member Chamber of Deputies.

14 POLITICAL PARTIES

In 1985, the Liberal Front Party (PFL) and the Party of the Brazilian Democratic Movement (Partido de Movimento Democrático Brasileiro—PMDB) formed the National Alliance, a coalition that won the 1985 elections. Although the PFL lost the 1989 presidential elections, it soon allied with President Collor.

Other parties include the Democratic Workers' Party (Partido Democrático Trabalhista—PDT), the Workers' Party (Partido dos Trabalhadores—PT), the Brazilian Workers' Party (Partido Trabalhista Brasileiro—PTB), and two communist parties.

15 JUDICIAL SYSTEM

The Supreme Federal Court is composed of 11 justices. It has final jurisdiction, especially in cases involving the constitution and the acts of state and local authorities. The Federal Appeals Court deals with cases involving the federal government. Immediately below it are federal courts located in the state capitals and in the Federal District, as well as military and

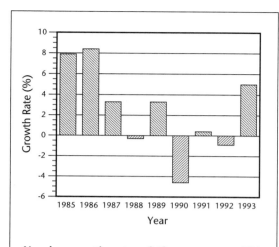

Yearly growth rate of the economy. This economic indicator tells by what percent the economy has increased or decreased when compared with the previous year.

labor courts. Each state and municipality has its own judicial system.

16 ARMED FORCES

The Brazilian armed forces had a total strength of 296,700 (128,500 draftees) in 1993. Military service for a minimum of one year is compulsory. Draftees are inducted at the age of 18.

The army, with about 60 brigades, had 196,000 personnel in 1993; the navy, 50,000 (including 15,000 marines and 700 naval airmen); air force personnel totaled 50,700, with 307 combat aircraft. In 1992, Brazil spent $2.12 billion on defense.

17 ECONOMY

The history of the Brazilian economy before World War II is characterized by six principal cycles, each centered on one particular commodity: brazilwood, livestock, sugar, gold, rubber, and, most recently, coffee. At the height of each cycle, Brazil led the world in production of that commodity. Even during the postwar era, variations in price and market conditions for coffee have largely determined the degree of national prosperity.

Attempts to diversify the economy through rapid industrialization have made Brazil one of the two leading industrial nations of South America, but uncontrolled inflation—close to 500% in 1986—has offset many of the economic advances.

The Brazilian economy was hit by a deep recession and record inflation in 1990. In March 1990, upon assuming office, President Collor announced sweeping economic reforms designed to stop inflation and integrate Brazil into the developed world economy. By mid-1990, the monthly inflation rate was around 10%, but by the end of the year it was in the 20% range.

After a second government economic program in 1991 failed to reduce inflation, high interest rates, combined with worsening inflation and political uncertainty, produced another recession in 1992.

18 INCOME

In 1992, Brazil's gross national product (GNP) was US$425,412 million at current prices, or US$2,930 per person. For the period 1985–92, the average inflation rate was 731.3%, resulting in a real growth rate in gross national product of 0.7% per person.

19 INDUSTRY

Major industries include iron and steel, automobiles, petroleum processing, chemicals, and cement. The Brazilian automotive industry is the major producer of vehicles in Latin America and the sixth-largest producer in the world.

Petroleum products include diesel oils, gasoline, and fuel oil. Brazil's developing petrochemical industry emphasizes the production of synthetic rubber. Other chemical products include distilled alcohol used for the nation's burgeoning alcohol-fuel fleet.

Brazil's electrical equipment industry manufactures television sets, transistor radios, refrigerators, air conditioners, and many other appliances. Brazil has the largest textile industry in South America.

20 LABOR

A 1990 estimate reported the economically active population of Brazil at 64,467,981. In 1990, 27% worked in agriculture, 42% in services, and 27% in industry. The economically active female population increased from about 18% of the labor force in 1960 to over 35% by 1990.

Except for young people working within the apprenticeship system, the minimum working age is 14. But in spite of the law, it is believed that millions of children in Brazil may be forced into working at unpleasant jobs with long hours and low pay. The Brazilian shoemaking indus-

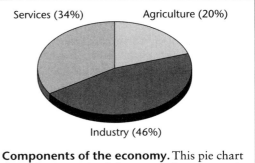

Components of the economy. This pie chart shows how much of the country's economy is devoted to agriculture (includes forestry, hunting, and fishing), industry, or services.

try is especially dependent on child labor. A report prepared in 1993 indicated that 40% of the shoe workers were children under 14, many of whom are exposed to hazardous and addictive fumes from the glue used in making shoes.

Steps are being taken to try to solve the problem of child labor, and to remove children from Brazil's work force.

21 AGRICULTURE

In 1992, the total crop area comprised 61.3 million hectares (152 million acres), and the number of farms was about 5 million. Except for grain (particularly wheat), of which some 2.8 million tons had to be imported in 1990, Brazil can supply almost all its own food. In 1990, Brazil ranked fifth in the export of cocoa beans at 118,126 tons. Almost 15% of all cocoa bean production came from Brazil in 1992. That same year, nearly 22% of the world's coffee came from Brazil.

Coffee, until 1974 Brazil's leading export, has been declining in importance since the early 1960s, while soybeans, sugarcane, cotton, wheat, and citrus fruits have shown dramatic increases. Sugarcane production, in which Brazil ranked first in the world in 1992, is used not only for refined sugar but also as a source of alcohol for fuel. Agricultural production in 1992 (in millions of tons) was: sugarcane, 270.6; oranges, 19.6; cassava, 22.6; soybeans, 19.1; rice, 9.9; coffee, 1.3; wheat, 2.8; cotton, 0.62; and cashews, 0.10.

22 DOMESTICATED ANIMALS

Brazil is a leading livestock-producing country, and 185,500,000 hectares (458,370,000 acres—more than one-fifth of the total national area) were devoted to open pasture in 1991. In 1992, there were an estimated 153 million head of cattle; 33 million hogs; and 19.5 million sheep. Of the other domestic animals raised commercially in 1992, there were some 12 million goats, 6.2 million horses, and 570 million chickens.

Meat production was estimated at 7.18 million tons in 1992, including 3 million tons of beef and veal. Estimated output of dairy products in 1992 included 15.5 million tons of fresh cow's milk and 1,455,000 tons of eggs. In 1992, livestock production expanded by 5.3%.

23 FISHING

Although Brazil has a seacoast of some 7,400 kilometers (4,600 miles) and excellent fishing grounds off the South Atlantic coast, the nation has never fully utilized its commercial potential. Swordfish is caught in large quantities off the coast of Natal and João Pessoa, and shrimp is caught and dried along the coasts of São Luis, Fortaleza, and Salvador. The annual fish catch is so modest that there has traditionally been a scarcity during Holy Week, about the only time when Brazilians eat much fish. The total catch in 1991 was 800,000 tons. Small quantities of lobster are exported.

24 FORESTRY

Nearly three-fifths of South America's forests and woodlands are in Brazil. Brazil's forests and woodlands cover 58% of the country's total area and are among the richest in the world, yielding timber, oil-bearing fruits, gums, resins, waxes, essential oils, cellulose, fibers, nuts, maté, and other products.

However, only a limited percentage of forestland is being exploited, in part because of a lack of adequate transportation. Brazil is one of the leading producers of tropical hardwood products. The hardwood trees of the Amazon rainforest are of excellent quality, but because of a thriving domestic furniture industry, they are used mainly locally.

Production of roundwood in 1991 was estimated at 264.6 million cubic meters. Sawn wood production was an estimated 17.1 million cubic meters. Brazil's production of rubber in 1991 was 304,082 tons. The natural rubber industry, once a world leader, was dealt a strong blow by the development of cheaper synthetics. Production of paper and woodpulp has expanded considerably since 1975. Exports of paper intensified between 1981

Photo credit: Susan D. Rock.

A family stands outside their home on the bank of the Amazon River, at Breves Narrows.

and 1991, from 337,000 tons to 840,000 tons.

25 MINING

Although Brazil has a vast potential of mineral wealth, little of it has been developed. Still, Brazil is the world leader in the production of bauxite, columbium, gemstones, gold, iron ore, kaolin, manganese, tantalum, and tin. Within Latin America, Brazil is a major producer of aluminum, cement, and ferroalloys.

Brazil's iron ore reserves total 19.2 billion tons. Iron ore production for 1991 increased to 150 million tons, and output of manganese was 2.5 million tons. Coal

production for that year was estimated at 7.2 million tons. There are important deposits of beryllium, chrome, graphite, magnesite, mica, quartz crystal, thorium, titanium, and zirconium. Major deposits of high-quality bauxite have been discovered in the Amazon region. Bauxite output has risen rapidly, from 6.5 million tons in 1987 to 10.3 million tons in 1991.

In 1991, production of diamonds amounted to 1,500 carats (6th in the world). Gold deposits found at Serra Pelada in 1980 raised gold production to 103,000 kg tons by 1989, making Brazil the world's sixth-largest producer; production averaged 90,380 kg during 1987–91, for a relative ranking of 7th in the world.

26 FOREIGN TRADE

The opening of the Brazilian market to foreign trade by former President Fernando Collor de Mello remains the cornerstone of Brazil's economic and trade policies. Over the last three years, most of Brazil's non-tariff barriers to trade, such as import limits, were eliminated or drastically reduced. Import duties were reduced from an average of about 50% in the late-1980s to an average of 14.2%.

Although the recessions of recent years have reduced the purchasing power of Brazilians by about 50% among the working and lower middle classes, the Brazilian market remains enormously attractive to US businesses.

In 1993, Brazil's exports totaled US$40 billion, and its imports totaled US$27 billion.

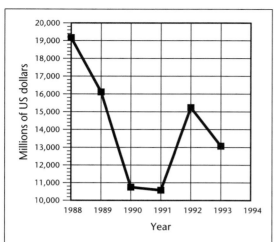

Yearly balance of trade measured in millions of US dollars. The balance of trade is the difference between what a country sells to other countries (its exports) and what it buys (its imports). If a country imports more than it exports, it has a negative balance of trade (a trade deficit). If exports exceed imports, there is a positive balance of trade (a trade surplus).

27 ENERGY AND POWER

Brazil's hydroelectric potential is thought to be among the world's largest. Great strides are being taken to increase production to keep pace with Brazil's expanding industries. In 1991, total installed capacity increased to 54.1 million kilowatts. Of that total, hydroelectricity accounted for 86%; conventional thermal plants for 13%; and nuclear plants for 1%.

Brazil has sharply scaled back its ambitious nuclear power program since 1983. Nuclear generation of electricity only accounted for about 1% of production in 1991. Estimates of uranium reserves were put at 163,000 tons in 1991, the fifth largest in the world.

Crude oil production in 1992 totaled 33 million tons, or 685,000 barrels per day. Natural gas production was 6.2 billion cubic meters in 1991.

28 SOCIAL DEVELOPMENT

In 1977, the National System of Social Security and Welfare was established. Benefits include modest insurance against accidents; old age, invalids', and survivors' pensions; funeral insurance; and medical, dental, and hospital coverage. Maternity benefits were introduced under the new constitution in 1988.

29 HEALTH

In 1993, Brazil's national health care system came to an end, chiefly due to widespread fraud by hospitals, physicians, and state and municipal agencies. The new Brazilian Minister of Health planned to introduce a new system.

The large cities have competent physicians, generally with advanced training abroad, but there is a shortage of doctors, hospitals, and nurses in most towns in the interior.

In 1990, there were 56 cases of tuberculosis per 100,000 inhabitants. The infant mortality rate is high, but it has declined over the last 10 years. The average life expectancy in is 67 years.

30 HOUSING

Despite major urban developments, both the housing supply and living conditions in Brazil remain inadequate. Large,

Selected Social Indicators

These statistics are estimates for the period 1988 to 1993. For comparison purposes, data for the United States and averages for low-income countries and high-income countries are also given.

Indicator	Brazil	Low-income countries	High-income countries	United States
Per capita gross national product†	**$2,930**	$380	$23,680	$24,740
Population growth rate	**1.8%**	1.9%	0.6%	1.0%
Population growth rate in urban areas	**0%**	3.9%	0.8%	1.3%
Population per square kilometer of land	**18**	78	25	26
Life expectancy in years	**67**	62	77	76
Number of people per physician	**681**	>3,300	453	419
Number of pupils per teacher (primary school)	**23**	39	<18	20
Illiteracy rate (15 years and older)	**18.9%**	41%	<5%	<3%
Energy consumed per capita (kg of oil equivalent)	**666**	364	5,203	7,918

† The gross national product (GNP) is the total dollar value of all goods and services produced by a country in a year. The per capita GNP is calculated by dividing a country's GNP by its population. The World Bank defines low-income countries as those with a per capita GNP of $695 or less. High-income countries have a per capita GNP of $8,626 or more. Less than 14% of the world's 5.5 billion people live in high-income countries, while almost 60% live in low-income countries.

> = greater than   < = less than

Sources: World Bank, *Social Indicators of Development 1995,* Baltimore: Johns Hopkins University Press, 1995. Central Intelligence Agency, *World Fact Book,* Washington, D.C.: Government Printing Office, 1994.

sprawling slums are widespread in the major cities, while most rural dwellers live without conveniences such as piped water and electricity. In 1992, there were 32,705,000 residences.

31 EDUCATION

Public education is free at all levels and non-profit private schools also receive public funding. In 1990, there were 37.6 million students: 3.9 million in preschool; 28.2 million at the elementary level; 3.8 million at the secondary level; and 1.7 million at the university level.

In 1990 there were 93 universities, including the Federal University of Rio de Janeiro and the universities of Minas Gerais, São Paulo, Rio Grande do Sul, Bahia, and Brasília. The federal government maintains at least one federal university in each state.

Although millions of Brazilians have received literacy training, adult illiteracy in 1990 was still 18.9% (males: 17.5% and females: 20.2%).

32 MEDIA

In 1992, Brazil had 1,223 AM radio stations and 112 commercial television stations. Some 58,500,000 radios and 31,400,000 television sets were in use in 1991. In that year, there were 14,059,524 telephones in use.

Brazil's leading dailies, with their estimated circulations in 1986 were *O Globo* (539,000); *Folha de São Paulo* (426,000); *O Dia* (425,000); *O Estado de São Paulo* (424,000); and *Jornal do Brasil* (216,000).

33 TOURISM AND RECREATION

Rio de Janeiro is one of the leading tourist destinations in South America. Notable sights around Rio de Janeiro include Sugar Loaf Mountain, with its cable car; the Corcovado, with its statue of Christ the Redeemer; Copacabana Beach, with its mosaic sidewalks; and the Botanical Gardens.

Brazil is also famous for its colorful celebrations of Carnival, especially in Rio de Janeiro. Eco-tourism attracts growing numbers of visitors to the world's largest rainforest in the North, the Iguacu Falls in the South, and the Mato Grosso wetlands in the Central West region.

A total of 1,352,000 tourists visited Brazil in 1991; 736,000 from South America and 163,000 from the US. Estimated tourism revenues were us$1.5 billion. As of 1990, there were 137,000 hotel rooms.

Soccer is by far the most popular sport. Brazil hosted the World Cup competition in 1950, and Brazilian teams won the championship in 1958, 1962, 1970, and 1994. Other favorite recreations include water sports, basketball, tennis, and boxing.

34 FAMOUS BRAZILIANS

The father of Brazilian independence was José Bonifacio de Andrada e Silva (1763–1838), a geologist, writer, and statesman. Pedro I (Antonio Pedro de Alcántara Bourbon, 1798–1834), of the Portuguese royal house of Bragança, declared Brazil independent and had himself crowned emperor in 1822. His Brazilian-born son, Pedro II (Pedro de Alcántara, 1825–91), emperor from 1840 to 1889, won respect as a diplomat, statesman, and patron of the arts and sciences. Brazilian aviation pioneer Alberto Santos Dumont (1873–1932) is called the father of flight for his invention of a gasoline-powered airship in 1901.

The painter and muralist Cândido Portinari (1903–62) is considered the greatest artist Brazil has produced. The greatest figure in Brazilian music is the composer and educator Heitor Villa-Lobos (1887–1959), who wrote in many styles and forms. One of the best-known Brazilians is soccer star Edson Arantes do Nascimento (b.1940), better known as Pelé.

35 BIBLIOGRAPHY

Burns, E. Bradford. *A History of Brazil.* 3rd ed. New York: Columbia University Press, 1993.
Ellis, William S. "Rondùnia: Brazil's Imperiled Rain Forest." *National Geographic,* December 1988, 772–799.
Haverstock, Nathan A. *Brazil in Pictures.* Minneapolis: Lerner, 1987.
McIntyre, Loren. "Urueu-Wau-Wau Indians: Last Days of Eden." *National Geographic,* December 1988, 800–817.
Mittermeier, Russell A. "Brazil's Monkeys in Peril." *National Geographic,* March 1987, 387–396.
Van Dyk, Jere. "The Amazon." *National Geographic,* February 1995, 2–39.
Vesilind, Priit J. "Brazil: The Promise and Pain." *National Geographic,* March 1987, 348–386.

BRUNEI DARUSSALAM

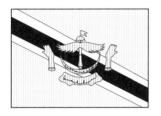

Nation of Brunei, Abode of Peace
Negara Brunei Darussalam

CAPITAL: Bandar Seri Begawan.

FLAG: On a yellow field extend three diagonal stripes of white and black, with the state emblem centered in red.

ANTHEM: National Anthem, beginning *Ya Allah lanjutkan usia* ("God bless His Highness with a long life").

MONETARY UNIT: The Brunei dollar (B$, or ringgit) of 100 cents is valued at par with, and is interchangeable with, the Singapore dollar. There are coins of 1, 5, 10, 20, and 50 cents, and notes of 1, 5, 10, 50, 100, 500, 1,000, and 10,000 Brunei dollars. B$1 = US$0.4941; (or US$1 = B$2.024).

WEIGHTS AND MEASURES: Imperial weights and measures are in common use, as are certain local units, but a change to the metric system is slowly proceeding.

HOLIDAYS: New Year's Day, 1 January; National Day, 23 February; Anniversary of the Royal Brunei Armed Forces, 31 May; Sultan's Birthday, 15 July. Movable holidays include the Chinese New Year and various Muslim holy days.

TIME: 8 PM = noon GMT.

1 LOCATION AND SIZE

Brunei occupies 5,770 square kilometers (2,228 square miles) on the northwestern coast of the island of Borneo. Comparatively, Brunei is slightly larger than the state of Delaware. It comprises two small areas separated by the Limbang River Valley, part of the Malaysian State of Sarawak. Brunei's total boundary length is 542 kilometers (337 miles). Brunei's capital city, Bandar Seri Begawan, is located in the northern part of the country.

2 TOPOGRAPHY

The land generally consists of tropical rainforest, with a narrow coastal strip in the western section. The eastern section is more hilly, rising to 1,850 meters (6,070 feet) at Mt. Pagon in the extreme south.

3 CLIMATE

The country has a tropical climate, with temperatures ranging from 23° to 32°C (73°–89°F). Humidity is high—about 80% all year round—and annual rainfall varies from about 275 centimeters (110 inches) along the coast to more than 500 centimeters (200 inches) in the interior.

4 PLANTS AND ANIMALS

The country is largely covered by mangrove and peat swamp, heath, and upland vegetation. The rainforest and swampland are inhabited by many small mammals, tropical birds, reptiles, and amphibians.

5 ENVIRONMENT

The forests are strictly protected by the government. Endangered species in 1987 included the estuarine crocodile.

6 POPULATION

The estimated population in 1991 was 260,482, with a density of 46 persons per square kilometer (117 per square mile). As of 1991, 46,229 Bruneians lived in the capital, Bandar Seri Begawan (formerly Brunei Town).

7 MIGRATION

There is little emigration except among the Chinese minority. The government is battling much illegal immigration, especially from Indonesia and Sarawak.

8 ETHNIC GROUPS

Malays formed 67% of the population in 1991. Minorities included an estimated 40,621 (16%) Chinese; 15,665 (6%) inhabitants of native descent—mainly Dusans, Kedayans, and Maruts; and 29,871 (11%) others.

9 LANGUAGES

Malay and English are the official languages. The principal Chinese dialect is Hokkien. Many native dialects are spoken as well.

Photo credit: Susan D. Rock.

Omar Ali Saifuddin Mosque.

10 RELIGIONS

Islam is the official religion. According to unofficial estimates, 63% of the population is Muslim. Another 14% is Buddhist, and 9% is Christian. The remaining 14% includes followers of other Chinese religions and of tribal religions.

11 TRANSPORTATION

There are only about 1,090 kilometers (677 miles) of main roads. In 1991, Brunei had 115,495 passenger cars and 13,019 commercial vehicles registered. A 13-kilometer (8-mile) railway is operated by the

Brunei Shell Petroleum Co. Two seaports, at Muara and Kuala Belait, offer direct shipping services to other Asian ports. The national carrier, Royal Brunei Airlines, operates regular flights to a number of Asian cities. Brunei International Airport is at Barakas, just outside the capital.

12 HISTORY

From the fourteenth to the sixteenth centuries, Brunei was the center of a powerful native sultanate (kingdom). By the nineteenth century, much of this empire had been reduced by war, piracy, and the colonial expansion of European nations. In 1888, Brunei became a British protectorate. By a 1959 agreement, Brunei was recognized as fully self-governing, with Britain retaining responsibility for defense and foreign affairs. Brunei's first elections in 1962 were won by militant nationalists who revolted against the sultan. Since then, the government has ruled by decree under a national state of emergency. In 1967, Sultan Omar abdicated in favor of his son, Muda Hassanal Bolkiah.

During the 1970s, Brunei's oil wealth made it the richest state in Southeast Asia. On 1 January 1984, the country attained full independence and membership in the British Commonwealth. During that year, Brunei joined both the Association of South-East Asian Nations (ASEAN) and the United Nations. In 1985, the Brunei National Democratic Party (BNDP) was formed, but government restricted its operation and, in 1988, arrested its top two leaders. Since that year, the state has emphasized a religious ideology called *Melayu Islam Beraja* (MIB). In 1991, the

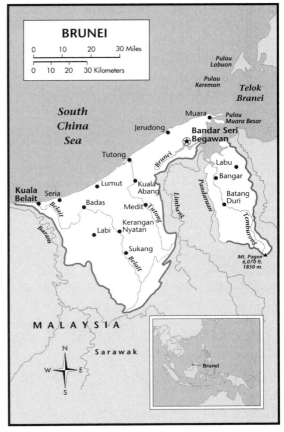

LOCATION: 4°2′ to 5°3′N; 114° to 115°22′E. **BOUNDARY LENGTHS:** Malaysia, 418 kilometers (260 miles); South China Sea and Brunei Bay coastlines, 161 kilometers (100 miles). **TERRITORIAL SEA LIMIT:** 12 miles.

import of alcohol and the public celebration of Christmas were banned.

His Majesty Sultan Haji Hassanal Bolkiah Mu'izzaddin Waddaulah celebrated 25 years on the throne in October 1992. As of 1993, *Fortune* magazine's estimate of the Sultan's personal wealth, $37 billion, indicates that he may be the richest man in the world. Brunei, along with the People's Republic of China, Vietnam, Malaysia, Taiwan, and the Philippines, is engaged in a regional dispute over claims to the Spratly Islands, situated in the South China Seas. The islands are militarily important and may have large oil reserves.

13 GOVERNMENT

Brunei is an independent Islamic sultanate. The 1959 constitution gives supreme executive authority to the sultan and provides for four Constitutional Councils to assist him. In 1992, the Sultan clearly stated his commitment to preserving Brunei's political system based on the concept of *Melayu Islam Beraja* (MIB), or Malay Islam Monarchy. Brunei has four administrative districts.

14 POLITICAL PARTIES

In 1988, political parties were banned and many of their leaders arrested. At that time, the political parties were the Brunei National Democratic Party (BNDP), the Brunei National United Party (BNUP), and the Brunei National Solidarity Party (BNSP).

15 JUDICIAL SYSTEM

There are five levels of courts, with the High Court at the top. Decisions of the High Court can be taken to the Court of Appeal. The Supreme Court consists of the High Court and the Court of Appeal.

16 ARMED FORCES

The Royal Brunei Armed Forces in 1993 consisted of an army of 3,600 men and women, a navy of 550, and an air force of 300. Brunei spent $233.1 million for defense in 1988.

17 ECONOMY

Brunei's economy depends almost entirely on oil and gas resources. The country's oil reserves are estimated to last another 20–25 years. The government is trying to make the economy more diverse and less oil-dependent.

18 INCOME

In 1992 the gross domestic product (GDP) was $3.5 billion in current dollars, or about $8,800 per person.

19 INDUSTRY

Industry is almost entirely dependent on oil and natural gas production. The small manufacturing section includes construction products, sawmills, and brick and tile factories.

20 LABOR

Brunei's severe labor shortage has drawn temporary workers from neighboring countries. Many of them are illegal immigrants. In 1991 there were about 85,000 persons in the labor force, of whom 6,000 were in the oil and gas industry.

21 AGRICULTURE

Rice production is low, and Brunei imports more than 80% of its requirements. Crops for home consumption include bananas, sweet potatoes, cassava, coconuts, pineapples, and vegetables.

22 DOMESTICATED ANIMALS

Cattle, buffalo, hogs, goats, and fowl are raised. The government owns a cattle station in Australia that is larger in area than Brunei itself.

23 FISHING

Traditional fishing has declined in recent years, with only 60% of home consumption provided by local fishers. The annual fish harvest in 1991 totaled 1,652 tons.

24 FORESTRY

Forest reserves constitute about 41% of the land area. There is a small sawmill and logging industry for local needs. From 1988 to 1990, Brunei produced about 294,000 cubic meters of roundwood annually.

25 MINING

Brunei's mining industry was involved only in the production and processing of crude oil and natural gas in 1991. Brunei's principal nonfuel mineral resource is silica sand of glassmaking quality.

26 FOREIGN TRADE

In 1991, liquefied natural gas exports were valued at about $940 billion; crude oil exports were valued at more than $980 billion. Principal imports are machinery and transport equipment, manufactured goods, and foodstuffs. In 1991, estimated exports totaled $2 million. In 1989, imports totaled about $840,000. In 1991, Brunei's major trading partners were Japan, Thailand, and Singapore.

27 ENERGY AND POWER

Production of crude oil in 1992 amounted to 9 million tons; output of natural gas was 10 billion cubic meters. In 1991 production of electricity totaled 1,242 million kilowatt hours.

28 SOCIAL DEVELOPMENT

The state provides pensions for the old and disabled, and financial aid for those living in poverty. A major social change in recent years has been the increasing influence of Islam as a way of life. Women are denied equal status with men in many areas, and citizenship is passed on through males only.

29 HEALTH

Medical personnel in 1991 included 197 physicians. Life expectancy in 1992 was estimated at 75 years. In 1990, 96% of the population had access to health care services. There is still some risk of filariasis and tuberculosis.

30 HOUSING

Development plans for 1986–90 included a public housing program, and government allocations for housing development totaled an estimated $46 million in 1985.

31 EDUCATION

In 1991, there were 149 primary schools, with 38,933 pupils and 2,543 teachers. Secondary schools had 25,699 students and 2,172 teachers. An estimated 95% of children and 71% of adults were literate. Brunei has a university and institutes of education and technology.

Selected Social Indicators

These statistics are estimates for the period 1988 to 1993. For comparison purposes, data for the United States and averages for low-income countries and high-income countries are also given.

Indicator	Brunei	Low-income countries	High-income countries	United States
Per capita gross national product†	$8,800	$380	$23,680	$24,740
Population growth rate	2.1%	1.9%	0.6%	1.0%
Population growth rate in urban areas	2.1%	3.9%	0.8%	1.3%
Population per square kilometer of land	46	78	25	26
Life expectancy in years	75	62	77	76
Number of people per physician	1,888	>3,300	453	419
Number of pupils per teacher (primary school)	16	39	<18	20
Illiteracy rate (15 years and older)	22%	41%	<5%	<3%
Energy consumed per capita (kg of oil equivalent)	7,687	364	5,203	7,918

† The gross national product (GNP) is the total dollar value of all goods and services produced by a country in a year. The per capita GNP is calculated by dividing a country's GNP by its population. The World Bank defines low-income countries as those with a per capita GNP of $695 or less. High-income countries have a per capita GNP of $8,626 or more. Less than 14% of the world's 5.5 billion people live in high-income countries, while almost 60% live in low-income countries.   > = greater than   < = less than

Sources: World Bank, *Social Indicators of Development 1995,* Baltimore: Johns Hopkins University Press, 1995. Central Intelligence Agency, *World Fact Book,* Washington, D.C.: Government Printing Office, 1994.

32 MEDIA

The only commercial daily newspaper serving Brunei is the English *Borneo Bulletin*, with a circulation of 32,000. Radio Television Brunei broadcasts radio programs in English, Malay, and Chinese, and television programs in Malay and English. In 1991, there were an estimated 71,000 radios and 62,000 television sets. In 1991, there were 49,036 telephones in use.

33 TOURISM AND RECREATION

Brunei attracts few tourists because of a lack of facilities. Among Brunei's newest sights is the sultan's 1,788-room palace, built at a reported cost of $300 million.

34 FAMOUS BRUNEIANS

Omar Ali Saifuddin (1916–86) was sultan from 1950 to 1967. His son, Muda Hassanal Bolkiah (Bolkiah Mu'izuddin Waddaulah, b.1946) has been sultan since 1967.

35 BIBLIOGRAPHY

Chalfont, Arthur Gwynne Jones, Baron. *By God's Will: a Portrait of the Sultan of Brunei.* 1st American ed. New York: Weidenfeld & Nicolson, 1989.

Major, John S. *The Land and People of Malaysia and Brunei.* New York, NY: HarperCollins, 1991.

Wright, D. *Brunei.* Chicago: Children's Press, 1991.

GLOSSARY

aboriginal: The first known inhabitants of a country. A species of animals or plants which originated within a given area.

acid rain: Rain (or snow) that has become slightly acid by mixing with industrial air pollution.

adobe: A brick made from sun-dried heavy clay mixed with straw, used in building houses. A house made of adobe bricks.

adult literacy: The ability of adults to read and write.

afforestation: The act of turning arable land into forest or woodland.

agrarian economy: An economy where agriculture is the dominant form of economic activity. A society where agriculture dominates the day-to-day activities of the population is called an agrarian society.

air link: Refers to scheduled air service that allows people and goods to travel between two places on a regular basis.

airborne industrial pollutant: Pollution caused by industry that is supported or carried by the air.

allies: Groups or persons who are united in a common purpose. Typically used to describe nations that have joined together to fight a common enemy in war.

In World War I, the term Allies described the nations that fought against Germany and its allies. In World War II, Allies described the United Kingdom, United States, the USSR and their allies, who fought against the Axis Powers of Germany, Italy, and Japan.

aloe: A plant particularly abundant in the southern part of Africa, where leaves of some species are made into ropes, fishing lines, bow strings, and hammocks. It is also a symbolic plant in the Islamic world; anyone who returns from a pilgrimage to Mecca (Mekkah) hangs aloe over his door as a token that he has performed the journey.

Altaic language family: A family of languages spoken in portions of northern and eastern Europe, and nearly the whole of northern and central Asia, together with some other regions. The family is divided into five branches: the Ugrian or Finno-Hungarian, Smoyed, Turkish, Mongolian, and Tunguse.

althing: A legislative assembly.

amendment: A change or addition to a document.

Amerindian: A contraction of the two words, American Indian. It describes native peoples of North, South, or Central America.

amnesty: An act of forgiveness or pardon, usually taken by a government, toward persons for crimes they may have committed.

Anglican: Pertaining to or connected with the Church of England.

animism: The belief that natural objects and phenomena have souls or innate spiritual powers.

annual growth rate: The rate at which something grows over a period of 12 months.

annual inflation rate: The rate of inflation in prices over the course of a year.

anthracite coal: Also called hard coal, it is usually 90 to 95 percent carbon, and burns cleanly, almost without a flame.

anti-Semitism: Agitation, persecution, or discrimination (physical, emotional, economic, political, or otherwise) directed against the Jews.

apartheid: The past governmental policy in the Republic of South Africa of separating the races in society.

appeasement: To bring to a state of peace.

appellate: Refers to an appeal of a court decision to a high authority.

applied science: Scientific techniques employed to achieve results that solve practical problems.

aquaculture: The culture or "farming" of aquatic plants or other natural produce, as in the raising of catfish in "farms."

aquatic resources: Resources that come from, grow in, or live in water, including fish and plants.

aquifer: An underground layer of porous rock, sand, or gravel that holds water.

arable land: Land that can be cultivated by plowing and used for growing crops.

arbitration: A process whereby disputes are settled by a designated person, called the arbitrator, instead of by a court of law.

archipelago: Any body of water abounding with islands, or the islands themselves collectively.

archives: A place where records or a collection of important documents are kept.

arctic climate: Cold, frigid weather similar to that experienced at or near the north pole.

aristocracy: A small minority that controls the government of a nation, typically on the basis of inherited wealth.

armistice: An agreement or truce which ends military conflict in anticipation of a peace treaty.

artesian well: A type of well where the water rises to the surface and overflows.

ASEAN *see* Association of Southeast Asian Nations

Association of Southeast Asian Nations: ASEAN was established in 1967 to promote political, economic, and social cooperation among its six member countries: Indonesia, Malaysia, the Philippines, Singapore, Thailand, and Brunei. ASEAN headquarters are in Jakarta, Indonesia. In January 1992, ASEAN agreed to create the ASEAN Free Trade Area (AFTA).

atheist: A person who denies the existence of God or of a supreme intelligent being.

atoll: A coral island, consisting of a strip or ring of coral surrounding a central lagoon.

atomic weapons: Weapons whose extremely violent explosive power comes from the splitting of the nuclei of atoms (usually uranium or plutonium) by neutrons in a rapid chain reaction. These weapons may be referred to as atom bombs, hydrogen bombs, or H-bombs.

austerity measures: Steps taken by a government to conserve money or resources during an economically difficult time, such as cutting back on federally funded programs.

Australoid: Pertains to the type of aborigines, or earliest inhabitants, of Australia.

Austronesian language: A family of languages which includes practically all the languages of the Pacific Islands—Indonesian, Melanesian, Polynesian, and Micronesian sub-families. Does not include Australian or Papuan languages.

authoritarianism: A form of government in which a person or group attempts to rule with absolute authority without the representation of the citizens.

autonomous state: A country which is completely self-governing, as opposed to being a dependency or part of another country.

autonomy: The state of existing as a self-governing entity. For instance, when a country gains its independence from another country, it gains autonomy.

average inflation rate: The average rate at which the general prices of goods and services increase over the period of a year.

average life expectancy: In any given society, the average age attained by persons at the time of death.

Axis Powers: The countries aligned against the Allied Nations in World War II, originally applied to Nazi Germany and Fascist Italy (Rome-Berlin Axis), and later extended to include Japan.

bagasse: Plant residue left after a product, such as juice, has been extracted.

Baha'i: The follower of a religious sect founded by Mirza Husayn Ali in Iran in 1863.

Baltic states. The three formerly communist countries of Estonia, Latvia, and Lithuania that border on the Baltic Sea.

Bantu language group: A name applied to the languages spoken in central and south Africa.

banyan tree: An East Indian fig tree. Individual trees develop roots from the branches that descend to the ground and become trunks. These roots support and nourish the crown of the tree.

Baptist: A member of a Protestant denomination that practices adult baptism by complete immersion in water.

barren land: Unproductive land, partly or entirely treeless.

barter: Trade practice where merchandise is exchanged directly for other merchandise or services without use of money.

bedrock: Solid rock lying under loose earth.

bicameral legislature: A legislative body consisting of two chambers, such as the U.S. House of Representatives and the U.S. Senate.

bill of rights: A written statement containing the list of privileges and powers to be granted to a body of people, usually introduced when a government or other organization is forming.

bituminous coal: Soft coal; coal which burns with a bright-yellow flame.

black market: A system of trade where goods are sold illegally, often for excessively inflated prices. This type of trade usually develops to avoid paying taxes or tariffs levied by the government, or to get around import or export restrictions on products.

bloodless coup: The sudden takeover of a country's government by hostile means but without killing anyone in the process.

boat people: Used to describe individuals (refugees) who attempt to flee their country by boat.

bog: Wet, soft, and spongy ground where the soil is composed mainly of decayed or decaying vegetable matter.

Bolshevik Revolution. A revolution in 1917 in Russia when a wing of the Russian Social Democratic party seized power. The Bolsheviks advocated the violent overthrow of capitalism.

bonded labor: Workers bound to service without pay; slaves.

border dispute: A disagreement between two countries as to the exact location or length of the dividing line between them.

Brahman: A member (by heredity) of the highest caste among the Hindus, usually assigned to the priesthood.

broadleaf forest: A forest composed mainly of broadleaf (deciduous) trees.

Buddhism: A religious system common in India and eastern Asia. Founded by and based upon the teachings of Siddhartha Gautama, Buddhism asserts that suffering is an inescapable part of life. Deliverance can only be achieved through the practice of charity, temperance, justice, honesty, and truth.

buffer state: A small country that lies between two larger, possibly hostile countries, considered to be a neutralizing force between them.

bureaucracy: A system of government that is characterized by division into bureaus of administration with their own divisional heads. Also refers to the inflexible procedures of such a system that often result in delay.

Byzantine Empire: An empire centered in the city of Byzantium, now Istanbul in present-day Turkey.

CACM *see* Central American Common Market.

candlewood: A name given to several species of trees and shrubs found in the British West Indies, northern Mexico, and the southwestern United States. The plants are characterized by a very resinous wood.

canton: A territory or small division or state within a country.

capital punishment: The ultimate act of punishment for a crime, the death penalty.

capitalism: An economic system in which goods and services and the means to produce and sell them are privately owned, and prices and wages are determined by market forces.

Caribbean Community and Common Market (CARICOM): Founded in 1973 and with its headquarters in Georgetown, Guyana, CARICOM seeks the establishment of a common trade policy and increased cooperation in the Caribbean region. Includes 13 English-speaking Caribbean nations: Antigua and Barbuda, the Bahamas, Barbados, Belize, Dominica, Grenada, Guyana, Jamaica, Montserrat, Saint Kitts-Nevis, Saint Lucia, St. Vincent/Grenadines, and Trinidad and Tobago.

CARICOM *see* Caribbean Community and Common Market.

carnivore: Flesh-eating animal or plant.

carob: The common English name for a plant that is similar to and sometimes used as a substitute for chocolate.

cartel: An organization of independent producers formed to regulate the production, pricing, or marketing practices of its members in order to limit competition and maximize their market power.

cash crop: A crop that is grown to be sold rather than kept for private use.

cassation: The reversal or annulling of a final judgment by the supreme authority.

cassava: The name of several species of stout herbs, extensively cultivated for food.

caste system: One of the artificial divisions or social classes into which the Hindus are rigidly separated according to the religious law of Brahmanism. Membership in a caste is hereditary, and the privileges and disabilities of each caste are transmitted by inheritance.

Caucasian: The white race of human beings, as determined by genealogy and physical features.

Caucasoid: Belonging to the racial group characterized by light skin pigmentation. Commonly called the "white race."

cease-fire: An official declaration of the end to the use of military force or active hostilities, even if only temporary.

CEMA *see* Council for Mutual Economic Assistance.

censorship: The practice of withholding certain items of news that may cast a country in an unfavorable light or give away secrets to the enemy.

census: An official counting of the inhabitants of a state or country with details of sex and age, family, occupation, possessions, etc.

Central American Common Market (CACM): Established in 1962, a trade alliance of five Central American nations. Participating are Costa Rica, El Salvador, Guatemala, Honduras, and Nicaragua.

Central Powers: In World War I, Germany and Austria-Hungary, and their allies, Turkey and Bulgaria.

centrally planned economy: An economic system all aspects of which are supervised and regulated by the government.

centrist position: Refers to opinions held by members of a moderate political group; that is, views that are somewhere in the middle of popular thought between conservative and liberal.

cession: Withdrawal from or yielding to physical force.

chancellor: A high-ranking government official. In some countries it is the prime minister.

cholera: An acute infectious disease characterized by severe diarrhea, vomiting, and, often, death.

Christianity: The religion founded by Jesus Christ, based on the Bible as holy scripture.

Church of England: The national and established church in England. The Church of England claims continuity with the branch of the Catholic Church that existed in England before the Reformation. Under Henry VIII, the spiritual supremacy and jurisdiction of the Pope were abolished, and the sovereign (king or queen) was declared head of the church.

circuit court: A court that convenes in two or more locations within its appointed district.

CIS *see* Commonwealth of Independent States

city-state: An independent state consisting of a city and its surrounding territory.

civil court: A court whose proceedings include determinations of rights of individual citizens, in contrast to criminal proceedings regarding individuals or the public.

civil jurisdiction: The authority to enforce the laws in civil matters brought before the court.

civil law: The law developed by a nation or state for the conduct of daily life of its own people.

civil rights: The privileges of all individuals to be treated as equals under the laws of their country; specifically, the rights given by certain amendments to the U.S. Constitution.

civil unrest: The feeling of uneasiness due to an unstable political climate, or actions taken as a result of it.

civil war: A war between groups of citizens of the same country who have different opinions or agendas. The Civil War of the United States was the conflict between the states of the North and South from 1861 to 1865.

climatic belt: A region or zone where a particular type of climate prevails.

Club du Sahel: The Club du Sahel is an informal coalition which seeks to reverse the effects of drought and the desertification in the eight Sahelian zone countries: Burkina Faso, Chad, Gambia, Mali, Mauritania, Niger, Senegal, and the Cape Verde Islands. Headquarters are in Ouagadougou, Burkina Faso.

CMEA see Council for Mutual Economic Assistance.

coalition government: A government combining differing factions within a country, usually temporary.

coastal belt: A coastal plain area of lowlands and somewhat higher ridges that run parallel to the coast.

coastal plain: A fairly level area of land along the coast of a land mass.

coca: A shrub native to South America, the leaves of which produce organic compounds that are used in the production of cocaine.

coke: The solid product of the carbonization of coal, bearing the same relation to coal that charcoal does to wood.

cold war: Refers to conflict over ideological differences that is carried on by words and diplomatic actions, not by military action. The term is usually used to refer to the tension that existed between the United States and the USSR from the 1950s until the breakup of the USSR in 1991.

collective bargaining: The negotiations between workers who are members of a union and their employer for the purpose of deciding work rules and policies regarding wages, hours, etc.

collective farm: A large farm formed from many small farms and supervised by the government; usually found in communist countries.

collective farming: The system of farming on a collective where all workers share in the income of the farm.

colloquial: Belonging to ordinary, everyday speech: often especially applied to common words and phrases which are not used in formal speech.

colonial period: The period of time when a country forms colonies in and extends control over a foreign area.

colonist: Any member of a colony or one who helps settle a new colony.

colony: A group of people who settle in a new area far from their original country, but still under the jurisdiction of that country. Also refers to the newly settled area itself.

COMECON see Council for Mutual Economic Assistance.

commerce: The trading of goods (buying and selling), especially on a large scale, between cities, states, and countries.

commercial catch: The amount of marketable fish, usually measured in tons, caught in a particular period of time.

commercial crop: Any marketable agricultural crop.

commission: A group of people designated to collectively do a job, including a government agency with certain law-making powers. Also, the power given to an individual or group to perform certain duties.

commodity: Any items, such as goods or services, that are bought or sold, or agricultural products that are traded or marketed.

common law: A legal system based on custom and decisions and opinions of the law courts. The basic system of law of England and the United States.

common market: An economic union among countries that is formed to remove trade barriers (tariffs) among those countries, increasing economic cooperation. The European Community is a notable example of a common market.

commonwealth: A commonwealth is a free association of sovereign independent states that has no charter, treaty, or constitution. The association promotes cooperation, consultation, and mutual assistance among members.

Commonwealth of Independent States: The CIS was established in December 1991 as an association of 11 republics of the former Soviet Union. The members include: Russia, Ukraine, Belarus (formerly Byelorussia), Moldova (formerly Moldavia), Armenia, Azerbaijan, Uzbekistan, Turkmenistan, Tajikistan, Kazakhstan, and Kirgizstan (formerly Kirghiziya). The Baltic states—Estonia, Latvia, and Lithuania—did not join. Georgia maintained observer status before joining the CIS in November 1993.

Commonwealth of Nations: Voluntary association of the United Kingdom and its present dependencies and associated states, as well as certain former dependencies and their dependent territories. The term was first used officially in 1926 and is embodied in the Statute of Westminster (1931). Within the Commonwealth, whose secretariat (established in 1965) is located in London, England, are numerous subgroups devoted to economic and technical cooperation.

commune: An organization of people living together in a community who share the ownership and use of property. Also refers to a small governmental district of a country, especially in Europe.

communism: A form of government whose system requires common ownership of property for the use of all citizens. All profits are to be equally distributed and prices on goods and services are usually set by the state. Also, communism refers directly to the official doctrine of the former U.S.S.R.

compulsory: Required by law or other regulation.

compulsory education: The mandatory requirement for children to attend school until they have reached a certain age or grade level.

conciliation: A process of bringing together opposing sides of a disagreement for the purpose of compromise. Or, a way of settling an international dispute in which the disagreement is submitted to an independent committee that will examine the facts and advise the participants of a possible solution.

concordat: An agreement, compact, or convention, especially between church and state.

confederation: An alliance or league formed for the purpose of promoting the common interests of its members.

Confucianism: The system of ethics and politics taught by the Chinese philosopher Confucius.

coniferous forest: A forest consisting mainly of pine, fir, and cypress trees.

conifers: Cone-bearing plants. Mostly evergreen trees and shrubs which produce cones.

conscription: To be required to join the military by law. Also known as the draft. Service personnel who join the military because of the legal requirement are called conscripts or draftees.

conservative party: A political group whose philosophy tends to be based on established traditions and not supportive of rapid change.

constituency: The registered voters in a governmental district, or a group of people that supports a position or a candidate.

constituent assembly: A group of people that has the power to determine the election of a political representative or create a constitution.

constitution: The written laws and basic rights of citizens of a country or members of an organized group.

constitutional monarchy: A system of government in which the hereditary sovereign (king or queen, usually) rules according to a written constitution.

constitutional republic: A system of government with an elected chief of state and elected representation, with a written constitution containing its governing principles. The United States is a constitutional republic.

consumer goods: Items that are bought to satisfy personal needs or wants of individuals.

continental climate: The climate of a part of the continent; the characteristics and peculiarities of the climate are a result of the land itself and its location.

continental shelf: A plain extending from the continental coast and varying in width that typically ends in a steep slope to the ocean floor.

copra: The dried meat of the coconut; it is frequently used as an ingredient of curry, and to produce coconut oil. Also written *cobra, coprah,* and *copperah.*

Coptic Christians: Members of the Coptic Church of Egypt, formerly of Ethiopia.

cordillera: A continuous ridge, range, or chain of mountains.

corvette: A small warship that is often used as an escort ship because it is easier to maneuver than larger ships like destroyers.

Council for Mutual Economic Assistance (CMEA): Also known as Comecon, the alliance of socialist economies was established on 25 January 1949 and abolished 1 January 1991. It included Afghanistan*, Albania, Angola*, Bulgaria, Cuba, Czechoslovakia, Ethiopia*, East Germany, Hungary, Laos*, Mongolia, Mozambique*, Nicaragua*, Poland, Romania, USSR, Vietnam, Yemen*, and Yugoslavia. Nations marked with an asterisk were observers only.

counterinsurgency operations: Organized military activity designed to stop rebellion against an established government.

county: A territorial division or administrative unit within a state or country.

coup d'ètat or coup: A sudden, violent overthrow of a government or its leader.

court of appeal: An appellate court, having the power of review after a case has been decided in a lower court.

court of first appeal: The next highest court to the court which has decided a case, to which that case may be presented for review.

court of last appeal: The highest court, in which a decision is not subject to review by any higher court. In the United States, it could be the Supreme Court of an individual state or the U.S. Supreme Court.

cricket (sport): A game played by two teams with a ball and bat, with two wickets (staked target) being defended by a batsman. Common in the United Kingdom and Commonwealth of Nations countries.

criminal law: The branch of law that deals primarily with crimes and their punishments.

crown colony: A colony established by a commonwealth over which the monarch has some control, as in colonies established by the United Kingdom's Commonwealth of Nations.

Crusades: Military expeditions by European Christian armies in the eleventh, twelfth, and thirteenth centuries to win land controlled by the Muslims in the middle east.

cultivable land: Land that can be prepared for the production of crops.

Cultural Revolution: An extreme reform movement in China from 1966 to 1976; its goal was to combat liberalization by restoring the ideas of Mao Zedong.

Cushitic language group: A group of Hamitic languages that are spoken in Ethiopia and other areas of eastern Africa.

customs union: An agreement between two or more countries to remove trade barriers with each other and to establish common tariff and nontariff policies with respect to imports from countries outside of the agreement.

cyclone: Any atmospheric movement, general or local, in which the wind blows spirally around and in towards a center. In the northern hemisphere, the cyclonic movement is usually counter-clockwise, and in the southern hemisphere, it is clockwise.

Cyrillic alphabet: An alphabet adopted by the Slavic people and invented by Cyril and Methodius in the ninth century as an alphabet that was easier for the copyist to write. The Russian alphabet is a slight modification of it.

decentralization: The redistribution of power in a government from one large central authority to a wider range of smaller local authorities.

deciduous species: Any species that sheds or casts off a part of itself after a definite period of time. More commonly used in reference to plants that shed their leaves on a yearly basis as opposed to those (evergreens) that retain them.

declaration of independence: A formal written document stating the intent of a group of persons to become fully self-governing.

deficit: The amount of money that is in excess between spending and income.

deficit spending: The process in which a government spends money on goods and services in excess of its income.

deforestation: The removal or clearing of a forest.

deity: A being with the attributes, nature, and essence of a god; a divinity.

delta: Triangular-shaped deposits of soil formed at the mouths of large rivers.

demarcate: To mark off from adjoining land or territory; set the limits or boundaries of.

demilitarized zone (DMZ): An area surrounded by a combat zone that has had military troops and weapons removed.

demobilize: To disband or discharge military troops.

democracy: A form of government in which the power lies in the hands of the people, who can govern directly, or can be governed indirectly by representatives elected by its citizens.

denationalize: To remove from government ownership or control.

deportation: To carry away or remove from one country to another, or to a distant place.

depression: A hollow; a surface that has sunken or fallen in.

deregulation: The act of reversing controls and restrictions on prices of goods, bank interest, and the like.

desalinization plant: A facility that produces freshwater by removing the salt from saltwater.

desegregation: The act of removing restrictions on people of a particular race that keep them socially, economically, and, sometimes, physically, separate from other groups.

desertification: The process of becoming a desert as a result of climatic changes, land mismanagement, or both.

détente: The official lessening of tension between countries in conflict.

devaluation: The official lowering of the value of a country's currency in relation to the value of gold or the currencies of other countries.

developed countries: Countries which have a high standard of living and a well-developed industrial base.

development assistance: Government programs intended to finance and promote the growth of new industries.

dialect: One of a number of regional or related modes of speech regarded as descending from a common origin.

dictatorship: A form of government in which all the power is retained by an absolute leader or tyrant. There are no rights granted to the people to elect their own representatives.

diplomatic relations: The relationship between countries as conducted by representatives of each government.

direct election: The process of selecting a representative to the government by balloting of the voting public, in contrast to selection by an elected representative of the people.

disarmament: The reduction or depletion of the number of weapons or the size of armed forces.

dissident: A person whose political opinions differ from the majority to the point of rejection.

dogma: A principle, maxim, or tenet held as being firmly established.

domain: The area of land governed by a particular ruler or government, sometimes referring to the ultimate control of that territory.

domestic spending: Money spent by a country's government on goods used, investments, running of the government, and exports and imports.

dominion: A self-governing nation that recognizes the British monarch as chief of state.

dormant volcano: A volcano that has not exhibited any signs of activity for an extended period of time.

dowry: The sum of the property or money that a bride brings to her groom at their marriage.

draft constitution: The preliminary written plans for the new constitution of a country forming a new government.

Druze: A member of a Muslim sect based in Syria, living chiefly in the mountain regions of Lebanon.

dual nationality: The status of an individual who can claim citizenship in two or more countries.

duchy: Any territory under the rule of a duke or duchess.

due process: In law, the application of the legal process to which every citizen has a right, which cannot be denied.

durable goods: Goods or products which are expected to last and perform for several years, such as cars and washing machines.

duty: A tax imposed on imports by the customs authority of a country. Duties are generally based on the value of the goods (*ad valorem* duties), some other factors such as weight or quantity (specific duties), or a combination of value and other factors (compound duties).

dyewoods: Any wood from which dye is extracted.

dynasty: A family line of sovereigns who rule in succession, and the time during which they reign.

earned income: The money paid to an individual in wages or salary.

Eastern Orthodox: The outgrowth of the original Eastern Church of the Eastern Roman Empire, consisting of eastern Europe, western Asia, and Egypt.

EC *see* European Community

ecclesiastical: Pertaining or relating to the church.

echidna: A spiny, toothless anteater of Australia, Tasmania, and New Guinea.

ecological balance: The condition of a healthy, well-functioning ecosystem, which includes all the plants and animals in a natural community together with their environment.

ecology: The branch of science that studies organisms in relationship to other organisms and to their environment.

economic depression: A prolonged period in which there is high unemployment, low production, falling prices, and general business failure.

economically active population: That portion of the people who are employed for wages and are consumers of goods and services.

ecotourism: Broad term that encompasses nature, adventure, and ethnic tourism; responsible or wilderness-sensitive tourism; soft-path or small-scale tourism; low-impact tourism; and sustainable tourism. Scientific, educational, or academic tourism (such as biotourism, archetourism, and geotourism) are also forms of ecotourism.

elected assembly: The persons that comprise a legislative body of a government who received their positions by direct election.

electoral system: A system of choosing government officials by votes cast by qualified citizens.

electoral vote: The votes of the members of the electoral college.

electorate: The people who are qualified to vote in an election.

emancipation: The freeing of persons from any kind of bondage or slavery.

embargo: A legal restriction on commercial ships to enter a country's ports, or any legal restriction of trade.

emigration: Moving from one country or region to another for the purpose of residence.

empire: A group of territories ruled by one sovereign or supreme ruler. Also, the period of time under that rule.

enclave: A territory belonging to one nation that is surrounded by that of another nation.

encroachment: The act of intruding, trespassing, or entering on the rights or possessions of another.

endangered species: A plant or animal species whose existence as a whole is threatened with extinction.

endemic: Anything that is peculiar to and characteristic of a locality or region.

Enlightenment: An intellectual movement of the late seventeenth and eighteenth centuries in which scientific thinking gained a strong foothold and old beliefs were challenged. The idea of absolute monarchy was questioned and people were gradually given more individual rights.

enteric disease: An intestinal disease.

epidemic: As applied to disease, any disease that is temporarily prevalent among people in one place at the same time.

Episcopal: Belonging to or vested in bishops or prelates; characteristic of or pertaining to a bishop or bishops.

ethnolinguistic group: A classification of related languages based on common ethnic origin.

EU *see* European Union

European Community: A regional organization created in 1958. Its purpose is to eliminate customs duties and other trade barriers in Europe. It promotes a common external tariff against other countries, a Common Agricultural Policy (CAP), and guarantees of free movement of labor and capital. The original six members were Belgium, France, West Germany, Italy, Luxembourg, and the Netherlands. Denmark, Ireland, and the United Kingdom became members in 1973; Greece joined in 1981; Spain and Portugal in 1986. Other nations continue to join.

European Union: The EU is an umbrella reference to the European Community (EC) and to two European integration efforts introduced by the Maastricht Treaty: Common Foreign and Security Policy (including defense) and Justice and Home Affairs (principally cooperation between police and other authorities on crime, terrorism, and immigration issues).

exports: Goods sold to foreign buyers.

external migration: The movement of people from their native country to another country, as opposed to internal migration, which is the movement of people from one area of a country to another in the same country.

fallout: The precipitation of particles from the atmosphere, often the result of a ground disturbance by volcanic activity or a nuclear explosion.

family planning: The use of birth control to determine the number of children a married couple will have.

Fascism: A political philosophy that holds the good of the nation as more important than the needs of the individual. Fascism also stands for a dictatorial leader and strong oppression of opposition or dissent.

federal: Pertaining to a union of states whose governments are subordinate to a central government.

federation: A union of states or other groups under the authority of a central government.

fetishism: The practice of worshipping a material object that is believed to have mysterious powers residing in it, or is the representation of a deity to which worship may be paid and from which supernatural aid is expected.

feudal estate: The property owned by a lord in medieval Europe under the feudal system.

feudal society: In medieval times, an economic and social structure in which persons could hold land given to them by a lord (nobleman) in return for service to that lord.

final jurisdiction: The final authority in the decision of a legal matter. In the United States, the Supreme Court would have final jurisdiction.

Finno-Ugric language group: A subfamily of languages spoken in northeastern Europe, including Finnish, Hungarian, Estonian, and Lapp.

fiscal year: The twelve months between the settling of financial accounts, not necessarily corresponding to a calendar year beginning on January 1.

fjord: A deep indentation of the land forming a comparatively narrow arm of the sea with more or less steep slopes or cliffs on each side.

fly: The part of a flag opposite and parallel to the one nearest the flagpole.

fodder: Food for cattle, horses, and sheep, such as hay, straw, and other kinds of vegetables.

folk religion: A religion with origins and traditions among the common people of a nation or region that is relevant to their particular life-style.

foreign exchange: Foreign currency that allows foreign countries to conduct financial transactions or settle debts with one another.

foreign policy: The course of action that one government chooses to adopt in relation to a foreign country.

Former Soviet Union: The FSU is a collective reference to republics comprising the former Soviet Union. The term, which has been used as both including and excluding the Baltic republics (Estonia, Latvia, and Lithuania), includes the other 12 republics: Russia, Ukraine, Belarus, Moldova, Armenia, Azerbaijan, Uzbekistan, Turkmenistan, Tajikistan, Kazakhstan, Kyrgizstan, and Georgia.

fossil fuels: Any mineral or mineral substance formed by the decomposition of organic matter buried beneath the earth's surface and used as a fuel.

free enterprise: The system of economics in which private business may be conducted with minimum interference by the government.

free-market economy: An economic system that relies on the market, as opposed to government planners, to set the prices for wages and products.

frigate. A medium-sized warship.

fundamentalist: A person who holds religious beliefs based on the complete acceptance of the words of the Bible or other holy scripture as the truth. For instance, a fundamentalist would believe the story of creation exactly as it is told in the Bible and would reject the idea of evolution.

game reserve: An area of land reserved for wild animals that are hunted for sport or for food.

GDP *see* gross domestic product.

Germanic language group: A large branch of the Indo-European family of languages including German itself, the Scandinavian languages, Dutch, Yiddish, Modern English, Modern Scottish, Afrikaans, and others. The group also includes extinct languages such as Gothic, Old High German, Old Saxon, Old English, Middle English, and the like.

glasnost: President Mikhail Gorbachev's frank revelations in the 1980s about the state of the economy and politics in the Soviet Union; his policy of openness.

global greenhouse gas emissions: Gases released into the atmosphere that contribute to the greenhouse effect, a condition in which the earth's excess heat cannot escape.

global warming: Also called the greenhouse effect. The theorized gradual warming of the earth's climate as a result of the burning of fossil fuels, the use of man-made chemicals, deforestation, etc.

GMT *see* Greenwich Mean Time.

GNP *see* gross national product.

grand duchy: A territory ruled by a nobleman, called a grand duke, who ranks just below a king.

Greek Catholic: A person who is a member of an Orthodox Eastern Church.

Greek Orthodox: The official church of Greece, a self-governing branch of the Orthodox Eastern Church.

Greenwich (Mean) Time: Mean solar time of the meridian at Greenwich, England, used as the basis for standard time throughout most of the world. The world is divided into 24 time zones, and all are related to the prime, or Greenwich mean, zone.

gross domestic product: A measure of the market value of all goods and services produced within the boundaries of a nation, regardless of asset ownership. Unlike gross national product, GDP excludes receipts from that nation's business operations in foreign countries.

gross national product: A measure of the market value of goods and services produced by the labor and property of a nation. Includes receipts from that nation's business operation in foreign countries

groundwater: Water located below the earth's surface, the source from which wells and springs draw their water.

guano: The excrement of seabirds and bats found in various areas around the world. Gathered commercially and sold as a fertilizer.

guerrilla: A member of a small radical military organization that uses unconventional tactics to take their enemies by surprise.

gymnasium: A secondary school, primarily in Europe, that prepares students for university.

hardwoods: The name given to deciduous trees, such as cherry, oak, maple, and mahogany.

harem: In a Muslim household, refers to the women (wives, concubines, and servants in ancient times) who live there and also to the area of the home they live in.

harmattan: An intensely dry, dusty wind felt along the coast of Africa between Cape Verde and Cape Lopez. It prevails at intervals during the months of December, January, and February.

heavy industry: Industries that use heavy or large machinery to produce goods, such as automobile manufacturing.

hoist: The part of a flag nearest the flagpole.

Holocaust: The mass slaughter of European civilians, the vast majority Jews, by the Nazis during World War II.

Holy Roman Empire: A kingdom consisting of a loose union of German and Italian territories that existed from around the ninth century until 1806.

home rule: The governing of a territory by the citizens who inhabit it.

homeland: A region or area set aside to be a state for a people of a particular national, cultural, or racial origin.

homogeneous: Of the same kind or nature, often used in reference to a whole.

Horn of Africa: The Horn of Africa comprises Djibouti, Eritrea, Ethiopia, Somalia, and Sudan.

housing starts: The initiation of new housing construction.

human rights activist: A person who vigorously pursues the attainment of basic rights for all people.

human rights issues: Any matters involving people's basic rights which are in question or thought to be abused.

humanist: A person who centers on human needs and values, and stresses dignity of the individual.

humanitarian aid: Money or supplies given to a persecuted group or people of a country at war, or those devastated by a natural disaster, to provide for basic human needs.

hydrocarbon: A compound of hydrogen and carbon, often occurring in organic substances or derivatives of organic substances such as coal, petroleum, natural gas, etc.

hydrocarbon emissions: Organic compounds containing only carbon and hydrogen, often occurring in petroleum, natural gas, coal, and bitumens, and which contribute to the greenhouse effect.

hydroelectric potential: The potential amount of electricity that can be produced hydroelectrically. Usually used in reference to a given area and how many hydroelectric power plants that area can sustain.

hydroelectric power plant: A factory that produces electrical power through the application of water-power.

IBRD *see* World Bank.

illegal alien: Any foreign-born individual who has unlawfully entered another country.

immigration: The act or process of passing or entering into another country for the purpose of permanent residence.

imports: Goods purchased from foreign suppliers.

indigenous: Born or originating in a particular place or country; native to a particular region or area.

Indo-Aryan language group: The group that includes the languages of India; also called Indo-European language group.

Indo-European language family: The group that includes the languages of India and much of Europe and southwestern Asia.

industrialized nation: A nation whose economy is based on industry.

infanticide: The act of murdering a baby.

infidel: One who is without faith or belief; particularly, one who rejects the distinctive doctrines of a particular religion.

inflation: The general rise of prices, as measured by a consumer price index. Results in a fall in value of currency.

installed capacity: The maximum possible output of electric power at any given time.

insurgency: The state or condition in which one rises against lawful authority or established government; rebellion.

insurrectionist: One who participates in an unorganized revolt against an authority.

interim government: A temporary or provisional government.

interim president: One who is appointed to perform temporarily the duties of president during a transitional period in a government.

internal migration: Term used to describe the relocation of individuals from one region to another without leaving the confines of the country or of a specified area.

International Date Line: An arbitrary line at about the 180th meridian that designates where one day begins and another ends.

Islam: The religious system of Mohammed, practiced by Moslems and based on a belief in Allah as the supreme being and Mohammed as his prophet. The spelling variations, Muslim and Muhammed, are also used, primarily by Islamic people. Islam also refers to those nations in which it is the primary religion.

isthmus: A narrow strip of land bordered by water and connecting two larger bodies of land, such as two continents, a continent and a peninsula, or two parts of an island.

Judaism: The religious system of the Jews, based on the Old Testament as revealed to Moses and characterized by a belief in one God and adherence to the laws of scripture and rabbinic traditions.

Judeo-Christian: The dominant traditional religious makeup of the United States and other countries based on the worship of the Old and New Testaments of the Bible.

junta: A small military group in power of a country, especially after a coup.

khan: A sovereign, or ruler, in central Asia.

khanate: A kingdom ruled by a khan, or man of rank.

kwashiorkor: Severe malnutrition in infants and children caused by a diet high in carbohydrates and lacking in protein.

kwh: The abbreviation for kilowatt-hour.

labor force: The number of people in a population available for work, whether actually employed or not.

labor movement: A movement in the early to mid-1800s to organize workers in groups according to profession to give them certain rights as a group, including bargaining power for better wages, working conditions, and benefits.

land reforms: Steps taken to create a fair distribution of farmland, especially by governmental action.

landlocked country: A country that does not have direct access to the sea; it is completely surrounded by other countries.

least developed countries: A subgroup of the United Nations designation of "less developed countries;" these countries generally have no significant economic growth, low literacy rates, and per person gross national product of less than $500. Also known as undeveloped countries.

leeward: The direction identical to that of the wind. For example, a *leeward tide* is a tide that runs in the same direction that the wind blows.

leftist: A person with a liberal or radical political affiliation.

legislative branch: The branch of government which makes or enacts the laws.

leprosy: A disease that can effect the skin and/or the nerves and can cause ulcers of the skin, loss of feeling, or loss of fingers and toes.

less developed countries (LDC): Designated by the United Nations to include countries with low levels of output, living standards, and per person gross national product generally below $5,000.

literacy: The ability to read and write.

Maastricht Treaty: The Maastricht Treaty (named for the Dutch town in which the treaty was signed) is also known as the Treaty of European Union. The treaty creates a European Union by: (a) committing the member states of the European Economic Community to both European Monetary Union (EMU) and political union; (b) introducing a single currency (European Currency Unit, ECU); (c) establishing a European System of Central Banks (ESCB); (d) creating a European Central Bank (ECB); and (e) broadening EC integration by including both a common foreign and security policy (CFSP) and cooperation in justice and home affairs (CJHA). The treaty entered into force on November 1, 1993.

Maghreb states: The Maghreb states include the three nations of Algeria, Morocco, and Tunisia; sometimes includes Libya and Mauritania.

maize: Another name (Spanish or British) for corn or the color of ripe corn.

majority party: The party with the largest number of votes and the controlling political party in a government.

mangrove: A tree which abounds on tropical shores in both hemispheres. Characterized by its numerous roots which arch out from its trunk and descend from its branches, mangroves form thick, dense growths along the tidal muds, reaching lengths hundreds of miles long.

manioc: The cassava plant or its product. Manioc is a very important food-staple in tropical America.

maquis. Scrubby, thick underbrush found along the coast of the Mediterranean Sea.

marginal land: Land that could produce an economic profit, but is so poor that it is only used when better land is no longer available.

marine life: The life that exists in, or is formed by the sea.

maritime climate: The climate and weather conditions typical of areas bordering the sea.

maritime rights: The rights that protect navigation and shipping.

market access: Market access refers to the openness of a national market to foreign products. Market access reflects a government's willingness to permit imports to compete relatively unimpeded with similar domestically produced goods.

market economy: A form of society which runs by the law of supply and demand. Goods are produced by firms to be sold to consumers, who determine the demand for them. Price levels vary according to the demand for certain goods and how much of them is produced.

market price: The price a commodity will bring when sold on the open market. The price is determined by the amount of demand for the commodity by buyers.

Marshall Plan: Formally known as the European Recovery Program, a joint project between the United States and most Western European nations under which $12.5 billion in U.S. loans and grants was expended to aid European recovery after World War II.

Marxism see Marxist-Leninist principles.

Marxist-Leninist principles: The doctrines of Karl Marx, built upon by Nikolai Lenin, on which communism was founded. They predicted the fall of capitalism, due to its own internal faults and the resulting oppression of workers.

Marxist: A follower of Karl Marx, a German socialist and revolutionary leader of the late 1800s, who contributed to Marxist-Leninist principles.

massif: A central mountain-mass or the dominant part of a range of mountains.

matrilineal (descent): Descending from, or tracing descent through, the maternal, or mother's, family line.

Mayan language family: The languages of the Central American Indians, further divided into two subgroups: the Maya and the Huastek.

mean temperature: The air temperature unit measured by the National Weather Service by adding the maximum and minimum daily temperatures together and diving the sum by 2.

Mecca (Mekkah): A city in Saudi Arabia; a destination of pilgrims in the Islamic world.

Mediterranean climate: A wet-winter, dry-summer climate with a moderate annual temperature range.

mestizo: The offspring of a person of mixed blood; especially, a person of mixed Spanish and American Indian parentage.

migratory birds: Those birds whose instincts prompt them to move from one place to another at the regularly recurring changes of season.

migratory workers: Usually agricultural workers who move from place to place for employment depending on the growing and harvesting seasons of various crops.

military coup: A sudden, violent overthrow of a government by military forces.

military junta: The small military group in power in a country, especially after a coup.

military regime: Government conducted by a military force.

military takeover: The seizure of control of a government by the military forces.

militia: The group of citizens of a country who are either serving in the reserve military forces or are eligible to be called up in time of emergency.

millet: A cereal grass whose small grain is used for food in Europe and Asia.

minority party: The political group that comprises the smaller part of the large overall group it belongs to; the party that is not in control.

missionary: A person sent by authority of a church or religious organization to spread his religious faith in a community where his church has no self-supporting organization.

Mohammed (or Muhammedor Mahomet): An Arabian prophet, known as the "Prophet of Allah" who founded the religion of Islam in 622, and wrote *The Koran*, the scripture of Islam. Also commonly spelled Muhammed, especially by Islamic people.

monarchy: Government by a sovereign, such as a king or queen.

money economy: A system or stage of economic development in which money replaces barter in the exchange of goods and services.

Mongol: One of an Asiatic race chiefly resident in Mongolia, a region north of China proper and south of Siberia.

Mongoloid: Having physical characteristics like those of the typical Mongols (Chinese, Japanese, Turks, Eskimos, etc.).

Moors: One of the Arab tribes that conquered Spain in the eighth century.

Moslem (Muslim): A follower of Mohammed (spelled Muhammed by many Islamic people), in the religion of Islam.

mosque: An Islam place of worship and the organization with which it is connected.

mouflon: A type of wild sheep characterized by curling horns.

mujahideen (mujahedin or mujahedeen): Rebel fighters in Islamic countries, especially those supporting the cause of Islam.

mulatto: One who is the offspring of parents one of whom is white and the other is black.

municipality: A district such as a city or town having its own incorporated government.

Muslim: A frequently used variation of the spelling of Moslem, to describe a follower of the prophet Mohammed (also spelled Muhammed), the founder of the religion of Islam.

Muslim New Year: A Muslim holiday. Although in some countries 1 Muharram, which is the first month of the Islamic year, is observed as a holiday, in other places the new year is observed on Sha'ban, the eighth month of the year. This practice apparently stems from pagan Arab times. Shab-i-Bharat, a national holiday in Bangladesh on this day, is held by many to be the occasion when God ordains all actions in the coming year.

NAFTA (North American Free Trade Agreement): NAFTA, which entered into force in January 1994, is a free trade agreement between Canada, the United States, and Mexico. The agreement progressively eliminates almost all U.S.-Mexico tariffs over a 10–15 year period.

nationalism: National spirit or aspirations; desire for national unity, independence, or prosperity.

nationalization: To transfer the control or ownership of land or industries to the nation from private owners.

native tongue: One's natural language. The language that is indigenous to an area.

NATO *see* North Atlantic Treaty Organization

natural gas: A combustible gas formed naturally in the earth and generally obtained by boring a well. The chemical makeup of natural gas is principally methane, hydrogen, ethylene compounds, and nitrogen.

natural harbor: A protected portion of a sea or lake along the shore resulting from the natural formations of the land.

naturalize: To confer the rights and privileges of a native-born subject or citizen upon someone who lives in the country by choice.

nature preserve: An area where one or more species of plant and/or animal are protected from harm, injury, or destruction.

neutrality: The policy of not taking sides with any countries during a war or dispute among them.

Newly Independent States: The NIS is a collective reference to 12 republics of the former Soviet Union: Russia, Ukraine, Belarus (formerly Byelorussia), Moldova (formerly Moldavia), Armenia, Azerbaijan, Uzbekistan, Turkmenistan, Tajikistan, Kazakhstan, and Kirgizstan (formerly Kirghiziya), and Georgia. Following dissolution of the Soviet Union, the distinction between the NIS and the Commonwealth of Independent States (CIS) was that Georgia was not a member of the CIS. That distinction dissolved when Georgia joined the CIS in November 1993.

news censorship *see* censorship

Nonaligned Movement: The NAM is an alliance of third world states that aims to promote the political and economic interests of developing countries. NAM interests have included ending colonialism/neo-colonialism, supporting the integrity of independent countries, and seeking a new international economic order.

Nordic Council: The Nordic Council, established in 1952, is directed toward supporting cooperation among Nordic countries. Members include Denmark, Finland, Iceland, Norway, and Sweden. Headquarters are in Stockholm, Sweden.

North Atlantic Treaty Organization (NATO): A mutual defense organization. Members include Belgium, Canada, Denmark, France (which has only partial membership), Greece, Iceland, Italy, Luxembourg, Netherlands, Norway, Portugal, Spain, Turkey, United Kingdom, United States, and Germany.

nuclear power plant: A factory that produces electrical power through the application of the nuclear reaction known as nuclear fission.

nuclear reactor: A device used to control the rate of nuclear fission in uranium. Used in commercial applications, nuclear reactors can maintain temperatures high enough to generate sufficient quantities of steam which can then be used to produce electricity.

OAPEC (Organization of Arab Petroleum Exporting countries): OAPEC was created in 1968; members include: Algeria, Bahrain, Egypt, Iraq, Kuwait, Libya, Qatar, Saudi Arabia, Syria, and the United Arab Emirates. Headquarters are in Cairo, Egypt.

OAS (Organization of American States): The OAS (Spanish: Organizaciûn de los Estados Americanos, OEA), or the Pan American Union, is a regional organization which promotes Latin American economic and social development. Members include the United States, Mexico, and most Central American, South American, and Caribbean nations.

OAS *see* Organization of American States

oasis: Originally, a fertile spot in the Libyan desert where there is a natural spring or well and vegetation; now refers to any fertile tract in the midst of a wasteland.

occupied territory: A territory that has an enemy's military forces present.

official language: The language in which the business of a country and its government is conducted.

oligarchy: A form of government in which a few people possess the power to rule as opposed to a monarchy which is ruled by one.

OPEC *see* OAPEC

open economy: An economy that imports and exports goods.

open market: Open market operations are the actions of the central bank to influence or control the money supply by buying or selling government bonds.

opposition party: A minority political party that is opposed to the party in power.

Organization of Arab Petroleum Exporting Countries *see* OAPEC

organized labor: The body of workers who belong to labor unions.

Ottoman Empire: An Turkish empire founded by Osman I in about 1603, that variously controlled large areas of land around the Mediterranean, Black, and Caspian Seas until it was dissolved in 1918.

overfishing: To deplete the quantity of fish in an area by removing more fish than can be naturally replaced.

overgrazing: Allowing animals to graze in an area to the point that the ground vegetation is damaged or destroyed.

overseas dependencies: A distant and physically separate territory that belongs to another country and is subject to its laws and government.

Pacific Rim: The Pacific Rim, referring to countries and economies bordering the Pacific Ocean.

pact: An international agreement.

Paleolithic: The early period of the Stone Age, when rough, chipped stone implements were used.

panhandle: A long narrow strip of land projecting like the handle of a frying pan.

papyrus: The paper-reed or -rush which grows on marshy river banks in the southeastern area of the Mediterranean, but more notably in the Nile valley.

paramilitary group: A supplementary organization to the military.

parasitic diseases: A group of diseases caused by parasitic organisms which feed off the host organism.

parliamentary republic: A system of government in which a president and prime minister, plus other ministers of departments, constitute the executive branch of the government and the parliament constitutes the legislative branch.

parliamentary rule: Government by a legislative body similar to that of Great Britain, which is composed of two houses—one elected and one hereditary.

parochial: Refers to matters of a church parish or something within narrow limits.

patriarchal system: A social system in which the head of the family or tribe is the father or oldest male. Kinship is determined and traced through the male members of the tribe.

patrilineal (descent): Descending from, or tracing descent through, the paternal or father's line.

pellagra: A disease marked by skin, intestinal, and central nervous system disorders, caused by a diet deficient in niacin, one of the B vitamins.

per capita: Literally, per person; for each person counted.

perestroika: The reorganization of the political and economic structures of the Soviet Union by president Mikhail Gorbachev.

periodical: A publication whose issues appear at regular intervals, such as weekly, monthly, or yearly.

petrochemical: A chemical derived from petroleum or from natural gas.

pharmaceutical plants: Any plant that is used in the preparation of medicinal drugs.

plantain: The name of a common weed that has often been used for medicinal purposes, as a folk remedy and in modern medicine. *Plaintain* is also the name of a tropical plant producing a type of banana.

poaching: To intrude or encroach upon another's preserves for the purpose of stealing animals, especially wild game.

polar climate: Also called tundra climate. A humid, severely cold climate controlled by arctic air masses, with no warm or summer season.

political climate: The prevailing political attitude of a particular time or place.

political refugee: A person forced to flee his or her native country for political reasons.

potable water: Water that is safe for drinking.

pound sterling: The monetary unit of Great Britain, otherwise known as the pound.

prefect: An administrative official; in France, the head of a particular department.

prefecture: The territory over which a prefect has authority.

prime meridian: Zero degrees in longitude that runs through Greenwich, England, site of the Royal Observatory. All other longitudes are measured from this point.

prime minister: The premier or chief administrative official in certain countries.

private sector: The division of an economy in which production of goods and services is privately owned.

privatization: To change from public to private control or ownership.

protectorate: A state or territory controlled by a stronger state, or the relationship of the stronger country toward the lesser one it protects.

Protestant Reformation: In 1529, a Christian religious movement begun in Germany to deny the universal authority of the Pope, and to establish the Bible as the only source of truth. (*Also see* Protestant)

Protestant: A member or an adherent of one of those Christian bodies which descended from the Reformation of the sixteenth century. Originally applied to those who opposed or protested the Roman Catholic Church.

proved reserves: The quantity of a recoverable mineral resource (such as oil or natural gas) that is still in the ground.

province: An administrative territory of a country.

provisional government: A temporary government set up during time of unrest or transition in a country.

pulses: Beans, peas, or lentils.

purge: The act of ridding a society of "undesirable" or unloyal persons by banishment or murder.

Rastafarian: A member of a Jamaican cult begun in 1930 as a semi-religious, semi-political movement.

rate of literacy: The percentage of people in a society who can read and write.

recession. A period of reduced economic activity in a country or region.

referendum: The practice of submitting legislation directly to the people for a popular vote.

Reformation *see* Protestant Reformation.

refugee: One who flees to a refuge or shelter or place of safety. One who in times of persecution or political commotion flees to a foreign country for safety.

revolution: A complete change in a government or society, such as in an overthrow of the government by the people.

right-wing party: The more conservative political party.

Roman alphabet: The alphabet of the ancient Romans from which the alphabets of most modern western European languages, including English, are derived.

Roman Catholic Church: The designation of the church of which the pope or Bishop of Rome is the head, and that holds him as the successor of St. Peter and heir of his spiritual authority, privileges, and gifts.

romance language: The group of languages derived from Latin: French, Spanish, Italian, Portuguese, and other related languages.

roundwood: Timber used as poles or in similar ways without being sawn or shaped.

runoff election: A deciding election put to the voters in case of a tie between candidates.

Russian Orthodox: The arm of the Orthodox Eastern Church that was the official church of Russia under the czars.

sack: To strip of valuables, especially after capture.

Sahelian zone: Eight countries make up this dry desert zone in Africa: Burkina Faso, Chad, Gambia, Mali, Mauritania, Niger, Senegal, and the Cape Verde Islands. *Also see* Club du Sahel.

salinization: An accumulation of soluble salts in soil. This condition is common in desert climates, where water evaporates quickly in poorly drained soil due to high temperatures.

Samaritans: A native or an inhabitant of Samaria; specifically, one of a race settled in the cities of Samaria by the king of Assyria after the removal of the Israelites from the country.

savanna: A treeless or near treeless plain of a tropical or subtropical region dominated by drought-resistant grasses.

schistosomiasis: A tropical disease that is chronic and characterized by disorders of the liver, urinary bladder, lungs, or central nervous system.

secession: The act of withdrawal, such as a state withdrawing from the Union in the Civil War in the United States.

sect: A religious denomination or group, often a dissenting one with extreme views.

segregation: The enforced separation of a racial or religious group from other groups, compelling them to live and go to school separately from the rest of society.

seismic activity: Relating to or connected with an earthquake or earthquakes in general.

self-sufficient: Able to function alone without help.

separation of power: The division of power in the government among the executive, legislative, and judicial branches and the checks and balances employed to keep them separate and independent of each other.

separatism: The policy of dissenters withdrawing from a larger political or religious group.

serfdom: In the feudal system of the Middle Ages, the condition of being attached to the land owned by a lord and being transferable to a new owner.

Seventh-day Adventist: One who believes in the second coming of Christ to establish a personal reign upon the earth.

shamanism: A religion of some Asians and Amerindians in which shamans, who are priests or medicine men, are believed to influence good and evil spirits.

shantytown: An urban settlement of people in flimsy, inadequate houses.

Shia Muslim: Members of one of two great sects of Islam. Shia Muslims believe that Ali and the Imams are the rightful successors of Mohammed (also commonly spelled Muhammed). They also believe that the last recognized Imam will return as a messiah. Also known as Shiites. (*Also see* Sunnis.)

Shiites *see* Shia Muslims.

Shintoism: The system of nature- and hero-worship which forms the indigenous religion of Japan.

shoal: A place where the water of a stream, lake, or sea is of little depth. Especially, a sand-bank which shows at low water.

sierra: A chain of hills or mountains.

Sikh: A member of a politico-religious community of India, founded as a sect around 1500 and based on the principles of monotheism (belief in one god) and human brotherhood.

Sino-Tibetan language family: The family of languages spoken in eastern Asia, including China, Thailand, Tibet, and Burma.

slash-and-burn agriculture: A hasty and sometimes temporary way of clearing land to make it available for agriculture by cutting down trees and burning them.

slave trade: The transportation of black Africans beginning in the 1700s to other countries to be sold as slaves—people owned as property and compelled to work for their owners at no pay.

Slavic languages: A major subgroup of the Indo-European language family. It is further subdivided into West Slavic (including Polish, Czech, Slovak and Serbian), South Slavic (including Bulgarian, Serbo-Croatian, Slovene, and Old Church Slavonic), and East Slavic (including Russian Ukrainian and Byelorussian).

social insurance: A government plan to protect low-income people, such as health and accident insurance, pension plans, etc.

social security: A form of social insurance, including life, disability, and old-age pension for workers. It is paid for by employers, employees, and the government.

socialism: An economic system in which ownership of land and other property is distributed among the community as a whole, and every member of the community shares in the work and products of the work.

socialist: A person who advocates socialism.

softwoods: The coniferous trees, whose wood density as a whole is relatively softer than the wood of those trees referred to as hardwoods.

sorghum (also known as Syrian Grass): Plant grown in various parts of the world for its valuable uses, such as for grain, syrup, or fodder.

Southeast Asia: The region in Asia that consists of the Malay Archipelago, the Malay Peninsula, and Indochina.

staple crop: A crop that is the chief commodity or product of a place, and which has widespread and constant use or value.

state: The politically organized body of people living under one government or one of the territorial units that make up a federal government, such as in the United States.

steppe: A level tract of land more or less devoid of trees, in certain parts of European and Asiatic Russia.

student demonstration: A public gathering of students to express strong feelings about a certain situation, usually taking place near the location of the people in power to change the situation.

subarctic climate: A high latitude climate of two types: *continental subarctic*, which has very cold winters, short, cool summers, light precipitation and moist air; and *marine subarctic*, a coastal and island climate with polar air masses causing large precipitation and extreme cold.

subcontinent: A land mass of great size, but smaller than any of the continents; a large subdivision of a continent.

subsistence economy: The part of a national economy in which money plays little or no role, trade is by barter, and living standards are minimal.

subsistence farming: Farming that provides the minimum food goods necessary for the continuation of the farm family.

subtropical climate: A middle latitude climate dominated by humid, warm temperatures and heavy rainfall in summer, with cool winters and frequent cyclonic storms.

subversion: The act of attempting to overthrow or ruin a government or organization by stealthy or deceitful means.

Sudanic language group: A related group of languages spoken in various areas of northern Africa, including Yoruba, Mandingo, and Tshi.

suffrage: The right to vote.

Sufi: A Muslim mystic who believes that God alone exists, there can be no real difference between good and evil, that the soul exists within the body as in a cage, so death should be the chief object of desire, and sufism is the only true philosophy.

sultan: A king of a Muslim state.

Sunni Muslim: Members of one of two major sects of the religion of Islam. Sunni Muslims adhere to strict orthodox traditions, and believe that the four caliphs are the rightful successors to Mohammed, founder of Islam. (Mohammed is commonly spelled Muhammed, especially by Islamic people.) (*Also see* Shia Muslim.)

Taoism: The doctrine of Lao-Tzu, an ancient Chinese philosopher (about 500 B.C.) as laid down by him in the *Tao-te-ching*.

tariff: A tax assessed by a government on goods as they enter (or leave) a country. May be imposed to protect domestic industries from imported goods and/or to generate revenue.

temperate zone: The parts of the earth lying between the tropics and the polar circles. The *northern temperate zone* is the area between the tropic of Cancer and the Arctic Circle. The *southern temperate zone* is the area between the tropic of Capricorn and the Antarctic Circle.

terracing: A form of agriculture that involves cultivating crops in raised banks of earth.

terrorism: Systematic acts of violence designed to frighten or intimidate.

thermal power plant: A facility that produces electric energy from heat energy released by combustion of fuel or nuclear reactions.

Third World: A term used to describe less developed countries; as of the mid-1990s, it is being replaced by the United Nations designation Less Developed Countries, or LDC.

topography: The physical or natural features of the land.

torrid zone: The part of the earth's surface that lies between the tropics, so named for the character of its climate.

totalitarian party: The single political party in complete authoritarian control of a government or state.

trachoma: A contagious bacterial disease that affects the eye.

treaty: A negotiated agreement between two governments.

tribal system: A social community in which people are organized into groups or clans descended from common ancestors and sharing customs and languages.

tropical monsoon climate: One of the tropical rainy climates; it is sufficiently warm and rainy to produce tropical rainforest vegetation, but also has a winter dry season.

tsetse fly: Any of the several African insects which can transmit a variety of parasitic organisms through its bite. Some of these organisms can prove fatal to both human and animal victims.

tundra: A nearly level treeless area whose climate and vegetation are characteristically arctic due to its northern position; the subsoil is permanently frozen.

undeveloped countries *see* least developed countries.

unemployment rate: The overall unemployment rate is the percentage of the work force (both employed and unemployed) who claim to be unemployed.

UNICEF: An international fund set-up for children's emergency relief: United Nations Children's Fund (formerly United Nations International Children's Emergency Fund).

universal adult suffrage: The policy of giving every adult in a nation the right to vote.

untouchables: In India, members of the lowest caste in the caste system, a hereditary social class system. They were considered unworthy to touch members of higher castes.

urban guerrilla: A rebel fighter operating in an urban area.

urbanization: The process of changing from country to city.

USSR: An abbreviation of Union of Soviet Socialist Republics.

veldt: In South Africa, an unforested or thinly forested tract of land or region, a grassland.

Warsaw Pact: Agreement made 14 May 1955 (and dissolved 1 July 1991) to promote mutual defense between Albania, Bulgaria, Czechoslovakia, East Germany, Hungary, Poland, Romania, and the USSR.

Western nations: Blanket term used to describe mostly democratic, capitalist countries, including the United States, Canada, and western European countries.

wildlife sanctuary: An area of land set aside for the protection and preservation of animals and plants.

workers' compensation: A series of regular payments by an employer to a person injured on the job.

World Bank: The World Bank is a group of international institutions which provides financial and technical assistance to developing countries.

world oil crisis: The severe shortage of oil in the 1970s precipitated by the Arab oil embargo.

wormwood: A woody perennial herb native to Europe and Asiatic Russia, valued for its medicinal uses.

yaws: A tropical disease caused by a bacteria which produces raspberry-like sores on the skin.

yellow fever: A tropical viral disease caused by the bite of an infected mosquito, characterized by jaundice.

Zoroastrianism: The system of religious doctrine taught by Zoroaster and his followers in the Avesta; the religion prevalent in Persia until its overthrow by the Muslims in the seventh century.